FINDING PURPLE AMERICA

EST. 75 YEARS 1938

THE UNIVERSITY OF GEORGIA PRESS 2013

Series Editors
Jon Smith, Simon Fraser University
Riché Richardson, Cornell University

Advisory Board
Houston A. Baker Jr., Vanderbilt University
Leigh Anne Duck, The University of Mississippi
Jennifer Greeson, The University of Virginia
Trudier Harris, The University of North Carolina, Chapel Hill
John T. Matthews, Boston University
Claudia Milian, Duke University
Tara McPherson, The University of Southern California

THE SOUTH
AND THE FUTURE
OF AMERICAN
CULTURAL STUDIES

FINDING
PURPLE
AMERICA

JON SMITH

THE UNIVERSITY OF GEORGIA PRESS   ATHENS AND LONDON

Parts of chapter 3 originally appeared in different form as "Growing Up and Out of Alt-country: On Gen X, Wearing Vintage, and Neko Case," by Jon Smith in *Old Roots, New Routes: The Cultural Politics of Alt. Country Music,* edited by Pamela Fox and Barbara Ching (Ann Arbor: The University of Michigan Press, 2008). © The University of Michigan Press. Parts of chapter 4 originally appeared in different form as "Faulkner, Metropolitan Fashion, and 'The South,'" by Jon Smith in *Faulkner's Inheritance: Faulkner and Yoknapatawpha 2005,* edited by Joseph R. Urgo and Ann J. Abadie (Jackson: University of Mississippi Press, 2007).

Set in Sabon MT Pro by Graphic Composition, Inc.,
    Bogart, Georgia.
Manufactured by Thomson-Shore
The paper in this book meets the guidelines for
permanence and durability of the Committee on
Production Guidelines for Book Longevity of the
Council on Library Resources.

Printed in the United States of America
17 16 15 14 13   P   5 4 3 2 1

Library of Congress Cataloging-in-Publication Data
Smith, Jon
    Finding purple America : the South and the future of
    American cultural studies / Jon Smith.
        pages cm. — (The new southern studies)
Includes bibliographical references and index.
ISBN 978-0-8203-3321-2 (hardcover : alk. paper) —
ISBN 0-8203-3321-2 (hardcover : alk. paper) —
ISBN 978-0-8203-4526-0 (pbk. : alk. paper) —
ISBN 0-8203-4526-1 (pbk. : alk. paper)
    1. Southern States—Study and teaching. 2. Southern States—Civilization.
3. United States—Study and teaching. 4. United States—Civilization. I. Title.
F208.5.S65 2013
975.07—dc23   2012047746

British Library Cataloging-in-Publication Data available

For my friends

CONTENTS

PREFACE

This did not start out to be a book about fantasies. It started out as an attempt to understand why a couple dozen literary scholars of my generation—scholars whose work would eventually be called the new southern
studies—didn't seem to fit in anywhere. Our experiences with American
studies could largely be summed up by an anecdote Katie Henninger related
a few years ago in the pages of *Contemporary Literature*: "in a job interview," Henninger recalled, she "was asked, 'Are you an Americanist who does
southern, or a southernist who does American?' asserting an unbridgeable
difference and implying that if I wanted a job teaching postmodern American
literature, I'd best be the former" (177n1). The idea among Americanists, apparently, was that if you worked on "the South," you must be the sort of
tweedy, backward "professional southernist" described decades ago by Paul
Bové. Yet we were hardly more welcome in southern studies; over and over
again, those of us who worked on "the South" from a progressive (non-neo-
agrarian) perspective found ourselves losing out in "southern literature" job
searches to candidates with much more traditional dissertations from much
more traditional places. Worse, even at Americanist journals and presses editors kept sending our work for peer review to, well, professional southernists,
who too often misunderstood it, resented that it didn't cite them or their
friends much (work that did, however, was praised in code as "judicious"),
sometimes feared it, and frequently tried to spike it.

In just the past three or four years, the situation has changed dramatically—sort of. The new southern studies is now decently represented in top-
twenty programs: Jennifer Greeson at Virginia, Riché Richardson at Cornell,
Melanie Benson Taylor at Dartmouth, Harry Stecopoulos at Iowa, Cole
Hutchison at Texas. (Long exceptional, Tara McPherson and Judith Jackson Fossett remain at the University of Southern California.) Even the south-

ern studies centers are starting to come around: the University of Mississippi recently made itself a playa by hiring to tenure both Leigh Anne Duck and Martyn Bone. (The latter has now returned to Copenhagen, citing in part, and perhaps in jest, Mississippi's new law permitting guns in college classrooms.) Nancy Grayson's vision in establishing the present book series at the University of Georgia Press has largely bypassed the "professional southernist" roadblock; other series routinely send the work of those southernists to us. (We try to be gracious.) Still, in writing this book, I have come to realize that "southern exceptionalism" remains much more than an academic disciplinary division. It is loaded with identitarian and ideological fantasies about who "we" are, and those fantasies can literally disrupt critics' and historians' ability to comprehend a scholarly argument. Moreover, by their very nature, those fantasies don't necessarily go away, even should the scholars on the conscious, logical level no longer endorse them.

This is why, I argue in the chapters that follow, "dynamiting the rails" of old southern studies didn't work, and why I advocate "shooting the jukebox" (disrupting the fundamental fantasy, as explained in chapter 1) instead. But this book is more about shooting the jukebox of American cultural studies. Almost a decade after Houston Baker and Dana Nelson decried southern exceptionalism in the preface to their special issue of *American Literature* on "Violence, the Body, and 'The South,'" Donald Pease published his book *The New American Exceptionalism*, which included a chapter about Roland Emmerich's rather obviously execrable Mel Gibson movie *The Patriot* and what Pease called the film's "Southernification of America." Pease never addresses the film's admittedly laughable attempts to distance its white southern landowner from slavery (the black laborers on the Revolutionary-era plantation owned by Gibson's character turn out to be free, paid employees! Who knew?), and to have its one (!) token racist, played by poor Donal Logue, learn to respect his one (!) token black co-rebel. But Pease isn't angry at such whitewashing. He's angry that the film "ostensibly restaged the emergence of the American nation within a geographical region that had formerly been all but excluded from the national symbolic order" (145). To be clear: he isn't even angry here at the national shame of slavery, racism, and segregation. He's angry that the film refuses to shame the region itself. In Pease's vision, "the South" is simply a "discredited region" (147) with a "discredited history" (147), an exceptional impurity that must be expelled, "excluded from the national symbolic order," and the horror of the film is that—*even though, however ridiculously and anachronistically, it explicitly condemns slavery and racism*—it "produced a fantasy that was designed to transmute the South from a discredited region to an exemplary geographical space" (147). Thus a book intended to critique "American exceptionalism" ends up embodying it.

It became clear to me that the proper response to this sort of thing could not be, yet again, to direct Pease to Baker and Nelson's essay, nor to Duck's *The Nation's Region*, nor to Greeson's *Our South*, nor to Matthew Lassiter and Joseph Crespino's excellent collection of historical essays *The Myth of Southern Exceptionalism*, which neatly takes down the whole "southernization" metaphor. Rather, I realized I needed to know what it is about "the South" that could so agitate a brilliant Americanist as to lead him into the same fallacy he had spent much of his career debunking. In Lacanian terms, what I wanted to know was the object-cause of Pease's desire. That desire, of course, is interesting not because it is peculiar to Pease but because it seems so expressive of many New Americanists' (baby boomers') continuing drive, in order to cling in fantasy (as "Americanists"?) to the very exceptional nation they consciously reject, to disavow "the South" as what Baker and Nelson called "an outland where 'we' know they live: all those guilty, white yahoos who just don't like people of color" (Baker and Nelson 235). For American studies not to keep getting blindsided over and over again by things like the 2004 and 2010 elections, however, we all need to see the nation in its senseless actuality: the reactionary suburban meat-and-potatoes Orange County tedium alongside the exciting urban gumbo of L.A.; racial and religious conservatism not expelled to a disavowed "South" but virtually everywhere. As the one segment of the nation that, despite its 100 million inhabitants, finds itself "all but excluded from the national symbolic order," or at least the New Americanists' version thereof, the South quite precisely tends to assume the place of the national Real. This is why, in refusing boomer disavowal of "the South," the new southern studies is ultimately neither a "critical regionalism" (yawn) nor a rebellion against old southern studies (yawn) but an attempt to fix a broken American studies, to disrupt boomer *Americanist* enjoyment of their symptom.

And it is, for the most part, a peculiarly boomer enjoyment. The very righteousness that provoked anger over civil rights abuses in those leftish boomers who eventually became academics, as opposed to the tut-tutting "can't legislate morality" attitude of many whites in the earlier George Herbert Walker Bush generation, seems to make it difficult for many boomers to look at the South, half a century later, in its senseless actuality; conversely, their tendency (observed by Lawrence Grossberg, among others) to see themselves as a generation of perpetual youth forever rebelling radically against The Man (Perry Miller, Gene Wise, etc.) seems to make it hard for them to step back and see how, as they alternately overlook, and look angrily at, Flyover Country, they appear to the generation of middle-aged people younger than they—a generation whose greatest achievement, if it comes about, will be, I argue in chapter three, simply to act like grownups rather than yet another narcissistic "youth culture." Of course, as I also argue, those Xers' generally more tolerant attitude toward the white South, enabled by their having no memory of Jim Crow and linked at least in part to the rather schlocky 1990s phenomena of alt-country and the hipster rehabilitations of Johnny Cash, Loretta Lynn, Merle Haggard, and so on, can reflect problematic fantasies of their own. I try to shoot that jukebox, too.

So this has become a book about fantasies. But it is also, I hope, a book about relative rationality and realism, about ways of living in modernity with Ruben Studdard, William Faulkner, and the older Neko Case instead of escaping into pre- or postmodern fantasy with the neo-agrarians, the religious Right, Johnny Cash, the L.A. school, or the editors of *American Quarterly*. Certainly this book was itself written in several different modernities. I drafted most of it while living in Birmingham, Alabama, and teaching at the University of Montevallo, but its overall concept gelled, and the composition began in earnest, in Dortmund, Germany, while I was on a Fulbright at Universität Dortmund and Ruhr-Universität Bochum. I finished it in Vancouver, British Columbia, on a very, very nice iMac looking out over Arthur Erickson's great midcentury modern garden at the center of the Academic Quadrangle of Simon Fraser University. When in Alabama I wrote a chapter somewhat critical of Pacific Northwest Gen X hipsters' "ironic" appropriation of country music, I never expected to find myself not merely living in Vancouver, but working in a department dominated by nearly two dozen very stylish Gen X assistant and associate professors. Something is definitely up when half your colleagues wear Fluevogs to work. I want to thank all the SFU English colleagues who supportively attended the talk I gave from chapter 1 in a departmental colloquium (and from chapter 5 as my job talk!) and who gave useful feedback, especially Susan Brook ("you're critiquing hipness and you're using *Žižek*?") and Anne Higgins. Special thanks go to the members of the Vancouver Lacan Salon, especially to geographer Paul Kingsbury and my English department colleague Clint Burnham, both of whom gave detailed and helpful readings of the most obviously Lacanian chapters of the book, those on Johnny Cash and the religious Right. Clint's comments on Slavoj Žižek on our runs up the Grouse Grind were also much appreciated, not least because they allowed me simply to focus on breathing. My colleague Christine Kim, an Asian Canadianist, "got" the project so well that she seemed to confirm my sense that people will comprehend this book in inverse proportion to how invested they are in the dominant fantasies of American studies or southern studies. On the other hand, she's also just really smart.

Further afield, my sister Alex Johnston put me up while I was doing fashion research at the library of the V&A Museum in London, while my cousin Ray York put me up while I was doing fieldwork in New York City. Jennifer Greeson and Russ Castronovo provided extremely generous feedback on two different versions of the introduction, and at a crucial point as I was grappling with reader reports late in the process, Jennifer, in a single eminently sensible phone call, got me back on track and, I think, made it possible for me to finish the project. Leigh Anne Duck, Martyn Bone, Cole Hutchison, and Scott Romine commented helpfully on both an early version of the introduction and the Johnny Cash chapter; Scott and Cole also helpfully responded to the religion chapter. Lisa Hinrichsen shared an excellent bibliography on trauma and melancholy that greatly strengthened the start of the Johnny Cash chapter. Riché Richardson and Katie McKee were, I believe, the only ones in the audience when I presented a very early version of the Ruben Studdard chapter on an 8:30 a.m. panel at one Society for the Study of Southern Literature convention; I appreciate their feedback, and, goodness knows, their company. Barbara Ching was a tremendously helpful and supportive reader of multiple drafts of the Neko Case chapter, and I wish to thank the University of Michigan Press for permission to reprint large parts of it; I also want to thank my four-time Montevallo undergraduate student Matt Roth for directing my attention to LCD Soundsystem. In addition, I wish to thank the students at the University of Montevallo as a whole: not only for the College Night dedication, which will always be the greatest honor of my career, but for being generally delightful people. Those were a good, if busy, five years. They were even busier for my colleagues Kathy King, Glenda Conway, and Glenda Weathers, who, when the administration refused to pay for an adjunct, *took over my classes for the final eight weeks of the spring 2005 semester* so I could take the Fulbright, which, because of the German academic calendar, began in March. Also at Montevallo, librarians Kathy Lowe and Rosemary Arneson helped me track down the photo of Ruben and Kristic Morgan Frazier, and they helped me overcome many of the challenges of working at a university without a research library. The University of Alabama, Birmingham library a mile from my house restricted me to ten books at a time and a two-week checkout period, but the book could not have been written without that access, and I am grateful for it. Scott Romine, Randy Boyagoda, Katie Henninger, and Deb Cohn all helped with the Great *Parade* Magazine Ad Hunt, responding to an email I sent on a hunch asking, "Hey, what's on the inside back cover of your *Parade* magazine today?" (Back then people still read newsprint.) The William Faulkner chapter benefited from comments by Richard Godden, Jack Matthews, and Judith Sensibar, who in particular directed me to references to fashion in Faulkner's letters. I thank the University Press of Mississippi for permission to reprint a large chunk of that chapter.

A quarter century ago, Pat Gill courageously and untenuredly taught the first cultural studies graduate course at the University of Virginia, and she shaped an entire generation of us a great deal more than the old boys then regnant ever did. Thanks, Pat. Immediately after grad school, I had the tremendous good fortune to be mentored by Gordon Hutner and Dale Bauer during a year's lectureship at the University of Wisconsin. It's an odd thing to say about a guy who works on good-but-not-great fiction, but Gordon's taste and high standards—for example, the vigor with which he once declared that the last thing *ALH* wanted was "another reading of 'Rappaccini's Daughter'"—have had a lasting impact on my own. They have also rendered me somewhat obnoxious to the sort of scholar who cranks out readings of "The Bear."

The experience of fighting for, and starting to attain, a place at the table tends to bond people pretty tightly, and over the years when things were not so easy (most of this book was written while I was teaching a 4–4 load, half of it freshman comp, and making less than $40,000 a year) I have drawn *tremendous* support from the group known sometimes by its detractors as the Puerto Vallarta Mafia (a.k.a. *la cosa nuestra*), after the 2002 conference there on postcolonial theory, the U.S. South, and new world studies, and sometimes (by those who enjoy irony) as what Tara McPherson dubbed us at the 2005 American Studies Association convention in Washington: the Radical Fringe Caucus of the Society for the Study of Southern Literature, or the RFC for short. Among senior folk, I want to thank Houston Baker, Patsy Yaeger, and Fred Hobson for their often vehement support, their intellectual rigor, and—especially in Patsy's and Fred's case—their letters of recommendation; though as this book makes clear, we sometimes disagree, I owe to them the fact I have had a career at all. Nancy Grayson is by far the best editor I have ever worked with. I am grateful to her vision some years ago regarding the need for this book series, which I believe has turned out rather well; for her support; and for her encouragement near the end of the project when the religion chapter seemed as though it would never be done. She has done more for the field of southern studies than all but a few scholars in it, and I am in awe. Among the RFC, I want to thank in particular Scott Romine (my best intellectual foil and a true friend despite his obvious Hobbesianism), Deb Cohn (for more than a decade of friendship), Leigh Anne Duck, Tara McPherson, Riché Richardson, Jack Matthews, Melanie Benson Taylor, George Handley, Jennifer Greeson, Adam Gussow, Katie McKee (whose floor I slept on countless times when I couldn't afford a hotel for the Faulkner conference), Annette Trefzer, Martyn Bone (whose floor I slept on in Nottingham and more than once in Copenhagen, where I could never afford a hotel), Judith Jackson Fossett, Katie Henninger, Hosam Aboul-Ela, Harry Stecopoulos, Cole Hutchison, and Bruce Brasell. They are staggeringly good company, and remain funnier and, for now, much better looking than most academics. Though not RFCers, I also want to thank—speaking of funny and good looking—my friends Christine Gerhardt, Jeanne Cortiel, Wolfgang Niehues, and Walter Grünzweig, who made Dortmund wonderful; my former Montevallo colleague and best-friend-at-work Kate Koppelman, now at Seattle University; and my wife Gail, best friend, period, through more than I can say. These people have made me happy when skies were gray, and I dedicate this book, quite insufficiently, to them.

FINDING PURPLE AMERICA

INTRODUCTION
What *Does* an American Studies Scholar Want?

What does it mean to be hip in the twenty-first century? If you're a baby boomer, particularly in academia, you may still think it has something to do with vocal countercultural politics, with sex, drugs, and rock 'n' roll, with rebelling against squares like Dwight Eisenhower and, say, Perry Miller. If you're an Xer (a term few use anymore), on the other hand, that whole thing has probably long looked kind of played. Back in the 1990s there's a good chance you read Douglas Coupland's *Generation X*, with its bitterness toward "bleeding ponytails" and other "sold-out" boomers who had succeeded simply through "fortunate birth" (21); you listened to Nirvana make fun of the Youngbloods' "Get Together"; and you tried to make cool all sorts of things the boomers had found square or otherwise offensive: country music, swing dancing, Mel Tormé, trucker hats, Skynyrd. And if you're a millennial, you probably spent more of the past decade than necessary loitering on hipster-bashing websites, from the pioneering, defunct *New York City Anti-Hipster Forum* (www.hipstersareannoying.com) up through *Look at This Fucking Hipster* (www.latfh.com). An abbreviated dialectic of the past forty years of hipness might look like this: hipness was hip, then unhipness was hip, now hipness itself is unhip.

Yet if you work in American cultural studies and are younger than fifty, like me you probably found it easier in your professional work to support the boomer project rather than continuing, as they had done, your own project of youthful rebellion and critique. Perhaps without fully realizing it, you too may well have made the Birmingham school's idea of Subcultures Resisting the Mainstream through Rituals into your own project of Countercultures Resisting the Man through Rituals; your work, you may have told yourself as you prospered in a difficult job market, constituted radical activism, and, like the New Americanists, you argued fiercely with those dead squares who had believed in American exceptionalism (Smith, "Postcolonial" 145; Smith and

Cohn, introduction 12). You were happy when your article on, say, Filipinas who resisted U.S. empire by making subversive textiles appeared in *American Quarterly*[1] and happier still when your Duke book on the same subject earned you tenure at a coastal research university. You were part of a generation that busily confirmed boomer insights that race matters, boundaries are problematic, and cyberspace offers possibilities for self-creation and subversion. When in 2009 an ad in *AQ* for membership in the American Studies Association declared that ASA "MEMBERS GET IT," you knew they were talking about you.

From a twenty-first-century perspective, however, this self-congratulatory "cool kids" ethos, derived (I will argue) from a simplification of Birmingham school principles and part of the reason for the past decade's exodus from the ASA of so many who work on places and times that don't fit a Centre for Contemporary Cultural Studies model, looks decidedly uncool. But I do not mean in what follows to supplant boomer American studies' tendency to reify (its own) 1960s-style hipness by shallowly reifying 2010s-style hipness, by offering up post-hipness as the Next Big Thing. Nor do I mean to denigrate the field's oft-stated commitment to social justice. My concern is that, with the exception of the Ruthie Gilmores and Angela Davises of this world, the most meaningful social justice work performed in the field is being done primarily by unglamorous people teaching critical thinking skills to first-generation college students, evangelical Christians, rural African Americans, and other graduates of horrible school systems out there in Flyover Country, working to make, as one former president of the University of Montevallo liked to put it, "a more enlightened Alabama." One doesn't hear from such folk— professional subalterns don't speak—in large part because they are too busy each semester teaching four courses and marking hundreds of compositions. In the ever more rarefied portions of contemporary American cultural studies where people actually have time to write—time usually obtained by exploiting the ever-growing ranks of part-time and graduate teaching labor— such a commitment is much more likely to operate, as in the arts, chiefly as a structure of feeling.[2] I thus want to examine, and maintain some critical distance from, the ways such disciplinary structures of feeling shape what we do.

I take such structures to be the fundamental piece missing from Russ Castronovo and Susan Gillman's generally solid critique of the field in the introduction to their recent essay collection, *States of Emergency*. "What," ask Castronovo and Gillman,

> does an American studies scholar want? At first glance, the answer is nothing sexy: theory and practice. But a closer look at alternative approaches to the field provided by this volume suggests that our desires to merge theory and practice, our fantasy to make our objects of study coincide with our political goals or objects, might be rather risqué. (3)

"What does an American studies scholar want?" of course echoes Sigmund Freud's famous "What does woman want?" For their opening question (they call it an "opening salvo"), "What is the object of American studies?" (1), I would therefore substitute a more psychoanalytic one: what is the *objet a* of American studies? What is it we take pleasure in continually circling without ever achieving? What is it, as Jacques Lacan would say, that is in those subversive textile makers, those medium-subverting Sauk Indian photographers and Asian American dramatists, those resistant Guatemalan peasants, those poor white country music makers in their trailers outside Austin, more than they are themselves? At first glance, irony notwithstanding, Castronovo and Gillman seem to answer *their* question with their own rhetoric: an American studies scholar wants to feel sexy, the subject of risqué fantasy: more, she or he wants sexy, militant, salvo-firing politics. If so, however, then Castronovo and Gillman have not moved past familiar boomer affect. (How many times, after all, have boomer scholars celebrated the putative transgressiveness of their own desires, the magical Marcusan convergence of self-indulgence and "praxis"?) And until we do get past it, I would argue, we will make no serious progress in either our theory or our practice.

To analyze our disciplinary structures of feeling, I will use Lacan a lot. I don't use him because over the past quarter century Slavoj Žižek has performed the remarkable feat of rendering the deliberately difficult French analyst trendy, even hip. Quite the reverse: I use Lacan because, properly understood, his style of psychoanalysis is poison for narcissism, for the radical or radical-chic posturings of hipsters of all ages. As Sherry Turkle argued a full decade before Žižek ever appeared on the scene, for Lacan "the role of both analyst and analytic theorist is to unrelentingly confront people with a vision of psychoanalysis as the unacceptable, the discourse that subverts everyday securities." And quite a few Americanist securities (to return to Castronovo and Gillman) look different if we shift the discussion, as Lacan would have us do, from desire to underlying drive. From a Lacanian perspective, we don't really derive pleasure from obtaining the object of our desire, we derive pleasure from getting all worked up about our desire, from the anxiety of not having the object, and what we fear is not "missing" the object but losing the excitation in us that circling it without ever attaining it provokes. The real goal is to feel something, even something as seemingly unpleasant as anger or melancholy, rather than nothing. From such a perspective, what American studies scholars want these days is precisely to live and work in a "state of emergency," and it doesn't matter whether we are in "crisis" because, as the New Americanists have been arguing in various forms for two decades (it's apparently a long crisis), the field is "divided between its original nationalist focus on the United States and new interests in the interrelations of the different nations and cultures of the western hemisphere" (Rowe 1), or because, as Castronovo and Gillman quite rightly argue in more modern form, "inclusiveness . . . [has] become a substitution for methodology" (3), or even because, as they also quite rightly argue, "the posture of critique has become an endgame, a substitute for self-criticism" (13). The irrelevance of the particular object of desire, the particular excuse for getting worked up, is why I wrote "subject" rather than "object" of risqué fantasy above: when we say someone's work is "sexy," what we desire is not that work (or the person doing it); what we really like is that it makes us feel desiring, agitated, stimulated. This is what drives want: not the goal, but the endless circling thereof. Try to imagine anyone getting major career traction—or even just a friendly reception at the annual ASA convention—by arguing that we are *not* in a state of crisis, for example, and you'll see what I mean. Nobody wants closure; the crisis fantasy has become central to our symbolic order: to how we work and, more fundamentally, how we work to feel about our work. In old southern studies, meanwhile, the crisis fantasy is about "forgetting"; we are supposed to be endlessly agitated about the loss of "memory" and hence "identity."

If you happen to work in new southern studies, your position between and outside these competing fantasies—one looking anxiously forward, the other anxiously backward—may not have been great for your career (since career advancement tends to depend on one's participating in more or less the same fantasies as peer reviewers and hiring and tenure committees, or at least on being able to fake it), but it has given you a bit of useful perspective. After all, such agitation is the precise opposite of what scholars, like analysands, are supposed to aspire to: we are supposed to learn to look at the world "in its senseless actuality," as Žižek likes to put it (*Looking Awry* 35), not fill it with our libidinal investments, our enjoyment. The reason is simple epistemology: you cannot act reasonably, and you are much less likely to succeed in enacting a progressive agenda (if that's your thing), if your actions are overdetermined by fantasy. Fantasy and enjoyment still lie within the pages of the present book, of course—it cannot be otherwise, and, as they say in *The Hipster Handbook*, "baby boomer bashing is fun" (Lanham 159). (So, as it turns out, are other forms of bashing.) Still, the book is intended, at least, as a scholarly exercise in Taking It Down a Notch.

It won't be universally received as such. The first section, "Disrupting Everyone's Enjoyment," is designed to do just that—and to do so "unrelentingly," as Turkle would say. The chapters in that section deal with (1) practitioners of old southern studies and recent enthusiasts of melancholy in contemporary theory and ethnography; (2) U.S. Christian fundamentalists; and (3) alt-country fans and performers (and Gen X more broadly). Though a very large segment of the United States and of academe, this of course still does not comprise "everyone," but I hope the chapters address a sufficiently wide range of subjects that one can see how their approach might be extended more broadly. The politics of this disruptive critical move have gotten more complicated in the twenty years since Žižek brought it to our attention in *Looking Awry*'s (8–9) famous reading of the Patricia Highsmith story, "Black House." In the story, a young engineer moves to a small town where all the men speak in awe of a "black house" outside town. The engineer goes to visit the house, and finds it's . . . just a house, that there is "nothing mysterious or fascinating about it" (Žižek, *Looking Awry* 9). When he announces this to the assembled men, one attacks him, he falls, and he dies. "The 'black house,'" Žižek explains,

> was forbidden to the men because it functioned as an empty space wherein they could project their nostalgic desires, their distorted memories; by publicly stating that the "black house" was nothing but an old ruin, the young intruder reduced their fantasy space to everyday, common reality. He annulled the difference between reality and fantasy space, depriving the men of the place in which they were able to articulate their desires. (9)

In early Žižek, such an act is generally heroic, aligned with the demystifying function of the analyst herself or himself. Later, Žižek grows a bit suspicious of this sort of heroism, and asks whether the child saying the new-clothed emperor is actually naked (the folktale closest to describing the disruption of a community's fundamental fantasy) isn't, in fact, generating a disaster. By *Living in the End Times*, disrupting someone's enjoyment even carries more than a whiff of Puritanism:

> Leftist libertarians see enjoyment as an emancipatory power: every oppressive power has to rely on libidinal repression, and the first act of liberation is to set the libido free. Puritan Leftists are, on the contrary, inherently suspicious of enjoyment: for them, it is a source of corruption and decadence, an instrument used by those in power to maintain their hold over us, so that the first act of liberation is to break its spell. The third position is that taken by [Alain] Badiou: *jouissance* is the nameless "infinite," a neutral substance which can be instrumentalized in a number of ways. (373)

(Žižek is himself taking it down a notch from Badiou, who with Gallic sweep had divided things into not "leftist libertarians" and "Puritan leftists" but, respectively, "the West" and "terrorists" ["Subject of Art"].)

I mention all this because, while I'm not a terrorist and I'm not sure I'm a "Puritan" leftist, I am certainly suspicious of academic enjoyment. I have reason to be. Žižek's own observation that "in our permissive times, when transgression itself is appropriated—even encouraged—by the dominant institutions, the predominant doxa as a rule presents itself as a subversive transgression" (*Did Somebody Say Totalitarianism?* 141) if anything applies even better to American cultural studies than to (as Thomas Frank has exhaustively argued) the culture at large. As many have noted, the past quarter century of cultural studies has seen boomer claims that everything from adultery (Kipnis) to watching soap operas with your daughter (Rapping) represents some kind of subversive transgression. Southern studies, on the other hand, has spent a much longer time conversely asking whether, as a result of modernity's instability, we have not Lost Something Very Important. (As I'll argue in the following chapter, this is a question designed never to be answered, so that it can be asked over and over and over again, which is where the enjoyment lies.) Even if these old forms of enjoyment once served a constructive scholarly purpose (I'm not sure they did), American studies and southern studies have been stuck in them for so long now that just about all of us in those fields under fifty (and, of course, a few over that age) have at some point felt a bit like Highsmith's young engineer, plopped down in the midst of a community overdetermined by fantasies, obsessions, and enthusiasms we not only don't share but can't in good faith ever bring ourselves to share.[3] So although the first part of this book is likely to anger people in direct proportion to how personally and professionally invested they are in enjoying their dominant disciplinary fantasy, what I really hope to have done is to have taken the sort of critique so many of us no-longer-young folks have been making over beers at our fields' conferences over the past few years—after yet another "radical" presidential address at the American Studies Association convention (almost always by someone with tenure and a six-figure income passionately insisting that the only thing standing between us and a return to the 1950s is a few more articles about subversive textiles)[4] or yet another celebration of "memory" at the Society for the Study of Southern Literature convention—and to ground that critique (to instrumentalize that enjoyment, if you will) in a sufficiently rigorous academic discourse that we can, perhaps, finally start to move on. Of course, I assume that future scholars will move beyond my (perhaps our) own enjoyment, the sooner the better. The aim of this book is at best to help break an impasse, not to establish a new order.

Although I use a lot of Lacan—and I will say more on disrupting enjoyment in the following chapter—I also draw heavily on two other traditions. The first is marketing theory because, I will argue, what we choose to "work" on as scholars is, perhaps paradoxically, more closely linked to the anxieties that drive people's consumption preferences than to any particular account of production. The second is the troublingly neglected strand of cultural studies that emerged in the iconoclastic 1990s work of Thomas Frank and Sarah Thornton. Thornton's icy characterization in *Club Cultures* of hipness as "subcultural capital" and Frank's discussion in *The Conquest of Cool* (and in his early essays for *The Baffler*) of coolness as always already owned by capitalism are, I think, fundamental to any attempt to move beyond the "cool kids" ethos American studies borrowed from (its imagined version of) the Birmingham school. (Though I will draw on its methodology less, the same must be said for Susan Fraiman's excellent 2003 book *Cool Men and the Second Sex*.) Yet I will also contend that (outside the work of Frank and Thornton, and particularly in pop culture) a 1990s Gen X sensibility too often replicated the very structure of feeling it thought it was repudiating. Things get more interesting in the 2000s, I argue, when Xers start to move beyond youth-cultural fantasies to celebrate quietly what, if this were a trade book and the phrase didn't already elicit 31,000 Google hits, I might dub The New Adulthood.

The second section, most of which was written first, is both less ambitious and less likely to disrupt anyone's enjoyment. Insofar as they tend to celebrate enjoyment and focus on the politics of cultural forms that don't, in fact, have much political impact—forms of resistance through rituals— the chapters in part II model a relatively old-fashioned, or at least uncontroversial, form of cultural studies. But there is a twist, however small, and it's a twist that derives from my background in new southern studies, that is, from my position as a relative outsider to both mainstream American cultural studies and mainstream southern studies. From that position, the *objets a* of both fields, the things that tend to get them excited, tend to look not like opposites—space versus place, the postmodern versus the premodern, fashion versus anti-fashion, self-invention versus fixed identity, the metropolis versus the province, cyberpunk versus the Southern Renascence, blue states versus red states, *Gesellschaft* versus *Gemeinschaft*, and so on—but like mirror images of each other, twin forms of antimodern fantasy. (Think of the redemptive functions of Dick Hebdige's notion of "subculture" in *Subculture: The Meaning of Style* [1979] and John Shelton Reed's in *The Enduring South: Subcultural Persistence in Mass Society* [1975] as both occupying the same place in the structure of the symbolic order.) So in these chapters, rather than dashing into the Westin Bonaventure or gobbling down potlikker—rather than embracing those aspects of the present that seem either to promise exciting glimpses of the future or to circle comforting residua of the past—I try to examine scenes in which people navigate conflicting tugs in both directions. This is the ambiguous, ambivalent set of alternative modernities—neither L.A. nor Mayberry—in which I live, even up here in hip, sublime Vancouver, and I suspect it's where most other North Americans live too. Although I focus on "my" Birmingham and William Faulkner's Memphis, I thus hold that my arguments work for most of the rest of the continent as well. Even if you live in L.A., you probably don't live in the "L.A." of the imagination of postmodern geographers; and even if you live in Mt. Airy, North Carolina—Andy Griffith's hometown model for Mayberry—you probably don't live in the South of the imagination of old southern studies. You live in between. And that's okay.

Disavowing Modernity

It's hardly controversial to note that, in the long wake of the Nashville agrarians, old southern studies has tended to define itself in opposition to fantasies of a disruptive, leveling modernity that intrudes from without, whether in the form of C. Vann Woodward's "bulldozer revolution," John Shelton Reed's "mass society," or Barbara Ladd's "national project of forgetting." Ladd herself rightly identifies the agrarian project as itself "a late-modernist critique of modernity" (1629), and I address the melancholia underlying this attitude, and its peculiarly durable replication across generations, at length in the following chapter. But it's also not terribly controversial to observe that American cultural studies has tended to reject modernity too, albeit from the other direction. "Sifting through the ever-expanding pile of samplers, summaries, introductions, and overviews of cultural studies," writes Rita Felski,

> one is easily persuaded that it is a field devoted entirely to the immediate present. . . . It is a field that is adamantly yoked to the new and the now, a method matched to its own moment, an approach tied to the epochal uniqueness of our own image-saturated, consumption-crazed, globally connected yet politically fragmented age. Since the mid-1980s, the lure of the word "postmodern" has proved almost irresistible; when "modernity" appears at all in cultural studies, it is often there to be refuted, derided, or denounced, a handy catch phrase for conservative politics, old hat metaphysics, and snobbish aesthetics. (501)

Michael Denning has rightly noted that "perhaps the central concept in the revival of American studies over the last two decades has been that of culture" (419), and it should not surprise anyone that at times the time and space and structure of feeling of American studies, too, seem to be folding into the time and space and structure of feeling of cultural studies described by Felski: not the present, but those aspects of the present that seem to promise exciting glimpses of the future; not the alternative modernities where things hang in the balance, but (our fantasies of) the hippest and most postmodern of urban metropoles. A 2004 issue of *American Quarterly*, for example, is entitled *Los Angeles Studies and the Future of Urban Cultures*; claiming the journal's move from an elite private university in Washington, D.C., to one in L.A. represents progress, the editors celebrate "the paradigmatic singularity and prognostic quality of metropolitan Los Angeles" (499). Yet such a claim makes just the fundamental error Arjun Appadurai warns against in *Modernity at Large*: the belief that "your present is their future (as in much modernization theory and in many self-satisfied tourist fantasies)" (31). Both politically and conceptually, the stakes of marginalizing the alternative spaces and places between the coasts—or within the Southern California "Southland" itself—are high. At the American Studies Association convention in Atlanta just after the 2004 elections, one German scholar asked, a bit plaintively, a bit rhetorically, whether any panel on the program could help explain the vote.[5] Four years later, the electoral triumph of California's Proposition 8 caught quite a few of us off guard as well. *Do* ASA members get it?

In calling out the field's tendencies toward urban, blue state narcissism[6] (which *is* still something of a step up from its earlier New England narcissism!), I am not interested here in merely restating the important (and largely ignored) arguments Barbara Ching and Gerald W. Creed made more than a decade ago in their introduction to *Knowing Your Place: Rural Identity and Cultural Hierarchy* about how cultural studies marginalizes the rural. Rather, I wish, loosely following Néstor García Canclini's work on Latin American "hybrid cultures" (206–63) in ways that might be expected of someone with a background in "hemispheric American studies," to question the urban/rural binarism itself. Certainly Ching and Creed's complaint that "in much postmodern social theory, the country as a vital place simply doesn't exist" (7) is as true—and relevant—now as ever. From my perspective, however, a greater concern is that scholars have found very few ways to talk about the vitality of spaces and places that lie—in scale, temporality, hipness, and consumption patterns, if not in literal geography—somewhere *between* Los Angeles and, say, Lockhart, Texas, the location featured in Aaron A. Fox's contribution to *Knowing Your Place* (or, for that matter, even to talk about spaces and places figuratively between Lockhart and its neighbor, überhip Austin, even as much of Austin's hipness derives from the borrowed authenticity of places like Lockhart). Instead, scholarship has tended to perpetuate surprisingly essentialized versions of Raymond Williams's ideological categories of the country and the city.

What Scholars Want: Consuming "Populist Worlds"

What is the appeal of these antimodern escapes? Until recently, subcultures, countercultures, and "the South," especially in their object manifestations, have also fulfilled for the academics who study them much the same function as what marketing theorist Douglas B. Holt calls populist worlds, whence come all iconic brands. "Icons," Holt writes, "come to represent a particular kind of story—an *identity myth*—that their consumers use to address identity desires and anxieties. Icons have extraordinary value because they carry a heavy symbolic load for their most enthusiastic consumers" (2). He goes on:

> Acting as vehicles of self-expression, the brands are imbued with stories that consumers find valuable in constructing their identities. Consumers flock to brands that embody the ideals they admire, brands that help them express who they want to be. The most successful of these brands become *iconic brands*. (3–4)

This iconicity derives in turn from the product's association with "populist worlds." Holt locates these "on the frontier, in bohemia communities, in rural backwaters, in immigrant and African American neighborhoods, [and] in youth subcultures" (59). Such worlds hold appeal, according to Holt, for the following reasons:

1. Populist worlds are perceived as "folk cultures"—their ethos is the collective and voluntary product of their participants. The ethos has not been imposed on them.
2. The activities within the populist world are perceived as intrinsically valuable to the participants. They are not motivated by commercial or political interests.
3. Reinforcing these perceptions, populist worlds are often set in places far removed from centers of commerce and politics. For worlds that have been commercialized (sports and music are key examples), these populist perceptions are much harder to maintain because the participants must fight off the commercial attributions. (58–59)

Like consumers, both conservative and progressive cultural scholars can tend to talk less about the "real" world than about populist ones, the sources of myths with which they desire to affiliate themselves. When in 1962, at the height of the civil rights movement, Louis D. Rubin Jr., paraphrasing the Nashville agrarians, described the South as "a society . . . in which leisure, tradition, aesthetic and religious impulses had not been lost in the pursuit of economic gain" and "a needed corrective to America's head-long materialism" ("Introduction" xxv), he was describing not the real world but a populist one, a potent source of identity myths for a certain sort of tweedy, out-of-touch, and very white mandarin.[7] What could be further from the aims of the hip urban editors of that recent special issue of *American Quarterly*? Yet here is Mike Davis, writing in 1990, on the L.A. school:

[B]y hyping Los Angeles as the paradigm of the future (even in a dystopian vein), [the "L.A. school" tends] to collapse history into teleology and glamorize the very reality they would deconstruct. [Edward] Soja and [Fredric] Jameson, particularly, in the very eloquence of their different "postmodern mappings" of Los Angeles, become celebrants of the myth. The city is a place where everything is possible, nothing is safe and durable enough to believe in, where constant synchronicity prevails, and the automatic ingenuity of capital ceaselessly throws up new forms and spectacles—a rhetoric, in other words, that recalls the hyperbole of [Herbert] Marcuse's *One-Dimensional Man*. (86)

Raúl Homero Villa and George J. Sánchez, the editors of the special issue, cite Davis, but manage to read him as saying exactly the opposite of this, adopting him against his will into the L.A. school "family": "Mike Davis, who is something of an outlaw cousin to the L.A. school proper, ascribes just such a prophetic quality to the study of Los Angeles in the title and method of his well-known book *City of Quartz: Excavating the Future in Los Angeles*" (499). For Villa and Sánchez as for Rubin, and for the hundreds of scholar-consumers in their fields who read their arguments without any sense that something is radically amiss, identitarian investment in a distinction-bestowing populist world must be strong indeed.[8]

American studies' present affinity for such worlds is not limited to one special issue of the field's flagship journal. For the next several years, nearly all of *American Quarterly*'s subsequent "cover stories," no doubt like many of the preceding ones, would take place in some sort of populist world (except, of course, the "rural backwater"): the frontier (Cadillac Ranch, March 2005; Legal Borderlands, September 2005; the Little Bighorn battlefield, December 2006), queer bohemia (lesbian pulp fiction, June 2005; the lavender scare, December 2005), immigrant and African American neighborhoods (Chinese exclusion, March 2006; New Orleans's Ninth Ward, September 2006; Connecticut Chinese, June 2007), and a different bohemia (Christo's *The Gates*, June 2006).[9] In the December 2010 issue, the new editor of *AQ* summarizes that issue's essays, which are situated in immigrant and African American neighborhoods (Wright's *Native Son*, the Mexican American civil rights movement)[10] and the early American frontier ("sermons and confessions regarding the execution of Native Americans"). She praises *AQ*'s "extraordinarily diverse scholarship" (Banet-Weiser vi), even as she notes that "the essays in this volume [all] address . . . some of the intersections of race and the state, of cultures and borders." Completing a kind of rhetorical hat trick, she even maintains the crisis rhetoric: "as has been true in the past, American studies . . . faces a critical and exciting juncture" (vi).

The fantasy is hardly limited to American studies. In her "Editor's Note" in the recent "Almost All-Asian Issue" of *PMLA*, Patricia Yaeger revels in the populist world of, well, "Asia": "Three years ago I was teaching a course on cities at the University of Beijing and waxing ecstatic about the transgressiveness of contemporary Chinese art," she begins (553). To his or her credit, a Chinese student, noting the gentrification of a nearby "hip art district" famous for its association with briefly jailed artist Ai Weiwei, challenges her claims about that art's transgressiveness. Yaeger concedes that "the relation between aesthetics and politics on global and local scales is contaminated and vexed," but the mood quickly passes: "What better way to begin this issue," she goes on to exult, "than with a glimpse of an exuberant, naked, leaping Ai Weiwei—his legs and tummy flailing in space, his genitals covered with a stuffed animal" (554). "The world," Yaeger writes, "demanded Ai's bodily freedom (during his imprisonment the Tate Modern bore a sign on its façade: 'RELEASE AI WEIWEI')" (554). Of course, the Tate Modern is not so much a *vox* of the globe's *populi* as, like *PMLA*, an elite institution anxious about its disconnect from popular struggle: three years earlier, in another attempt to bridge this gap, the Tate had adorned its façade with the work of "street artists" from Europe, the United States, and Brazil.[11] In Yaeger's enjoying hands, the complexities of Ai's art and struggles become an updated version of the standard boomer narrative of a libidinal ("exuberant, naked") 1960s counterculture pitted against repressive 1950s conformity, here in the form of the "Communist Party Central Committee" (554). If Yaeger's reduction seems a stretch, a false equivalence, a narcissistic fantasy, what are we to make of her closing summons to radical activism in—where else?—the United States, a call that appears, out of nowhere, in the final sentence? "We need to work collectively to protect the rights of artists who lose their voice in China," she concludes, reaffirming our state of crisis, "*as well as the rights of citizens returning from prison in the United States who also lose a crucial voice: their right to vote*" (554, italics added). Asian issue or no, Americans, in the end it is, apparently, still all about *your* crisis.

Over the past twenty years most of us have gotten so used to these rallying cries that we have almost forgotten they were once daring rather than de rigueur. (Boomers, I suspect, still imagine them as daring.) But talk is cheap, and is it really progressive anymore—not to speak of "critical and exciting"—simply to produce and consume more articles in which artistic countercultures fight the man, and borders are shown to be problematic, and crises need immediate addressing, or to travel—in our scholarship and in our real life—to populist worlds to consume exciting, authentic, naked rebellious art? And does this sort of leisure class—leisure to write, leisure to travel—scholarship really effect political interventions, or does it function more like consumption choices that, in turn, help to maintain a certain structure of feeling, like shopping at Whole Foods (or, as one could also do at the time, receiving a "Limited Edition 3–D Ai Weiwei T-shirt by Ali Hossaini" in exchange for a one hundred-dollar donation to "Where Is Ai Weiwei")? Almost a decade earlier, in their introduction to *The Futures of American Studies* (note the title), Donald Pease and Robyn Wiegman had declared those titular futures to lie in affiliation with "new social movements" (15) and "socially transformative projects" (19) that in fact turned out to be . . . "the sixties counterculture" (17). Perhaps less a spatial world than a temporal one, "the sixties" nevertheless remains for many boomers the most powerful populist world of all; in such an imaginary, and regardless of whether New England or Los Angeles functions as the Americanist "paradigm," the imagined space and time of "the South" (whether as the displaced locus of a disavowed slavery or as the disavowed epicenter of repressive "fifties" racism, sexism, and conformity) remain something less than the objects of academic fandom.

But fandom, I've been arguing, shouldn't be the issue, and over the past decade, not coincidentally as post-boomers have moved into academe, strains of both cultural studies and southern studies have emerged that are arguably more sophisticated and certainly less fantastically, consumeristically invested in their objects of study. (*States of Emergency* may represent a slightly belated similar turn in American studies.) I am painting with a necessarily broad brush here. In both southern studies and cultural studies, the work of feminists and minority critics long ago complicated what in both cases was a largely white male narrative, and in southern studies, at least, there was always a minoritarian tradition of focusing on the "bad South," as Fred Hobson has put it. (One thinks, for example, of W. J. Cash or Hobson's own early, approbatory work on H. L. Mencken.) In cultural studies, too, Lawrence Grossberg, for example, spent most of the 1990s trying "to understand how the popular defines at least one set of the conditions of possibilities for the increasing appeal of a new conservatism" (*Dancing in Spite of Myself* 9). Yet it is much too easy to overstate the radicalness of many of these revisions, which frequently involve less a critical stance toward southernness or punk (say) than what Tara McPherson in the southern context calls "an easy old-school liberal humanism, most recently packaged as multiculturalism" (30), and which leaves the fundamental assumptions of the field largely untouched. In cultural studies, the otherwise excellent *Pretty in Punk*, by Gen Xer Laraine Leblanc, offers a classic example of a text that, while rightly critiquing the subculture from a feminist perspective, overwhelmingly allies itself with punk as a critique of modernity. In southern studies, as late as 2005, Barbara Ladd could, in the pages of *PMLA*, simultaneously declare race and gender the "most salient problematics" of southern studies and reinscribe southern exceptionalism: in her account, the South is different from (and by implication better than) the rest of the nation because of its resistance to the "national project of forgetting" (1630, 1637). And despite Ladd's stated desire not to "reify" the old categories, that resistance, we are told, still takes the form of "memory, history, place, family, kinship, and community" (1636).

Yet for increasing numbers of scholars in both disciplines, the 1980s are as dead as the 1960s. Whereas the affinity of leftist Birmingham school sociologists for punk, for example, was so strong that later scholars such as Rupert Weinzierl and David Muggleton could characterize such work as overinvested in "subcultural heroism" (6–7), some younger scholars have been much more critical than many of their CCCS predecessors of simple oppositions between putatively rebellious, "hip" subcultures and some alleged conformist, "square" mainstream. Hence, they have been much less likely to affiliate themselves with the former. "In thinking through [Pierre] Bourdieu's theories in relation to the terrain of youth culture," writes Sarah Thornton,

I've come to conceive of "hipness" as a form of *subcultural capital*. . . . Subcultural capital confers status on its owner in the eyes of the relevant beholder. In many ways it affects the standing of the young like its adult equivalent. Subcultural capital can be *objectified* or *embodied*. Just as books and paintings display cultural capital in the family home, so subcultural capital is objectified in the form of fashionable haircuts and well-assembled record collections (full of well-chosen, limited edition "white label" twelve-inches and the like). Just as cultural capital is personified in "good" manners and urbane conversation, so subcultural capital is embodied in the form of being "in the know," using (but not overusing) current slang and looking as if you were born to perform the latest dance styles. (11–12)

At least two points are worth noting here. First, if "for the baby boomers," as Grossberg argued back when Gen Xers could still be called twenty-somethings, "youth is something to be held onto by cultural and physical effort" (*We Gotta Get Out of This Place* 183), those Gen X scholars such as Thornton who are not invested in continuing the boomer project seem much less interested in such increasingly strained affiliation. Second, by the early twenty-first century, this scholarly critique of hipness as subcultural capital (and by implication as unimaginative and conformist, hence as *failing* to bestow meaningful distinction, in effect repositioning the subculture as a form of groupthink against which the scholar rebels) had itself crossed over into popular culture. 2003's *The Hipster Handbook* sets out to describe hipness quite precisely in the unflattering terms of subcultural capital, even listing acceptable haircuts (52–55) and mentioning limited-edition vinyl (32). A joke circulating on the Internet in the early 2000s, including a comment posted at *The New York City Anti-Hipster Forum*, asks the following: "How many hipsters does it take to screw in a light bulb? What . . . you don't know!?!"

Similarly, a new generation of southern studies scholars, and of southerners at large, has begun to turn away from its predecessors' striving for organic intellectualism. In 1988, Michael O'Brien could still argue that "the southern intellectual has masked his intellectuality in order to survive" in an anti-intellectual culture: "he has become folksy" (213). By 1999, however, after decades of neo-agrarian celebration of folkish community, a celebration that one might fairly call "southern cultural heroism," Scott Romine noted the nakedness of that emperor. In celebrating community, Romine dryly observed, Cleanth Brooks (and his neo-agrarian ilk) had "made a mistake so obvious that, like [Edgar Allan] Poe's purloined letter, it threatens to go unnoticed: the commonly held view of reality to which he refers is a fantasy and always has been. . . . [T]he first law of community . . . I take to be this: insofar as it is cohesive, a community will tend to be coercive" (*Narrative Forms* 2). Nine years later, he would declare the "real South" to be "the fake South, which . . . becomes the real South through the intervention of narrative" (*Real South* 9). In 2000, some years before assuming the editorship of *PMLA*, Patricia Yaeger similarly proclaimed she was "tired" of the "rather ordinary expectations about the South and what we will find in southern literature" (*Dirt and Desire* ix). No small number of the contributors to the 2002 collection *South to a New Place*—not least Romine and Amy J. Elias— similarly called attention to the *in*authenticity of various highly mediated aspects of southern cultures. My own essay in that volume dismissed such clichés of southern identity as place, community, and the presence of the past as kinds of object-cathexes, symptoms of a profound cultural narcissism, evidence of not a stable identity but—following Scott Romine and, for that matter, W. J. Cash—a desperate lack of it. The turn away from organicism was not, I argued, limited to academics. Looking at the punk roots both of the band Southern Culture on the Skids and of the broader 1990s phenomenon of southern surf guitar (Teisco Del Rey, Los Straitjackets, Man or Astroman?, the Penetrators, etc.), I concluded (with too much faith, I now believe, in the redemptive functions of subcultures) that "by foregrounding the arbitrariness of cultural codes, punk may—for those young white southerners alert to the implications—have freed white southern identity from its long, narcissistic gaze at its own ancestral navel" (95). More recent works such as Leigh Anne Duck's *The Nation's Region*, Jennifer Greeson's *Our South*, and Matthew Lassiter and Joseph Crespino's collection of historical essays *The Myth of Southern Exceptionalism* all explore the constitutive cultural work that disavowing "the South" has performed in the national imagination.

What has come to pass thus may be just what Fredric Jameson predicted as he contemplated an observation in *Cultural Studies* by Simon Frith:

"if, as variously suggested in this book, fans are 'popular' (or organic) intellectuals, [writes Frith,] then they may well have the same anxieties about being fans (and take comfort from the same myths) as the rest of us" (182). This is to underscore a peculiarly Derridean turn in the transformation of the "people" into "fans": where the first of these was a primary substance, calmly persisting in its essence, and exercising a powerful gravitational effect on the insubstantial intellectuals who fluttered near it, the new version opens up a hall of mirrors in which the "people" itself longs to be a "people" and be "popular," feels its own ontological lack, longs for its own impossible stability, and narcissistically attempts, in a variety of rituals, to recuperate a being that never existed in the first place. That would, to be sure, lead us on to a more psychoanalytic view of groups and ethnic conflict (perhaps along the lines proposed by Slavoj Žižek); but it would also considerably dampen the enthusiasm of popular intellectuals for a collective condition not much better than their own. ("On Cultural Studies" 43)

If scholars in the edgier quadrants of southern and cultural studies are now much less likely to be narcissistic "fans" of what they study, why do they keep studying it? The short answer is, I suspect and hope, to break the spell of narcissism that keeps people conceiving of their selves as lacks, thus remaining overinvested in the Next Big Radical Thing (for the hip) or the Lost Loved Object (for the melancholy white southerner). It might be said that the best cultural studies and southern studies (especially that sort of southern studies that tries to intervene in American studies) now aspire to serve as a kind of cultural therapy, often very much "along the lines proposed by Slavoj Žižek," but also along those proposed by Vamik Volkan. Anthropologist James Peacock, for example, makes this therapeutic aim clear at the beginning of his 2007 book *Grounded Globalism*, which suggests an incipient global orientation in the U.S. South may be able to mitigate or even heal the region's longstanding narcissistic insecurities:

> Among other things, grounding openness and global outreach in human-scale traditions and other regional norms can transform a crippling oppositional identity that has led the South or, at least, some southerners, to feel different from, opposed to, even scorned by the rest of the nation. (x)

Yet such therapy is also appropriate for the nation beyond merely "the South" and hip urban neighborhoods (where subcultural capital matters a bit too much), as it also may be for academics beyond cultural studies and southern studies. Quite precisely following Žižek, Houston A. Baker Jr. and Dana D. Nelson argue that

> [i]n order for there to exist a good union, there must be a recalcitrant, secessionist "splitter." To have a nation of "good," liberal, and innocent white Americans, there must be an outland where "we" know they all live: all the guilty, white yahoos who just don't like people of color. Slavoj Žižek has described this agreeable splitting and projection as the "kernel of pleasure" that organizes nationalism's joy in "wholeness." (235)

In such a vision, the new southern studies brings the national patient to terms with that patient's narcissism, its unhealthy acts of projection and introjection. It disrupts our smug national enjoyment. If the quest for populist worlds of pre-, post-, or antimodern subjects has been driven by a sense that the merely modern self presents a lack (often of authenticity) to be filled elsewhere—on the farm or in the perfect pair of vintage earrings, in the Philippines or among the Hopi, up in the old, weird Appalachia or down in the Delta—the best cultural and southern studies thus appear to work on behalf of others from something resembling a position of happiness or relative fulfillment. This therapeutic approach seems a large part of why so many of us find Žižek's older work—perhaps especially his fundamental, even banal, injunction in *Looking Awry* that "instead of running after the impossible, we must learn to consent to our common lot and to find pleasure in the trivia of our everyday life" (8)—so bracing.

Speaking thus of narcissism, fulfillment, and therapy suggests we have also reached the point in the opening chapter at which one is supposed to talk about oneself, to lay one's own identification cards on the table, as it were, in order to avoid the false "voice from nowhere" of much twentieth-century social science. I usually enjoy reading these brief accounts, perhaps especially in southern studies: I like reading about Houston Baker's childhood fears of the "Blue Man"; I laugh with Tara McPherson that she's named after *that* Tara; I feel with Patricia Yaeger when she writes that her "identities and sympathies, then, are all with the southern grotesque, having been one and known more than a few" (2), even as, knowing her, I fail to find the grounds for her alleged grotesquerie. (Notably, her account closely resembles the "vitriolic prologue" that begins *Pretty in Punk*.) Yet even in three of the best books about southern literature and culture of this young century, I worry that such accounts can wind up reinscribing kinds of essential southern identity that the books' own arguments work strenuously and productively against. As David Simpson cogently argues in *Situatedness, or, Why We Keep Saying Where We're Coming From*, situatedness offers "an instance of the governing rhetoric of late capitalist entrepreneurial culture," and "situatedness arguments . . . could be taken to imply a basic comfort with the terms of our culture, which only need to be twiddled around and polished up to produce positive outcomes" (245). For years, for example, even into the twenty-first century, the annual Southern Focus Polls conducted by the University of North Carolina's Odum Institute for Research in Social Science would ask respondents, in English, "Do you consider yourself a southerner, or not?" I cannot answer the question as posed. A little like the millions of mixed-race people who prior to 2000 had no category to check on the census, I find myself, no matter how I try, forced   disciplined—into a conceptual box that does not fit. Baker, McPherson, and Yaeger, for all their grievances with the region and its interpretive history, are all willing, in their autobiographical sections, to check "southerner."

Appadurai, by contrast, argues that "the past is now not a land to return to in a simple politics of memory. It has become a synchronic warehouse of cultural scenarios, a kind of temporal central casting, to which recourse can be taken as appropriate, depending on the movie to be made, the scene to be enacted, the hostages to be rescued" (30). So general a postmodern point is hardly unique to him. But even though Appadurai himself begins *Modernity at Large* with an account of his "own early life in Bombay" grounded in the body ("I begged my brother at Stanford [in the early 1960s] to bring me back blue jeans and smelled America in his Right Guard when he returned" [1]), I cannot in good faith do the same. If I pull out of central casting the big southern family on my father's side that would later appear to have walked en masse out of a Peter Taylor story (by the time they appeared so, however,

I was in graduate school and most of them were dead) and the trips in the Chevy II from Charlottesville down to visit that family in Greensboro and Roaring Gap, then I leave out my father's English first wife, my Caribbean-born English and Australian half-sisters, and my mother's family, once old New York money, now a decidedly middle-class assortment of racist Southern California fundamentalists. If I speak of attending a conservative southern all-boys' and nearly all-white prep school on scholarship, and hating it, I leave out attending Yale on scholarship, loving it, being shaped by it, feeling intellectually "at home" as I had never felt in "the South," and meeting my midwestern wife there. If I speak of Charlottesville's particularities, the nooks and crannies of Albemarle County where I would swim, bike, and run, I leave out my much greater childhood consumption of, and participation in, national and international mass culture: *Three's Company*, *Star Wars*, triathlon, punk.[12] And if I speak of "southern" at all, how do I register the colossal differences between Charlottesville and the Deep South where I taught for twelve years, the differences between Mississippi and Alabama, Birmingham and Atlanta, even the differences between adjacent Alabama counties, adjacent Birmingham suburbs?

And those are just the problems with "southern." Except for the punk reference, we haven't talked about "hip": how until recently I bought most of my clothes at charity and vintage shops in London and Barcelona and Antwerp and Copenhagen and New York, what that Gogol Bordello concert at the Nick was like (or, for the younger folk, that Dirty Projectors show at Richard's on Richards), where I "found" that kitchen table, how long I've subscribed to *Dwell*, where I got those *shoes*—but on the other hand knowing exactly where I was (the weight room at Marquette University in Milwaukee) when news came over Kurt Cobain had died *and I didn't know who he was*. On top of that, I garden, I am not really skinny anymore, and my best friend looked at me funny when I didn't recognize the Belle and Sebastian song she used as a soundtrack to a movie-slideshow she made about my dog on her Mac. Those are all pretty much deal-breakers. I did not even meet my first 1990s hipster, an art teacher who wore 1960s vintage and was into swing dancing a full six months before the Louis Prima Gap ad, until I was in my early thirties and living in Wisconsin. That none of those things is still hip as you read this is part of my point. When you add to that the fact I'm now a permanent resident of Canada, intend to apply for dual citizenship (speaking of complicated identities), and, moreover, live happily in a decidedly Pacific Rim metropolis in *western* Canada (there's a difference!)—well, things get complicated.

What I am trying to do here is not simply to convey the difficulty in defining identity as (sigh) "southern" or (sigh) "hip"—don't even start on (sigh) "Canadian"—but rather to keep my subject position both unreified and in line with the argument of this book. If the people who need therapy—fans with populist worlds where their politics should be—are those who narcissistically cathect either southernness or hipness (one's own or that of someone or something else) as bestowing distinction and hence identity, then achieving a degree of happiness and fulfillment may necessitate a both/and sensibility about space and place, hipness and squareness, change and stability, *Gesellschaft* and *Gemeinschaft*, popular culture and folk culture, and so on. In unflattering terms, one might call this the exquisitely bourgeois strategy of hedging one's bets, diversifying one's portfolio, not putting all one's eggs in a single basket-cathexis: quite literally a strategy of guarding against loss.

I am hard-pressed to find much heroic about so middling a situation—perhaps because I am not much of a Kierkegaardian, perhaps because I am—but that, too, is part of the point: rather than generating a "populist world" where people are more authentic than they are "here" or at the extremes, I hope to come closer to describing how most people actually construct identity—at least a precursor, I would humbly suggest, to doing "progressive" work (perhaps even to making "progressive" art). Needless to say, the modern ambivalence I am attempting to describe, and which varies from individual to individual, is very different from the banal notion of "both loving and hating the land" that long animated mainstream southern studies. A century ago, Georg Simmel argued that society (and fashion in particular) comes about because of the tension between identification (our desire to feel part of a group, to be like everybody else) and differentiation (our desire to feel unique). In "Ambivalence, and Its Relation to Fashion and the Body," Anne Boultwood and Robert Jerrard argue that

> it is as unacceptable to be strikingly unfashionable as it is to be outrageously fashionable. In our striving to fulfill both needs, we are driven to seek a compromise. Paradoxically, what we achieve is mediocrity. . . . The conflicting, sometimes contradictory, attitudes that characterize much of our emotional and psychological experience are encapsulated in the concept of ambivalence. It is a concept that pervades our late twentieth-century cultural and personal experience. Cultural ambivalence is apparent in the meeting of different cultures: ideas are borrowed, and recycled in the arts, philosophy, and lifestyles; yet at the same time there is a need to maintain cultural identity. (308)

If much of this seems obvious, recall that it took fifteen years for Jameson to start to move away from his famous, if premature, claim in *Postmodernism* that as of the 1980s we had let one side of this dualism go forever: "in modernism . . . some residual zones of 'nature' or 'being,' of the old, the older, the archaic, still subsist. . . . Postmodernism is what you have when the modernization process is complete and nature is gone for good" (ix). Instead, in 2002's *A Singular Modernity* (the title expresses his resistance to Appadurai's concept of alternative ones), he finds himself reluctantly coming to terms with what he calls "the return to and reestablishment of all kinds of old things" (1).

Thus if some consortium of southern sociologists and postmodern geographers began telephone polling North Americans and asking (after explaining their terms), "Do you consider yourself a person who exults in postmodern space, or one who revels in premodern place?" odds are that most North Americans, at least, would not be able to answer the question as posed. Regardless of the universal, totalizing declarations of so many 1980s postmodern theorists, today as then most people still seek, and enjoy, some way to combine the freedom of space and change with the security of place and continuity. This pleasure—sought and not infrequently attained by people of all backgrounds, even under "late capitalism"—paradoxically reflects a kind of ambivalence, but it also offers an example of what I mean by living in a very real modernity that nevertheless occupies what until now has been a kind of theoretical limbo somewhere between "the new and the now" of cultural studies and "the presence of the past" of southern studies.[13]

To assume this ambivalence necessarily leads to mediocrity, however, is to assume falsely that the mechanism at work must always be one of averaging. Combinations, juxtapositions, and simultaneities are also always in play. Reviewing Toni Cade Bambara's posthumous novel *Those Bones Are Not My Child*, for example, bell hooks praises Bambara's "wild mixture of down home basic blackness and a rare, strange, all-over-the-place complex global consciousness" (16, cited in Bone 241). As I touch-type these words, my eyes flit back and forth between the monitor (where a little earlier I was reading *McSweeney's*) and the ruby-throated hummingbird at the agapanthus out the window. In fact, it is fair to say that the present book arises less out of any unresolved childhood issues with the region (or with mass culture) than the fact that a decade ago we moved to Birmingham, Alabama, and to my surprise, I *loved* the combinations and juxtapositions available there. If I stood up in front of the monitor and looked out the window to my left, I saw my midcentury-modern neighborhood tumbling down the north slope of Red Mountain, the urban grid reasserting its right angles at the base of the ridge, the Birmingham skyline in the middle ground three miles off and, in the background, the gentle ridges on the far side of Jones Valley. If I looked out the window to my right, I saw the terraced slopes of my garden, and behind it the dense second-growth Appalachian hardwood forest that runs two hundred feet higher up to the crest of the mountain. This site neither averaged nor fetishized urban space and rural place; it partook of both at the same time. (The same might be, and has been, said of the Simon Fraser University campus atop Burnaby Mountain where I revised this introduction: from some parts of the exquisite midcentury-modern campus—nestled in a wildlife preserve where bear sightings are common—I can see both the cosmopolitan splendor of Vancouver and the raw wilderness of the Coast Mountains just across Burrard Inlet. Unfortunately, while the campus is indeed beautifully sited, a house in Vancouver, the world's second most expensive housing market, costs seven times as much as one in Birmingham.)[14]

Even more interesting and pleasurable than combination or juxtaposition, however, is dialectic. The desire and ability to synthesize postmodern hipness with what hipsters (and others) call "realness" have generated some of the most striking and compelling cultural productions of the post-postmodern era, as Hal Foster first intimated in 1996 in *The Return of the Real: The Avant-Garde at the End of the Century*, and as his former student Miwon Kwon argued in 2002 in *One Place After Another: Site-Specific Art and Locational Identity*, to which I will return. Although in the present book I focus chiefly on Birmingham and Alabama, lying as they do about halfway between Atlanta, usually figured as a kind of L.A. lite,[15] and Mississippi, usually figured as, well, Mississippi (i.e., as all that is implied in George Lipsitz's description of California as "the Mississippi of the 1990s"), there is still much I could not consider. I do not discuss, for example, the assemblage art of Thornton Dial, which is at the forefront of a kind of Alabama vernacular art being described, in places like the *Souls Grown Deep* volumes, as "the visual equivalent of jazz." (Jazz, especially hard bop, serves for me as a kind of paradigm for the successful synthesis of lasting [funky black southern] identity with a rigorous, urbane modernism—two tendencies African American studies has too often seen as necessarily opposed, as in, say Hazel Carby's discomfort with grounding African American identity in southern black folk culture.)[16] I analyze neither the poetry of C. D. Wright, Yusef Komunyakaa, and Charles Wright, nor the Rural Studio architecture of the late MacArthur "genius grant" winner Samuel Mockbee, who incorporated recycled materials and an avant-garde aesthetic as he and his students built houses and community centers for poor people in Alabama's Black Belt. I do not consider the Provence-inflected southern cuisine of Frank Stitt's Highlands Bar and Grill, a Birmingham restaurant consistently near the top of *Gourmet* magazine's national rankings. Nor do I discuss hick hop.

But that's the point: in its second section, this book seeks not to be definitive of anything (least of all "identity"), but to model an approach that might more fruitfully be applied to such hybrid cultural phenomena—and they are as rich and omnipresent inside the United States as outside it—than those currently featured in the repertoires of either American cultural studies or southern studies. Almost all of the previous paragraph's examples of synthesis and fusion, of hybrid culture, come from Alabama, generally considered an almost hysterically conservative—perhaps the most hysterically conservative—state. After all, in 2008 Barack Obama captured but 10 percent of the white vote there, the lowest in the country. Gazing westward from his current position at Emory University in Atlanta, historian Allen Tullos has recently described the state as "encased in social amber like an ancient insect, stuck in repetitive loops of uneven development, rife with ol' boy prejudices and debilitating habits of judgment, dishing out foreclosed futures to its young" (1). Yet even Tullos acknowledges Alabama's active presence in "the circulating currents of global capital, manufacturing, biomedical research, military R&D, cultural tourism, and human rights" (1). Gazing metaphorically eastward from "Mississippi," on the other hand (as in Malcolm X's "Mississippi is anywhere in the United States south of the Canadian border"), Houston Baker sees a bright future of black modernism: a movement beyond "zones of discipline and confinement and through time to the righteous civil rights motions of the black-South body. We find ourselves in the extraordinary company of Mrs. Rosa Parks and Dr. Martin Luther King" (98).

"Alabama," these examples suggest, looks different depending on whether you're looking from an elite liberal university in a major city or (at least metaphorically) from deep in Flyover Country. There are bits of both Alabamas in this book: Tullos's most obviously in the Faulkner chapter, Baker's in the chapter on Ruben Studdard. In the main, however, what I hope lies in these pages is a much less extraordinary, but perhaps much less predictable, Alabama. Indeed, the working title of this book was long *Alabama and the Future of American Cultural Studies*, as "the South" is, for me, a meaningless term, naming nothing but fantasies: either a great, 100-million-resident void at the heart of American studies, or a ridiculously strained attempt at identity politics at the heart of old southern studies. "Alabama" is more coherent and manageable as a site of modernity, one where the tugs of past and future, place and space, and so on mingle in very complicated ways. If the working title was a joke at the expense of aging New Americanist pretentions to futurity and radical youth, even as it was also a marketing concession to the profession's insatiable appetite for crisis rhetoric, future talk, and the Next Big Thing, the current subtitle represents a further concession: nobody, several elder Americanists have argued to me, wants to read a book merely about "Alabama." (After all, even Baker, whose book climaxes with the differences between metaphorical Mississippi and metaphorical Alabama, still titled his book *Turning South Again*.) My own title now comes from the press's marketing department, so I should be clear: this is not a work of political science. I am generally much less interested in who voted for whom than in the larger, but not unrelated, question of how North Americans inhabit their several, and very complex, alternative modernities. To "find" that America—neither L.A. nor Mayberry—I also needed to move beyond the methodologies, and structures of feeling, of both American studies and old southern studies. For the purposes of this book, then, "purple" substantively denotes hybridity and temporal ambivalence, and methodologically denotes a consequent impatience with disciplinary ideologies, still surprisingly strong, of national and regional exceptionalism and purity. However, even if you picked up this book because of the title or because that "future" in the subtitle implied its contents might help you maintain the professional hipness you worry about, I hope it might still lead you, if you have gotten this far, to question your enjoyable participation in—and your interpellation by—disciplinary fantasy.

The chapters that follow offer generally contrarian takes on melancholy, religion, maturity, the present, commodity culture, and gardening. They argue against antimodern fantasies of both the Left and the Right, of both baby boomers and Gen Xers, and advocate strategies for living in modernity rather than getting stuck circling the past or the future. Yet for all its cautions against antimodern fantasies, the book also celebrates those who, like William Faulkner, Ruben Studdard, and the better sort of Gen Xer, eventually try to be adults rather than somebody's idea of "youth culture," to live in an actual present, to synthesize the demands of change and continuity, and, as best they can, to behave rationally, rather than narcissistically, in a world of other people.

I am hardly alone in valuing and desiring these sorts of syntheses, which at worst may make me some sort of organic intellectual of the temporally ambivalent bourgeoisie, whether they be a small-town Mississippi writer lingering in Greenwich Village, an urban hipster listening to Johnny Cash, or those whose ambivalence does indeed lead to mediocrity. (I simplify: there is no reason the small-town Mississippi writer cannot also be the urban hipster. Increasingly, in figures like Donna Tartt, she has been just that. For that matter, it is hardly clear that the desire for temporal—and spatial—synthesis or rapprochement is exclusively bourgeois.) In the 2002 movie *Sweet Home Alabama*, Reese Witherspoon's character, a fashion designer, is set to marry the son of the mayor of New York City. She returns to Alabama to finalize her divorce from her estranged and very, very "southern" stillhusband, as Faulkner might put it, played by Josh Lucas. The surprise is that, to win her back, the husband—who to some degree stands for "the South" or the province, just as the fiancé, as the mayor's son, stands for New York City or the metropole—has become a successful artist. In two senses, it is the *nature* of the art that matters here: the husband drives metal poles into the beach when thunderstorms are predicted. When lightning strikes a pole, it fuses the sand below into a giant and beautiful splash of glass. The *old* hubby, who appears on first meeting to be merely a flannel-shirted redneck who accessorizes with hound dogs and slamming screen doors, is not enough to keep ambitious designer Melanie, but hubby 2.0—with his synthesis of southern authenticity and sophisticated artsiness, of what is figured as nature and culture—is able to win her back from the merely cosmopolitan New Yorker (played by Patrick Dempsey), who wears stylish turtlenecks with very, very high necks. The synthesis goes on even at the level of a kind of marriage subplot, in which Melanie's very out black gay fashion associate (who also wears high turtlenecks) and her closeted white childhood friend who has stayed in Alabama (and flannel) fall instantly for each other, yet again combining, we are led to believe, the best of both worlds. The film has grossed more than $180 million worldwide.

Less successful but also telling was the short-lived magazine *deep*, headquartered in the Atlanta suburb of Decatur, marketed to "hip southern women," and apparently aimed at a niche market put off by the conservatism of *Southern Living*. The July/August 2006 issue, for example, offered Janisse Ray, author of *Ecology of a Cracker Childhood*, as a "soul model" and had a story on the Greensboro Truth and Reconciliation Commission—even as it also offered tips on how to be a "hip southern bride" and where to go shopping in Savannah: "After decades of flying elsewhere for our fashion finds, Savannah fashionistas are living the designer dream, right here at home" (12). It is easy to look down on Savannah fashionistas—the phrase conjures drawling *Sex and the City* wannabes—and, at least in the South, to this day "living the dream" has very different connotations thanks to Dr. King. Yet as I hope the Faulkner chapter shows, consumerist dreams are not always shallow, and the hope that one might finally be able to fulfill them without leaving the region matters more than might immediately be apparent.

One can go on almost indefinitely: in July 2006, the *Washington Post* reported that "Virginia's Blue Ridge from Middleburg to Charlottesville is . . . becoming urbane without the urban. Or even suburban. It is becoming a place where people can make city-quality money, and satisfy city-quality tastes, without the city" (Garreau). Conversely, when I visited Earwax Records at hipster ground zero on Bedford Avenue in Williamsburg, Brooklyn, in May 2004, a little past the peak of the alt-country boom, they were offering for sale more Johnny Cash records than Bob Dylan, more Steve Earle than the Clash. In July 2006, the Associated Press reported that the top arcade game in New York City hipster bars was "Big Buck Hunter" (Goldman); seven months later, the *New York Times* reported that red velvet cake, a signature southern dessert whose rich hue comes from copious artificial coloring, was "suddenly all the rage" in that city (Fabricant). The following summer, Memphis-born Justin Timberlake opened his theme restaurant Southern Hospitality on the Upper East Side. ("First it was sexy, and now, Justin Timberlake plans to bring southern back," enthused *Spin*.) The restaurant was sufficiently successful that the following year his agents began scouting for a location in Chicago, with openings in several other cities under consideration. (The Great Recession appears to have deferred those openings.) In 2010, Conan O'Brien closed out his run on the *Tonight Show* with a Will Ferrell-led rendition of "Freebird." In 2005, White Trash Fast Food, Berlin's hippest club, was in the habit of projecting *Smokey and the Bandit* on all four walls and offering an exhibit of photos taken at U.S. southern livestock shows. The following year, *Vice* magazine published, with quite unironic approval, a cartoon by Flannery O'Connor. Just before it folded, the hip British fashion magazine *The Face* instructed its readers (correctly) when to use "fuck all y'all" instead of "fuck y'all." The *Guardian*, of all places, fawned over the Kings of Leon as "the redneck Strokes," and gushed, "While many of Caleb's lyrics are surreal in a William Faulkner kind of way, it's clear these preacher's sons are singing about indulging in the unholy pleasures of the flesh and leaving before the cock crows. Consider 'showing off your something shaved and lacy' in the rollicking 'Velvet Snow.' Or, 'I'd pop myself in your body, I'd cum all over your party but I'm soft' in the staggering-home-drunk dosie-do 'Soft.' Or the song title 'Pistol of Fire.'" With their *relative* absence of shtick, bands such as the Drive-by Truckers or the North Mississippi All-Stars seem unable to crack the British appetite for the sorts of stereotypes that populate populist worlds—preachers' sons, dosie-dos, the southern grotesque—and overdetermining drive to call awful lyrics Faulknerian. (In any event, they probably meant Caldwellian.)

It is hard to say where all this is going, especially when one is leery of fetishizing the Next Big Thing or offering one's present as someone else's future. Describing the two separate worlds in which he has spent most of his life, the Mayberry-ish South he grew up in and the once-vast global spaces he traversed to do anthropological fieldwork in Sukarto's Indonesia, Peacock observes that in the past decade or two the boundaries between those worlds seem to have collapsed. To describe what the South is becoming, he proposes the notion of "grounded globalism," the idea "that global can synergize with local, specifically that a sense of place could be preserved under globalism, creating a sort of grounded globalism that might resonate with yet also transform the south's traditional emphasis on place" ("South and Grounded Globalism" 271). Yet in the same volume as Peacock's essay, Donald Nonini looks at globalization not as rationalization or increasing consumer choices but as the product of labor exploitation. Thus the South, long considered backward, in fact "historically may have led in constructing, and its elites certainly anticipated and led in creating, the design of the features of the neoliberal political and economic order that currently prevails more widely in the United States" (256). As "postmodernism" recedes into 1980s fantasy, both Peacock's utopia for consumers and Nonini's dystopia for laborers may indeed be (in) everybody's future instead. Or not. For now, we might simply (and, for now, neutrally) observe that, however paradoxically, for much of the past fifteen or twenty years the South, in large part because of its perceived authentic, backward abjection, has been hip: consumed avidly (if often ironically) by transnational postmodern urban youth and popular culture as a "populist world," even if in sometimes weird forms; and increasingly productive of its own kinds of much-desired modern—and modernist—temporal syntheses. That hipness seems to have faded by the late 2000s along with alt-country, southern hip-hop, and any lingering Gen X claims to constituting a youth culture. But that is precisely the point, I will argue, at which things get interesting.

So I will eschew the grand pronouncements that so often bestow distinction in the academic marketplace and insist, a little wryly, that what I am trying to do in this book is just to tell a kind of story that so far has not really been told in cultural studies, American studies, or southern studies. Speaking chiefly of the introduction to *Look Away! The U.S. South in New World Studies*, but also of his own work, George Handley has cautioned me that when you try to make an argument (admittedly, I am of course also making an argument) from a position that represents neither one side of a debate nor the other, partisans of each side will see you as siding with the other. Still, I would hope careful readers of this book might find in it a way to move beyond the fantastic populist worlds to which academics, be they tweedy mandarins or narrow-bespectacled hipsters, are drawn just like other consumers. I am trying, like a few other people, to write a post-heroic, post-hip, American cultural studies. How hard could that be?

PART I

DISRUPTING EVERYONE'S ENJOYMENT

ONE

SONGS THAT MOVE HIPSTERS TO TEARS
Johnny Cash and the New Melancholy

Is there anything behind the symbols of modern "country," or are the symbols themselves the whole story? Are the hats, the boots, the pickup trucks, and the honky-tonking poses all that's left of a disintegrating culture? Back in Arkansas, a way of life produced a certain kind of music. Does a certain kind of music now produce a way of life? —Johnny Cash, *Cash: The Autobiography* (1997)

Could the writer in [the South of the late 1960s] write with the same intensity and conviction that drove [George Washington] Cable and [Lillian] Smith and [W. J.] Cash—or, in a different way, [William] Faulkner? Had what was once natural become stylized, what was deeply and painfully experienced become ritualized?
— Fred Hobson, *The Southern Writer in the Postmodern World* (1991)

Has the Southern heritage become an old hunting jacket that one slips on comfortably while at home but discards when he ventures abroad in favor of some more conventional or modish garb? Or is it perhaps an attic full of ancestral wardrobes useful only in connection with costume balls and play acting—staged primarily in Washington, D.C.? —C. Vann Woodward, "The Search for Southern Identity" (1958)

From its very beginning, people have believed that the South, defined against an earlier South that was somehow more authentic, more real, more unified and distinct, was not only disappearing but also declining. [Thomas] Jefferson's South declined into the delusion of [John C.] Calhoun's South, which declined into the incompetency of Jefferson Davis' South, which declined into the corruption of the carpetbaggers' South, which declined into the poverty and inbreeding of [William] Faulkner's South, which declined into the race baiting of George Wallace's South, which declined into the scandals of Jim Bakker and Jimmy Swaggart.
—Edward J. Ayers, "What We Talk About When We Talk About the South" (1996)

My tears spoiled my aim. —John Shelton Reed, *My Tears Spoiled My Aim* (1993)

In her afterword to the 2004 essay collection *Loss*, Judith Butler applauds "a new kind of scholarship that seeks to bring theory to bear on the analysis of social and political life, in particular, to the temporality of social and political life" (467). As it turns out, this "new" scholarship is interested in concepts that are far from new to southern studies: the presence of the past, the experience of defeat, and the sense of community. "The past is not actually the past," she writes, not only channeling William Faulkner's Gavin

Stevens but also, as she continues, deconstructively glossing him, "in the sense of 'over,' since it continues as an animating absence in the presence, one that makes itself known precisely in and through the survival of anachronism itself." "Loss," she goes on, "becomes condition and necessity for a certain sense of community, where community does not overcome the loss, where community *cannot* overcome the loss without losing the very sense of itself as community" (468). Indeed, when Butler writes, "The presumptions that the future follows the past, that mourning might follow melancholia, that mourning might be completed are all called poignantly into question in these pages" (467), she could also be speaking of nearly any work of old southern studies, from Michael Kreyling's 2010 book *The South That Wasn't There: Postsouthern Memory and History* and Barbara Ladd's 2005 *PMLA* review essay, with their reifications of "memory," all the way back to *I'll Take My Stand* itself. Kreyling's book begins with a scary epigraph warning that "loss of memory destroys our sense of self. It severs the connection with the past and with other people" (1); Ladd fears a "national project of forgetting" (1629).[1] (See also John Crowe Ransom's praise of "nostalgia" [6], which operates for him as melancholy does for Butler; Lyle Lanier's critique of "progress" [122–54]; and so on.) The same year *Loss* appeared, Columbia ethnomusicologist Aaron Fox lauded in his book *Real Country* the culture of country music fans in Lockhart, Texas, as "almost folkloric in its residuality, its orientation towards a collectively imagined past, and the pervasive orality that symbolizes that orientation" (318); opposed that culture to an "uncertain global postmodernity" (the twenty-first-century correlate of the uncertain national modernity against which the agrarians rebelled) that appears to "disdain the distinctiveness of place" (320); praised its "poetic obsession with loss and the looming presence of the past" (318); and, in good old southern studies fashion, lamented how "in the years since I left Texas, that scene has itself declined in coherence and quality, with many of its principle [sic] actors scattered on the winds of time and rapid social change" (319). From a new southern studies perspective, however, if the New Black means to celebrate folklore, orality, the presence of the past, the sense of place, and the sense of community, and to lament the scattering winds of time and change, then the New Black looks way too much like the Old White.

Which is to say it looks like a Lacanian fantasy space, an antimodern populist world not unlike "Dixie" as Scott Romine sees it: "a territory associated, in my mind at least, with a white quasi nation always, already consigned to an irretrievable past—a place where a certain *kind* of I *wishes* that it were" (*Real South* 1). If the goal of this book is to examine the sorts of present people actually live in, rather than to continue to consume fantasies overdetermined by symbolic investments in the future or the past, then Jacques Lacan's distinction between the real and the symbolic has quite a bit to offer. "What can a Lacanian approach tell us about the ecological crisis?" asks Slavoj Žižek. "Simply that we must learn to accept the real of the ecological crisis in its senseless actuality, without charging it with some message or meaning" (*Looking Awry* 35). "The only proper attitude," he continues, "is that which fully assumes this gap [between the real and the symbolic] as something that defines our very *condition humaine*, without endeavoring to suspend it through fetishistic disavowal" (36).[2] What can a Lacanian approach tell us about the affects with which we approach "the South"?

To answer this question, the present chapter extends Žižek's later critique of melancholy in particular (in "Melancholy") to three linked fields: the melancholy ideology of many old-school southern white people, both inside academia and out; the melancholic consumption of that melancholy ideology by young, urban, mainly white people from the late 1980s into the 2000s (the "long 1990s"); and the scholarship that is starting to be produced as alumni of that urban youth culture have grown up, entered middle age, and published work in cultural studies that, unawares, attempts to reanimate agrarian melancholy (as an "authentic" response to postmodernity) at the precise moment new southern studies—far more experienced in these matters— finally seems to be killing it off.

This chapter has three goals. The first is to analyze old southern studies' melancholy not as a lament over the loss of white male privilege[3] but more fundamentally as a free-floating Lacanian drive. The second is to suggest (again, with a degree of postcolonial irony) that if the turn to melancholy is not arrested, old southern studies' present may well be American cultural studies' future, so that attending to new southern studies may, if nothing else, save the larger field a few years. This temporal argument is not grounded in (or interesting to me because of) the mere contingency that melancholy is still, for the moment, fashionable. Houston A. Baker Jr. and Dana D. Nelson famously argued that "the South" is the nation's "abjected regional Other," but I am more interested here in the academic correlative of that observation, in how old southern studies functions as American cultural studies' disavowed, abjected Other. After all, Baker and Nelson's foundational insistence on the need for a "new" southern studies leaves *that* disavowal very much intact. (An extended Lacanian reading of the Symbolic aspects of our field's construction of "bad" scholarship, even as high-status theory repeats the errors of a low-status subfield, is, unfortunately, beyond the scope of this book.) It is precisely this disavowal of old southern studies that I wish to avoid by very unhiply troubling to engage at some length with this body of work. Structurally, I will argue, old southern studies differs very little from the hippest, edgiest deployments of postmodern theory; this is precisely why melancholy can so easily fill the space of the New Black, can so easily become fashionable—and also why it has (in other contexts) so easily been disavowed as unfashionable.

Finally, the third goal of the chapter is to register with dismay the way melancholy both old and new, posited as a guarantor of authenticity and maturity by fans who feel a narcissistic lack of both, seems inevitably to slide into bathos: the slippery slope of affect that takes us from Butler's "poignancy" through Reed's and Cash's copious tears and such sentimental clichés as "scattered on the winds of time" back to, as we shall see, more tears. The problem is not sentiment itself but the bad faith of that sentiment, and the solution is not to reinscribe a false masculinist objectivity. Still, at the present juncture the "only proper attitude" toward the demise of postmodernism cannot consist simply of a return to its melancholy apparent antithesis, however fashionable (or, more precisely, fashionably unfashionable). Scholars, like everybody else, must instead strive toward an honest engagement with the complex temporality of the present "in its senseless actuality."

White Southern Melancholy as Lacanian Drive

At the end of *American Dreams in Mississippi: Consumers, Poverty, and Culture, 1830–1998*, Ted Ownby observes that

> [w]riters do not seem to tire of asking whether a South still exists. Perhaps the time has come that we should. The question tends to construe a few key elements in a regional past as the essence of the South and then judges whether industrialization or agricultural mechanization or the Sun Belt economy or migration or the civil rights movement or two-party politics or something else has challenged, eroded, or overcome these essential elements. (159)

Like Ayers, Ownby is a southern historian, not a psychoanalytic critic, but like Ayers he calls attention to the curiously *symptomatic* repetitiveness of much mainstream southern studies. With no small frustration, Ayers conveys it by repeating the phrase "which declined into," while Ownby repeats a simple "or," culminating in "or something else," suggesting that *what* is posited as the loss is much less relevant to this apparently endless scholarly circuit than the grieving over it. Such a pattern enacts precisely Lacan's refinement, in *The Four Fundamental Concepts of Psycho-analysis*, of Sigmund Freud's notion of *das Trieb* (the drive): "if one distinguishes, at the outset of the dialectic of the drive, Not from *Bedürfnis*, need from the pressure of the drive—it is precisely because no object of any *Not*, need, can satisfy the drive" (167). Žižek explicates this "Lacanian distinction between a drive's *aim* and its *goal*" as follows:

> The goal is the final destination, while the aim is what we intend to do, i.e., the way itself. Lacan's point is that the real purpose of the drive is not its goal (full satisfaction) but its aim: the drive's ultimate aim is simply to reproduce itself as drive, to return to its circular path, to continue its path to and from the goal. The

real source of enjoyment is the repetitive movement of this closed circuit. (*Looking Awry* 5)

Hence the interrogative form Ownby notes, the form also of this chapter's first three epigraphs: the pleasure (which paradoxically derives from the ginning up of anxiety) lies in the inquiry, the perpetual reopening of and circling around the question, not in any closure that might, say, lead such scholars out of melancholy and into mourning.[4] In such a context, the tears of southern humorist and sociologist John Shelton Reed, no less than those of his country music speaker in this chapter's fifth epigraph, who has found his woman with another man, operate the same way: far from spoiling his "aim," they guarantee it by preventing him from firing the shot that would have reached his goal.[5] Hence, too, the eerie tirelessness Ownby shrewdly observes ("writers do not seem to tire"): Žižek's favorite pop culture image of pure drive is the horror movie figure of the "undead" (zombies, vampires, etc.), a figure he sees operating in science fiction as well. Speaking of *The Terminator*, he observes that "the horror of [the title] figure consists precisely in the fact that it functions as a programmed automaton who, even when all that remains of him is a metallic, legless skeleton, persists in his demand and pursues his victim with no trace of compromise or hesitation. The terminator is the embodiment of the drive, devoid of desire" (*Looking Awry* 22).

Such an approach may help explain how, in the present era, so many in old southern studies have shifted effortlessly from melancholy over the loss of black labor[6] to melancholy, however many decades after the fact, over the loss of (mainly) black civil rights martyrs, a shift whose political progressivism—relative to firehoses and police dogs—masks its continued structural investment in reactionary fantasy, its continued inability to live in the present-day South. Kreyling began 1998's *Inventing Southern Literature* by evoking "[Michael] Schwerner, [James] Chaney, and [Andrew] Goodwin [sic]—how many Mississippi ghosts or burning movies later?—still dead, and still powerful" (xi); a recent Minrose Gwin project entitled "Mourning Medgar" invites, as Gwin lingers over the details of Medgar Evers's last weeks and minutes, a simple observation: if you are still mourning someone forty-five years later, you may well have been engaged less in mourning than in melancholy—a concept curiously absent from Gwin's meditations, affecting though they be. (It is also absent from Gwin's introduction to the 2008 special issue of *The Southern Literary Journal* on "History, Memory and Mourning in Southern Literature," except in reference to Éva Tettenborn's essay on Randall Kenan, an essay that unsurprisingly attempts to *validate* melancholy.)[7] In 2010's *The South That Wasn't There*—a book that appeared after this chapter was drafted but usefully confirms its claims—Kreyling appears unable to transcend what even he realizes is a pretty weird compulsion to talk about memory again: "the twin subjects of the South and memory are dusty common-places in the history of southern literary studies" (x), he concedes, repeating a few pages later that "history and memory are not an unlikely couple in southern studies, and there have been many times in the writing and revising of this book that I have thought that one more iteration is too many" (5).

Drives are nothing if not iterative, however, and melancholy's *Triebheit* in old southern studies is precisely what seems to invalidate any attempt to stop it by dynamiting its rails. Intellectually speaking, the rails have been dynamited for a decade or more, but the fantasy train of white southern melancholy does not run on the rails of logic, so the critic's task today must be, less glamorously, to show what it does run on. Sadly, given the nature of drives, one might predict that, heedless of the past decade's massive deconstruction of old southern studies, no small percentage of the coming generations of "southernists," scholars too young to remember the Clarence Thomas hearings, much less the civil rights movement, will symptomatically find, through a combination of training and the personal predilections that led them to that training, something else to be melancholy about—perhaps the loss of melancholy itself as an organizing principle of the field. Yet one must also hope that a greater percentage will, in time, learn to break this cycle: learn not to "forget" a lost loved object or southern "essence" (as the issue has historically been presented) but to come to understand what leads them to seek out such objects in the first place and invest so much in them.

The *Objet Petit a* of White Southern Melancholy

If the specific object of melancholy is, as Lacan puts it, "indifferent" (*Four Fundamental Concepts* 168), what, as one imagines countless outsiders to old southern studies asking themselves over the years, makes melancholy so appealing? For Lacan, the technical answer is the *objet petit a*: that thing in the desired object that leads us to desire it even as we may not know the reason for our desire, even as we may imagine we desire the object in spite of that thing. Thus in dealing with melancholy, the theoretical problem is that, as Žižek puts it, "lack is not the same as loss":

> In so far as the object-cause of desire [thanks to the *objet petit a*] is originally, in a constitutive way, lacking, melancholy interprets this lack as a loss, as if the object lacking were once possessed and then lost. In short, what melancholy obfuscates is the fact that the object is lacking from the very beginning, that its emergence coincides with its lack, that this object is *nothing but* the positivization of a void/lack, a purely anamorphic entity which does not exist "in itself." The paradox, of course, is that this deceitful translation of lack into loss enables us to assert our possession of the object: what we never possessed can also never be

lost, so the melancholic, in his unconditional fixation on the lost object, in a way possesses it in its very loss. ("Melancholy" 142–43)

To understand this rather dense argument, we might consider a remark of John Shelton Reed on the Public Radio International program *Whad'Ya Know?* hosted by Wisconsinite Michael Feldman. In a show broadcast on October 5, 2002, from Chapel Hill, Feldman asks Reed, "Among Southerners, is the Civil War still an issue?" Reed replies, "Among some it is. . . . I always tell people, 'Bring the spoons back and we'll forget all about it.'"[8] The legatee of processes of deferral well described by David Blight in *Race and Reunion*, Reed narrates the Civil War as a well-worn tale of Yankee depredation. Indeed, the now-predictable argument here would be to note, *pace* Harriet Jacobs's famous description of how her mistress's silver candelabra embodied her grandmother's stolen labor, that the stolen, implicitly silver spoons again substitute for the "real" trauma, the loss of unfree black labor. (While Reed mentions cotton and Dixie several times in his interview with Feldman, he does not mention slavery once, not even when discussing the Civil War.) However, the more subtle yet more broadly structural problem lies in what Žižek calls "the very logic of melancholic identification, in which the object is overpresent in its very unconditional and irretrievable loss" ("Melancholy" 144). These spoons will not be forgotten—they are constantly overpresent to the resentful white southerner—until they are returned, and thus the Civil War is indeed "still an issue." Of course, while Reed's reference to spoons makes restitution—reparation!—for this 140-year-old alleged traumatic wound seem simple, it in fact makes healing impossible. *The spoons are never coming back, so the spoons are always present.*

Perhaps the most fundamental error of the old southern studies (and one American cultural studies would do well not to repeat) thus lies in its debilitating and nearly universal confusion between "the presence of the past," which it sees as opposed to the imagined absence of any past, and the pathological, melancholy *over*presence of the past, of the lost loved object. Ironically enough, on this issue the thrust of old southern studies has always already embodied what Žižek calls the "predominant doxa" of contemporary academe: a "politically correct" disposition toward melancholy ("Melancholy" 140–41). "With regard to mourning and melancholy," he observes,

the predominant doxa is as follows: Freud opposed "normal" mourning (the successful acceptance of loss) to "pathological" melancholy (where the subject persists in his or her narcissistic identification with the lost object). Against Freud, one should [in this doxa] assert the conceptual *and* ethical primacy of melancholy: in the process of loss, there is always a remainder which cannot be integrated through the work of mourning, and the ultimate fidelity is fidelity to this remainder. Mourning is a kind of betrayal, the "second killing" of the (lost) object, while the melancholic subject remains faithful to the lost object, refusing to renounce his or her attachment to it. (141)

In *My Tears Spoiled My Aim*, for example, Reed describes an early 1980s meeting with some young Germans:

> I suggested that we had something in common: How did it feel to them, I asked, to have lost a war, to recognize that the world may [sic] be a better place for it, but nevertheless to know that you lost? They simply did not understand the question. They seemed to have no sense that *they* had lost a war, no sense of identification with the generation that had happened to. For some reason, I found that disturbing. (48)

Insisting on fidelity to the remainders of regional or national loss, Reed quite precisely inverts Freud's claim that mourning is normal, melancholy pathological.[9] So, too, does Rebecca Mark in "Mourning Emmett," one of the essays in Gwin's special issue:

> After [Hurricane Katrina], I drove from my evacuation home in Perdido Key, Florida to Tuscaloosa, Alabama for an Emmett Till conference. . . . The discussion had all the energy of academic competition, detective sleuthing, and journalistic scooping. At another time and place I might have been interested. But at this moment I was in shock from Katrina. All I could hear was the silence. There was no moaning, no mourning or grieving for Emmett. . . . All I could feel at the moment was that this academic and legal pursuit was serving some intellectual purpose, some safety valve of white liberalism, but after the Convention Center and the Superdome, one for which I had no tolerance. There was no keening, or caring, or emotion of any kind. (130)

For Mark, the loss of Till, who died two months before she was born, is insufficiently *over*present at the conference, the scholars (like Reed's young Germans) insufficiently melancholy, the whole event a betrayal and even a second killing. When a student in one of her undergraduate courses asks Mark the obvious question about her melancholy, namely why in her class they have to read what Mark herself states is "about six books on Emmett Till" (129), her response (in addition to composing a prose poem) provides the climactic final sentence of her essay: "We are reading these books because I love Emmett and I want everyone to know how furious and sad I am that he is dead" (136). Yet this in itself, as Faulkner's *Absalom, Absalom!* characters might say, "does not explain." The real question for the student-analyst (and no student should ever be placed in such a position) is the logical next one: not "Why do you hate the South?" anymore, but "Why—out of all the possible traumatized victims of history or human malevolence, if that's your thing—do you love Emmett? What is the object-cause of your desire?"

To return to an earlier question that might help us answer this one: what do we make of Žižek's claim that fixating on such objects is a fundamentally compensatory gesture? How can it be that the older white southerner "never had" the spoons? Here, the Lacanian reading does not refer to the likelihood that the spoons literally never existed, nor even to the fact that, if they did exist, they were "lost" well before Reed was born, and hence lost by somebody else—the whole structure of feeling evoked by Marianne Hirsch's notion of "postmemory," say. (This distinction is perhaps clearer in the example of the subsequent generation of southernists: the dead civil rights workers really existed, and in many boomers' lifetimes, even if they did not know them personally.) Rather, we are brought back to the relative unimportance of *what* is lost, an insight Žižek calls

> the fundamental lesson of Lacan: while it is true that any object can occupy the empty place of the Thing, it can do so only by means of the illusion that it was always already there, i.e., that it was not placed there by us but *found there as an "answer of the real."* Although any object can function as the object-cause of desire—insofar as the power of fascination it exerts is not its immediate property but results from the place it occupies in the structure—we must, by structural necessity, fall prey to the illusion that the power of fascination belongs to the object as such. (*Looking Awry* 33, Žižek's italics)

Everybody feels desire because of some kind of narcissistic lack; the problem with the melancholic is that she or he tries to fill that void (and winds up circling around it) by treating it not as a constitutive lack, but as a prior wholeness that has been lost, and, on top of that, fails to grasp the object-cause for which that particular lost loved object was selected by the melancholic. The first ethical problem here is that the subject is rendered unable to live in the present; the second is the lie that the subject was ever whole.

In other words—and in conflating two different arguments of Žižek, I am arriving at this conclusion by a slightly different route than he does—"melancholy is not simply attachment to the lost object, but attachment to the very original gesture of its loss" ("Melancholy" 144). Speaking of someone's moving from a place in which that person has lived all his or her life, Žižek notes that "[w]hat makes me sad is the fact that I am aware that, sooner or later—sooner than I am ready to admit—I will integrate myself into a new community, forgetting the place which *now* means so much to me. In short, what makes me sad is the awareness that I will lose my desire for (what is now) my home" (149). Or, as he explains in a note to this passage, "At its most radical, anxiety is not the anxiety of losing the desired object, but the anxiety of losing desire itself," that is, it is "a defense mechanism against the much more horrifying prospect of passive indifference, of *not desiring at all*. . . . For example, when we are separated from our lover for a year or two, what we fear most is not the pain of separation itself but the prospect of indifference, of becoming accustomed to the absence of the beloved" (265, 266, Žižek's italics). This fear of passive indifference, of losing loss itself, of the cessation of one's melancholy circling, I would submit, is the fundamental anxiety of old southern studies, a field whose most passionate critiques of successful mourning, bulldozer revolutions, national projects of forgetting, and the like thus stand among its most self-deceptive moments.[10]

So Why Isn't Old Southern Studies Youth Culture?

Though in hindsight, the 1990s increasingly appears as a brief window of relative peace and prosperity between the Cold War and the "War on Terror," the period's youth culture tended to view the decade through a lens of remarkable melancholy. The characters in Douglas Coupland's 1991 novel *Generation X*, the *locus classicus* of Gen X rhetoric, for example, exude sadness and rage toward their elders, the baby boomers. Envying boomers' "fortunate births" and decrying "bleeding ponytails" ("elderly sold-out baby boomer[s] who pin[e] for hippie or pre-sellout days"), they are convinced, among other things, that there will be no Social Security left for them. One character tells a boomer, "You'd last about ten minutes if you were my age these days, Martin. And I have to endure pinheads like you rusting above me for the rest of my life, always grabbing the best piece of cake first and then putting a barbed wire fence around the rest. You really make me sick" (21). Chapters bear such upbeat titles as "Our Parents Had More" and "Dead at 30 Buried at 70." The rock band Smashing Pumpkins, meanwhile, cannily named their multiplatinum 1995 album *Mellon Collie and the Infinite Sadness*; its hit single featured the radio-friendly couplet "Despite all my rage / I am still just a rat in a cage." Less angry but more effectively pathetic was Uncle Tupelo's cover of the Carter Family's "No Depression in Heaven" on their 1990 album *No Depression*—a record that was, rightly or wrongly, widely taken as launching the alt-country movement. Indeed, country music—because of its melancholy, and for other reasons outlined in the following chapter, including its association with a culture found profoundly uncool by the baby boomers, the white South—was tailor-made for such a cultural moment, and in his 2002 essay "Why Isn't Country Music Youth Culture?" Trent Hill succinctly ties a Gen X youth culture sensibility to the melancholy southern working-class culture of country music that urban hipsters were rediscovering in the 1990s: "the cultural politics of alternative country are premised less on the possibilities of flight, freedom, and mobility than on immobility or downward mobility" (183), he writes, positing moreover that alt-country fans "imagin[e] an alternative culture, . . . one that might allow new affective and political alliances to understand the experience of 'working man's blues,' regardless of whether that working man is a truck driver or an office temp, a college-town bohemian or army vet" (183).

At least two things are worth observing about Hill's fantasy of alliance (an alliance that was deferred, to say the least, during the divisive Bush years). First, work and immobility are figured as the antithesis of boomer youth culture's reification of "flight, freedom, and mobility." In fact, at first glance, what the Xers were melancholy for appears to have been adulthood itself. This lack manifested itself in part as the loss of any adult role models under the ideological regime of what Christopher Lasch had labeled the "culture of narcissism." As early as 1992—at the dawn of what would appear to many to be sixteen consecutive years of a narcissistic, perpetually adolescent boomer occupying the Oval Office[11]—Lawrence Grossberg observed (as noted in the previous chapter) that "for the baby boomers, youth is something to be held onto by cultural and physical effort" (*We Gotta Get Out of This Place* 183)— no matter, many Xers might add, how indecorous this effort became. (Pop culture made by Gen Xers is full of this sort of observation. One thinks, for example, of Joss Whedon's 1999 *Buffy the Vampire Slayer* episode "Band Candy," produced in the immediate wake of the Monica Lewinsky scandal, in which the parental figures all begin acting like teenagers unable to defer gratification, with potentially disastrous effects that must be headed off by their children who, like Buffy herself, find themselves prematurely shouldering decidedly adult responsibilities; of the apparently disastrous legacies of all the appallingly bad fathers in J. J. Abrams's series *Lost*; of Kurt Cobain's lament in "Serve the Servants" that "I tried hard to have a father / But instead I had a Dad"; even of the Lemony Snicket novels.)[12] Yet the dominant Xer affect also, and more important, appears chiefly to have been experienced as a melancholy for Xers' *own* adulthood, an adulthood that—in good melancholic fashion—they had not lost yet, but kept overpresent precisely by bemoaning its loss: that vanished social security (in a double sense), those forty vanished years from age thirty to age seventy, that "Martin" perennially rusting over their heads.

Yet the backlash against the perpetual postmodern youth culture of "the generation which arrives at the gate in the 1960s" (Jameson, "Postmodernism and Consumer Culture" 112) seems to have led, second and a bit naively, to a desire for its antithesis, a wistfully premodern white southern "structure of feeling" that in various ways goes back at least to Edwin Alderman's discussion of the experience of defeat, an experience C. Vann Woodward would link to a kind of cultural adulthood. Having imagined a shared melancholic maturity, Xers such as Hill then seem actually to have expected it to trump traditional, obvious, and powerful political differences on such issues as war, abortion, gay marriage, gun rights, and the like, and expected it to do so largely because of a shared opposition to—that is, expected it to produce alliances against—what? The simplest answer would appear to be "the effects of globalization," which for all its flashy rhetoric regarding increased mobility (of both labor and capital) has quite obviously, in its turn toward increasing income inequality, led to diminished mobility both for the U.S. white working class and for many Gen Xers. In the face of these changes (and, for the white working class, in the face of changes wrought by the civil rights movement), and given the notorious difficulty involved in comprehending globalization itself, both groups have predictably enough constructed—and had constructed for them—an Other who has, in Lacan's terms, "stolen their *jouissance*." For Xers, that Other is the baby boomers (who have taken "the best piece of cake"). Unsurprisingly, then, when Hill asserts that alt-country's "musicians are not, unlike the urban, college-graduate hillbillies of the folk revival, interested in recovering an authentic past so much as articulating a set of connections and alliances within a marginalized present" (183), his argument suggests disavowal of its own boomer traits, as alt-country's fan base and performers consisted almost entirely of "urban, college-graduate hillbillies." The U.S. white working class, on the other hand, generally prefers to name its fantastic Other "liberal elites," "secular humanists," and so on: classes that very much include college-town bohemians, despite the latter's professed aversion to hippies-cum-yuppies. The fundamental problem here is not simply that—to put a Colbertian spin on Lacan—the Real has a well-known liberal bias. The fundamental problem is that the very narcissistic lack that drew Xers in the 1990s to a fantasy of truck driver-bohemian alliance blinded them to the most fundamental pathology of the melancholic: the complete inability to enter into new affective alliances because he or she is still circling endlessly around the Lost Loved Object.

The North American Furtwängler

We would seem to be back in the situation suggested by Fredric Jameson in the previous chapter: a group (Xers) as narcissistic fans of a "people" who themselves turn out to be narcissistically incomplete. Yet when it comes to melancholy, the situation may be more complicated. Of classical music fans' passion for the German conductor Wilhelm Furtwängler, Žižek writes,

> [i]t is not only that we are fascinated by Furtwängler's "naïve," immediately organic passion, which no longer seems possible in our era. [Rather,] the very lost object of our fascination already involves a certain loss—that is to say, Furtwängler's passion was infused with a kind of traumatic intensity. . . . So what we are longing to recapture in old Furtwängler recordings is not the organic immediacy

of classical music but, rather the organic-immediate experience of the loss itself that is no longer accessible to us—in this sense, our fascination with Furtwängler is melancholy at its purest. ("Melancholy" 145)

In the rather less highbrow North American context, we might do better to say our fascination with the lost traumatic intensity of classic country—Hank Williams, Johnny Cash, the Carter Family, Merle Haggard, Loretta Lynn, even Patsy Cline—represents "melancholy at its purest." But if we can imagine a melancholic longing for melancholic longing, can we not imagine a still purer melancholic longing for melancholic longing for melancholic longing? Ah, how I miss the good old days when we used to listen to Furtwängler! Or: how I miss the good old days when we used to listen to Furtwängler conduct Mahler! Or even: how I miss the good old days when we used to listen to Furtwängler conducting Fischer-Dieskau singing Mahler—on vinyl! Etc. In a potentially infinite series—logically, a necessarily infinite series—no single state can be melancholy's purest form: there is always another state one further, seemingly adulterating remove from the imagined original traumatic loss. Put differently, every melancholic state might be seen as *always already* a state whose object-cause is infinitely receding. Ah, how I miss the good old days when we used to listen to that 8-track of Johnny Cash performing live at a prison a version of his earlier studio performance of a convict weeping daily because of a train whistle that suggests his own melancholy!

But as the recursive nature of the previous example might suggest, might it not also be possible—as a kind of formal manifestation of the drive's own circular structure—to construct a sort of Moebius strip of melancholy? If so, such is the brilliant strategy behind Rick Rubin's persuading Johnny Cash to cover Trent Reznor's teen-angst ballad "Hurt," to produce the purest (to date) fantasy of hipster melancholia, in which, in Žižek's terms, Cash/Furtwängler sings improbably of cutting himself: "I hurt myself today / to see if I still feel. / I focus on the pain, / the only thing that's real," etc., etc. Cash has a long history of melancholically performing someone else's melancholy—a long way of saying, perhaps, that he is no stranger to schmaltzy tearjerkers. "Folsom" is just the tip of the iceberg; though the list is nearly endless, for example, one might consider how, in "Long Black Veil," a song written in 1959 to sound much older, he expertly takes on the challenging task of singing, from the point of view of a dead man of some unspecified earlier era, about his best friend's wife whose decidedly ill-founded good reputation he dies to save, a woman who "cries o'er my bones." Yet the melancholy Cash performs on "Hurt" has a particular 1990s youth culture tinge to it even apart from the song's being a Nine Inch Nails cover. In *Welcome to the Desert of the Real!* Žižek reminds us of the 1990s phenomenon of "'cutters' (people, mostly women, who experience an irresistible urge to cut themselves with razors or otherwise hurt themselves). . . . Far from being suicidal, far from indicating a desire for self-annihilation, cutting is a radical attempt to (re)gain a hold on reality, or (another aspect of the same phenomenon) to ground the ego firmly in bodily reality, against the unbearable anxiety of perceiving oneself as nonexistent" (10). The irony is that this perception of nonexistence is, in the Lacanian view, existentially accurate, so that cutting is actually an *escape* from the Real. As Žižek asks rhetorically a few pages later, "if the true opposite of the Real is reality, what if, then, what [cutters] are actually escaping from is not simply the feeling of unreality, of the artificial virtuality of our lifeworld, but the Real itself which explodes in the guise of uncontrolled hallucinations which start to haunt us once we lose our anchoring in reality" (20)?

On one level, cutting yourself and listening to country music (like lamenting lost spoons and long-dead civil rights figures) *do* operate the same way: both allow you to escape from the Real into circling a much more manageable substitute trauma. "Bubba Shot the Jukebox," the Mark Chesnutt hit released a year before Reed published *My Tears Spoiled My Aim*, precisely illustrates this Lacanian principle: "Bubba shot the jukebox last night / Said it played a sad song that made him cry." It is not that Bubba cannot bear the sad reality brought to him by the jukebox, but the reverse: Bubba disrupts the melancholy circling of the bar's entire clientele, a community that, in Judith Butler's terms, "*cannot* overcome the loss without losing the very sense of itself as community" (468). He disrupts this community's "reality" by properly disposing of the jukebox, the *objet petit a*, "a quite ordinary, everyday object that, as soon as it is 'elevated to the status of the Thing,' starts to function as a kind of screen, an empty space on which the subject [here, the entire bar community] projects the fantasies that support his desire" (*Looking Awry* 133). Bubba's tears do *not* spoil his aim: "Reckless discharge of a gun / That's what the officers were claiming / Bubba hollered, 'Reckless! Hell! / I shot just where I was aiming.'" Moreover, unlike the young engineer in Žižek's interpretation of "Black House," Bubba is no technocratic outsider to the community but its ultimate insider: the redneck's redneck (as his name suggests) who knows exactly how to handle his .45. The most authentic response to white southern melancholy, Chesnutt (or his songwriter Dennis Linde) slyly suggests, is to confront the jukebox "in its senseless actuality"—a response the community, of course, finds unbearably "reckless." No wonder the song's first-person-plural narrator figures Bubba as not "mentally stable."

Rather less slyly, Johnny Cash's "Hurt" video sends the opposite message about melancholy. In "Hurt," Cash, the abjected regional Other, the object of hipster desire partly because he appears capable of deep—bass baritone—passion (even better when he's old and melancholy for when he was young and angry) and partly because he sings of, and as, people trapped in their own melancholy (people who cry, cry, cry), sings melancholically of being . . . an affectively deprived hipster. The award-winning video of the song (which in July 2011, www.nme.com, the website of the British fanboy magazine *NME*, pronounced the best music video of all time) tries to make it less about affective deprivation and more about *sic transit gloria mundi*: Cash's "empire of dirt" turns out, Ozymandias-style, to be all the stuff inside the shuttered House of Cash Museum—a framed gold record (for *At San Quentin*) whose glass has been shattered, a mix of clips from Cash's film career, and so on. (Do you remember how we used to watch that melancholy music video featuring old film footage of Johnny Cash in his lost young adulthood melancholically revisiting the dilapidated home of his lost childhood in melancholy rural Arkansas?) And here, of course, the contemplative gaze of the Other is rendered by June Carter Cash, the loving wife—and, arguably, codependent in chief—who looks with great love and concern and enabling forgiveness at her husband as he reflects with bitterness on the career that, alas, has brought him naught but fame, great wealth, and an estate on Jamaica. (Here, at least, the line "I will make you hurt" may be read as reflecting a degree of guilt over the narcissist's use of that Other, though it's a bit puzzling why the presence of June seems not to console Johnny.) When the song was recorded, of course, she was living disproof of the lines "everyone I know / goes away in the end," though her death shortly thereafter, and just a little before Johnny's, gave the whole thing an uncanny, yet highly satisfying, feel. The same may be said for Cash's strangely theatrical gestures, such as his ritually spilling some wine from what looks like a goblet. Is this some kind of seder?

In trying to bridge the gap between hipster melancholy and country music melancholy, between cutters and jukebox weepers, and in trying to validate both, the "Hurt" video inadvertently calls attention to the structural homology between the "passion for the real" (Žižek's concern in *Welcome to the Desert of the Real*) and melancholy (his concern in "Melancholy and the Act"). In both, that is, the pursuit of authentic emotion arrives instead at spectacular fakery. Of the passion for the real, Žižek notes that "the 'passion for the real' . . . culminates in its apparent opposite, in a *theatrical spectacle*—from the Stalinist show trials to spectacular terrorist acts" (*Welcome to the Desert* 9, Žižek's italics). Of melancholy, we learn that "the melancholic's *refusal* to accomplish the work of mourning thus takes the form of its very opposite: of a faked spectacle of *excessive, superfluous mourning* even before this object is lost" ("Melancholy" 146, Žižek's italics). I am still just a rat in my cage. I hurt myself today. I want everyone to know how furious and sad I am. I have to endure pinheads like you. I hang my head and cry.

Songs That Move Hipsters to Tears

The irony of the epigraph with which this chapter began—Johnny Cash asking whether there is anything behind the symbols of modern country— is that from a Lacanian perspective Cash himself occupies exactly such an empty position within the symbolic order. In Pitchfork Media's 2006 feature "The 200 Greatest Songs of the 1960s," for example, Cash's live-at-Folsom version of "Folsom Prison Blues" clocks in at an astounding number eight. Reviewer Stephen M. Deusner gushes, "'Hello. I'm Johnny Cash.' That opening line, so deadpan and needless—everybody, especially in Folsom, knows who Johnny Cash is—may be the genesis of the Man in Black myth, even more so than the song 'Man in Black.' Making such a humble introduc-tion, Cash sounds larger than life—definitely larger than prison" (Deusner, "Johnny Cash"). Two years later, when Columbia released the "Legacy Edi-tion" of that concert, Deusner faced a difficult moment:

> Columbia/Legacy's new set relegates [the "Hello, I'm Johnny Cash" line] to the actual moment in the show, well after Carl Perkins and the Statler Brothers have warmed up the crowd. Here it's revealed to be a rehearsed moment:
>
> > HUGH CHERRY: I need your help. When John comes out here, he will say—and which will be recorded—"Hi there. I'm Johnny Cash." When he says that, then you respond. Don't respond to him walking out. Welcome him after he says, "Johnny Cash." I'll have my hands up, and you just follow me.
> > JOHNNY CASH: Hello, I'm Johnny Cash.
> > CROWD: Goes nuts. (Deusner, Rev. of *Johnny Cash at Folsom Prison*)

Deusner's response? "Call it staged if you want, but the moment comes across as genuine, as if the emcee had told the prisoners what they had planned to do anyway." In response to the widely acknowledged difference in quality between the two shows Cash performed at Folsom that day, moreover, Deusner claims, "The liners suggest that Cash was simply tired, but it seems more likely that the worst of it was over and he knew he had nothing left to prove at that point." Even the scandalous inauthenticity of Cash's perform-ing as a convict to convicts gets acknowledged, only to be beaten back down by Deusner's will-to-idolatry:

> of course, Cash never really did all the hard time he sang about in "Folsom Prison Blues"; his violations were largely misdemeanors (picking flowers in Starkville, Mississippi) rather than outright felonies (shooting a man in Reno just to watch him die). But his lackluster rap sheet doesn't make these two shows any less re-warding or meaningful. Rather, they have the force of empathic endeavors, as if he were doing penance for his notorious bad habits. Having courted his own prison sentences—both literally and metaphorically—Cash knew how little sepa-rated the free and the condemned, so he turned his angst into raucous country

music during his first performance and breathed a deep sigh of relief during his second.

As art historian John Berger was fond of saying, "This is mystification." Deusner's "as ifs" and his "seems more likely" allow him to report his own overdetermined subjective responses to Cash "as if" they were objective traits of Cash's own performance.

Such reportage is symptomatic of Cash's status as the Pitchfork hipster's *objet petit a*. Looked at straight on, Johnny Cash is one of many significant mass culture performers: at the University of Mississippi's 2006 southern music conference, country music scholar Diane Pecknold dryly observed of her childhood (and the same holds true for mine), "in our house, it was Johnny Cash and *The Lawrence Welk Show*."[13] Looked at straight on, Cash is a fake convict (unlike, say, David Allan Coe or Merle Haggard); looked at straight on, his deadpan trademark "Hello, I'm Johnny Cash," on which Deusner has hung all the "Man in Black" myth of authenticity, is carefully staged; looked at straight on, the Man in Black is worn out by his second show (the first, after all, had begun at 9:40 in the morning). Looked at awry, however, with the fairy dust of hipster anamorphosis glittering upon him, Cash, remade as "larger than life," fills out the void of the Thing.

More worryingly, he serves the same function in Aaron Fox's 2004 scholarly book *Real Country: Music and Language in Working-Class Culture*:

> low and gravelly and accented and weary and dour, Johnny Cash's voice will always signify pain and entrapment and struggle, the sonic equivalent of the black garments he always wore in solidarity with the poor and oppressed of the world. "Folsom Prison Blues," in particular, will be forever associated with its canonical performance on an album recorded live at California's Folsom Prison in 1968, where the prisoners unleashed a mighty cheer as [guitarist Luther] Perkins' opening riff sounded out. (310)

This is Pitchfork prose, and as such it must struggle to maintain its anamorphic gaze on Cash. Indeed, much of its symptomaticity lies in the worst aspects of the writing itself: the cliché "unleashed a mighty cheer" reminds us of how weirdly both Fox and Deusner invest convicts, of all people, with an unproblematic authenticity, while "forever" and the repetition of "always," both so lacking in scholarly caution, attempt to divert our attention away from the obvious temporality, and by implication the arbitrariness, of Cash's current popularity: how very uncool he was in the 1970s, when country music was definitely not youth culture; how hipsters resuscitated his reputation in the late 1980s; how Rick Rubin cannily marketed in the 1990s what those hipsters had "discovered"[14]; and how very unlikely it is that the presently hegemonic notion of what Cash's voice "signifies" will outlive people like Fox and Deusner. (Ironically enough, the transience of fame is precisely the major motif of the "Hurt" video.) If Fox's work anywhere engaged directly with the massive body of work on authenticity cited, for example, in Pamela Fox's and Barbara Ching's introduction to their recent collection *Old Roots, New Routes: The Cultural Politics of Alt.country Music* (24–25n33), to which Fox contributes, this approach might not seem so egregious. Absent such engagement, Fox's claims for country music's "authenticity" appear to reflect not country music or its fans but Fox's own fantasy (in the strict Lacanian sense).

Indeed, reviewing *Real Country* in *American Quarterly*, Jonathan Silverman gently notes the book "feels a bit romanticized," and compares Fox's experiences with working-class Texans to Silverman's own infatuation, as an outsider like Fox come to Texas for graduate study, with quarter horse racing culture: "I was more fascinated with its peculiarities and less concerned with its politics. . . . Fox may be suffering from the same type of fascination with his subject" (549). Romanticizing the working class is nothing new in bourgeois culture or scholarship. What is remarkable, however, is Fox's bourgeois-hipster disavowal of alt-country bourgeois hipsters, whom he rather oddly conflates with the phenomenal success of the *O Brother, Where Art Thou?* soundtrack. In "'Alternative' to What? *O Brother*, September 11, and the Politics of Country Music," an essay that appeared a year after *Real Country* but that is cited in it, Fox sets out the contrast in some detail:

> For artists like [obscure rural working-class musician Randy] Meyer and Shania Twain, the ideological categories within which they craft their respective arts offer few if any alternatives to gendered musical conventions. Their socially located performance styles are overdetermined by working-class identity politics, and by each artist's working-class background. Conversely, *O Brother* embodies bourgeois ease: the freedom to cultivate, curate, dabble in, and reconfigure the alternatives offered up in the commodity form by modern American culture. The social crossing, passing, and constitutive irony of the project . . . complement the claim to adjudicate the boundaries of vernacular authenticity assumed by the *O Brother* project.
>
> Johannes Fabian has famously said of anthropology that the discipline "emerged and established itself as an allochronic discourse; it is a science of other men in another Time. It is a discourse whose referent has been removed from the present of the speaking/writing subject. This 'petrified relation,'" he writes, quoting [Karl] Marx, "is a scandal" (1983, 143). *Mutatis mutandis*, the same could be said of the present condition of some contemporary alternative constructions of the vernacular. It is not as simple as deciding whether any particular gesture of cultural minstrelsy is respectful or not, authentic or not, popular or not, commercial or not. I am passing no judgment on any of those questions. Rather, I am interrogating the class politics of alternative identities. . . . Th[e] point, in summary, is that the answer to the question "'alternative' to what?" . . . might best be rephrased as "alternative to—and for—whom?" (188)

Of course, Fox *is* "passing judgments": "cultural minstrelsy" is not exactly a nonjudgmental phrase. The real problem here appears to be that *O Brother* seems to threaten Fox's own claim in *Real Country* to "adjudicate the boundaries of vernacular authenticity." On the very first page of *Real Country*, Fox writes, "My central assertion—that country music is an authentic working-class art of enormous value to its blue-collar constituency—is straightforward and perhaps obvious, though it is an argument of a kind currently out of fashion in popular music scholarship. I hope this book is a convincing critique of such fashions" (ix). Yet Fox's own ethnography and musical tastes replicate precisely what he rails against. The son of a college professor, Fox grows up in Cambridge, Massachusetts, and, he tells us, discovers country music while working as a furniture mover during a period when he has dropped out of Harvard. Fox is free to come and go not only between being a mover and being a Harvard student but also later between Lockhart, Texas, site of his fieldwork, and Austin, where he attends graduate school (and later between Lockhart and Seattle and New York, where he lands positions at prestigious research universities); he is free to "cultivate, curate, dabble in" country music and engage in "social crossing [and] passing"; and—most disturbingly—he is free to petrify country as "a trope of alternativity to the modern" ("Alternative" 167), stuck in "the postwar class compromise" (*Real Country* 319), its desires "modulated by a poetic obsession with loss and the looming presence of the past" (*Real Country* 318).

In short, the working-class white South operates as an authentic, antimodern populist world every bit as much for Fox as it does for the consumers of the *O Brother, Where Art Thou?* soundtrack. Or, in Lacanian terms, in its "passion for the real," Fox's work spectacularly embodies bourgeois academic fashion: the lingering 1990s fashion for melancholy and abjection, which no less a trend-watcher than art historian Hal Foster first wrote about back in 1996 in *The Return of the Real*: "for many in contemporary culture truth resides in the traumatic or abject subject, in the diseased or damaged body" (166). The final chapter of *Real Country* is entitled "'I Hang My Head and Cry,'" and it describes a moment when, performing a cover of "Folsom Prison Blues," a working-class fellow named "Big Joe" sings that line:

> Joe lowered his large head iconically and bellowed the line, word for word, with the most incredible amount of gravity, sinking down to the resonant low E on the last word, sung with enough *profundo* power that it vibrated our bones, the way only a few singers besides Johnny Cash can do. Suddenly, Johnny Cash *was* in the room with us. (314)

Joe then forgets some of the words, but, concludes Fox, "Knowing all the words did not mean knowing a song. The right words had to be saturated with the sweat and specificity of a particular body, a particular life, and a particular voice" (315).

The story does not end there, however. A few years later, on a blog Fox set up to promote the book, a York University graduate student named "Gillian T." commented, "Just wanted to let you know that I just cried through the end of the book, something that I rarely do with an ethnography." Apparently, that is, Gillian T. wept at Fox's depiction of Big Joe's impersonation of Johnny Cash performing live at a prison a version of his earlier studio performance of a convict weeping daily because of a train whistle. The "passion for the real"—here, the bourgeois Canadian academic's mediated consumption of a rural backwater populist world where people are more authentic than they allegedly are in Toronto—culminates yet again in a *"theatrical spectacle."*

Shooting the Jukebox

The essays in *Loss*—only one of which, Vilashini Cooppan's, deals with Lacan more than in passing, and none of which engages with Žižek's devastating critique of melancholy first published four years earlier—seem to slide between a strong set of claims about melancholy and a weaker but, I think, more compelling set. When Judith Butler writes approvingly of a place "where community does not overcome the loss, where community *cannot* overcome the loss without losing the very sense of itself as community" (468), she expresses the stronger argument, one in which melancholy is imagined as in itself productive. On the matter of melancholy, I have tried (following Žižek) to show how, in practice, scholarship fascinated by this affective dimension falls rapidly into bathos; on the matter of community, one very much wishes Butler had read Scott Romine's masterful deconstruction of such communities in his 1999 book *The Narrative Forms of Southern Community*. More broadly, one wishes that queer theory (like ethnography) had from the start been more interested in Flyover Country and the recent scholarship on (and from) it, which has more to offer than some coastally based scholars seem to think.[15] Had that been the case, those fields' practitioners might be less inclined now to praise, like Butler and Fox, such communities' exotic poignancy—less inclined, in postcolonialist terms, to indulge in the romance of Otherness.

At points in their introduction to the volume, David L. Eng and David Kazanjian do offer a more moderate view. Following Freud, and Butler's somewhat earlier work, they figure melancholia as important not least because it facilitates both subject formation *and mourning itself* (4). In other places, however, they go so far as to suggest that "avowals of and attachments to loss can produce a world of remains as a world of new representations and alternative meanings. . . . Ultimately, such counterintuitive understandings of loss apprehend the modern and postmodern epoch of loss . . . as full of volatile potentialities and future militancies rather than as pathologically bereft and politically reactive" (5).

As I argue throughout this book, however, most people—despite Cold War modernization theory—live neither in a world of "future militancies" nor in a world that is "pathologically bereft and politically reactive." Most of us muddle through a very complex present. Under such circumstances, if scholars, in theory or practice, end up circling either the *objet petit a* of a radical futurity or that of a reactionary pastness, the critic—"Puritan leftist" or not—has a singular responsibility, in Lacan's terms, to "traverse the fantasy." At such a point, that is, the critic needs to brace himself or herself for the inevitable (and, for Žižek, inevitably "catastrophic" [*Plague* 29]) accusations of recklessness, even madness—and shoot the jukebox.

TWO

GERMAN LESSONS
On Getting Over a Lost Supremacy

Psychoanalysis is much more severe than Christianity: ignorance is *not* a sufficient reason for forgiveness since it conveys a hidden dimension of *enjoyment*. Where one doesn't (want to) know, in the blanks of one's symbolic universe, one enjoys, and there is no Father to forgive. —Slavoj Žižek, *For They Know Not What They Do*, 1991

Every good Christian ought to kick Falwell right in the ass.[1] —Barry Goldwater, 1981

From a White Man's Country to a Christian Nation

As displacements of irresponsible white melancholy, the escapist enjoyments of old southern studies scholars and of melancholy hipsters are hardly the worst responses to modernity one encounters. As I was finishing this book, the news was filling with reports about the proposed Ugandan "Anti-Homosexuality Bill," known to the U.S. Left as the "Kill the Gays" bill. The bill's reasoning derived in part from the writings and statements of "ex-gay" Richard Cohen and others on the U.S. religious Right, including both Rick Warren (who in 2008 had declared Uganda the world's second official "purpose-driven nation,"[2] and who was very late to denounce the legislation) and Warren's old dissertation director at Fuller Theological Seminary in Pasadena, C. Peter Wagner. Although the *New York Times* reported the immediate impetus for the legislation was a visit by antigay evangelicals Scott Lively, Caleb Lee Brundidge, and Don Schmierer, "who were presented as experts on homosexuality" at a series of talks attended by "thousands of Ugandans including police officers, teachers and national politicians" who "listened raptly to the Americans" (Gettleman), the story also involved a weird, almost Skull and Bones-like organization of religious conservatives called "The Family," the subject of the 2008 bestseller of that name by *Harper's* contributing editor Jeff Sharlet. The Ugandan legislation's sponsor, David Bahati, is a member of the group, as are past and present U.S. Senators John Ensign, James Inhofe, Chuck Grassley, and Tom Coburn, along with former Representative Bart Stupak, among many others.[3]

These global connections, along with other aspects of the surprisingly close financial, ideological, and personal links between the legislation and the U.S. Christian Right described in recent news reports, may represent the true face of what James Peacock describes as progress in his usually excellent book *Grounded Globalism: How the U.S. South Embraces the World*:

> Anglicans from the American South who are joining the global south are allying themselves with African colleagues who would previously have been regarded as subordinate or alien: they are black, they were colonized, and they are citizens of a continent that provided slaves. And in this allegiance, the U.S. southerners bypass the northeastern United States, which was formerly the source of liberal thinking about race relations and civil rights, and go straight to the global sphere. In so doing, the southern U.S. Anglicans repeat a certain pattern of the past: they secede from a northern union. (62)

Even given the national, rather than just regional, makeup of the Christian Right, which is strong everywhere except in the nation's two most secularized regions, the Northeast and the Pacific Northwest (and which is even growing in Canada, whose prime minister, Stephen Harper, is a conservative evangelical), Peacock's comparison of the two secessions is astute in ways he may not have intended since he is thinking about the civil rights only of blacks, not gays (whose ordination is, of course, a major driver of the Anglican split). A decade ago, when I reviewed Scott Romine's excellent first book, *The Narrative Forms of Southern Community*, about the only thing I could take issue with was his conclusion, which—like most other southern studies of the past twenty or thirty years—made a mistake similar to Peacock's. After having shown by the second page of that book that "insofar as it is cohesive, a community will tend to be coercive" (2), Romine ultimately waffled, suggesting that community might still be possible if "the old ideals of responsibility, connectedness, and manners" (211) were extended across racial lines. However, citing the mid-1990s Pontotoc, Mississippi, case in which a Lutheran woman had moved there from Wisconsin, protested the prayers that issued forth from the loudspeakers of her children's public school, become thereby the object of concerted opposition by an alliance of white and black preachers, and received death threats, I suggested in the review that biracial communities just tend to become coercive in different ways, most likely religious ones (Rev. of *The Narrative Forms of Southern Community* 331–32).

Regionally, nationally, and globally, we are well along in just such a transition, but most of us in global/U.S./southern literary studies have not adapted very well to this present. Christian conservatism is not the only form of conservatism, of course, and it may or may not itself be fracturing these days, but it nevertheless remains the single biggest and best-organized conservative force in the country, and we need to think about this secessional shift. Despite the protests of religious studies scholars—more on which below—one could do worse than to begin with psychoanalytic theory. The United States, including the U.S. South, is hardly the first national culture to deal with the perceived loss of a racial supremacy, and postwar Germany, I argue in this chapter, offers a highly relevant case study in the mourning and working-through of that loss. Germany owes its relative success in getting over the narcissistic loss of its "Aryan supremacy" in large part to the efforts of psychoanalytically minded intellectuals like Alexander and Margarete Mitscherlich and Jürgen Habermas to create a space, a public sphere, for that mourning and working-through. The United States, however, has, with few exceptions, preferred to dodge such an experience, and, as a result, many of its whites keep identifying as victims. The cycle of endless displacement—from "this is a white man's country" to "this is a Christian nation" to something else—will not be broken until we stop dodging that experience. Yet the solution to this problem will not be arrived at by "moderation," as some contemporary scholars see it, nor by gentle compromise with—enabling of—racial and religious irrationality. Indeed, the argument that the religious live in a "different modernity" than the rest of us do and hence should be accommodated precisely echoes the arguments that perpetuated Jim Crow segregation. What we need, instead, are arguments that rationally disrupt the mindless circling of conservative drive, that shoot the conservative jukebox.

Nine years ago in *A Stone of Hope*, the revisionist civil rights historian David Chappell, breaking with the rather heroic accounts of baby boomers about why the civil rights movement succeeded, looked instead at why its conservative opposition failed. He argued that racism "fail[ed] to solidify a conservative coalition" and that "it would remain for a later conservative movement, one that sublimated the racism of the southern white masses and built its power within the churches, to hammer together a radical (and largely successful) conservative insurgency" (178). Contemporary conservatives have "learned the lessons of history" from the deeply religious civil rights movement, he argued, concluding, "historians need to catch up with them" (178).

So do the rest of us. But the Ugandan example suggests something more complicated is going on than can be explained by Chappell's vaguely Freudian concept of "sublimation." "Sublimation" suggests the redirection of a deep primacy; it is something we do with the sex or death drive, for example. It might work as a general, less technical notion of unconscious substitution, if, for example, you happen to believe, as I do not, that calling Obama a "Muslim" is nothing more than code for, or sublimation of, calling him black, or that "this is a Christian nation" is nothing more than the same for "this is a white man's country."[4] But Chappell's own account of how relatively easily a racist status quo not firmly grounded in religion collapsed in the face of an antiracist movement that was, not to mention the ease and speed with which the Right's focus has shifted, in the Ugandan example, from racist secession to the homophobic sort, reminds us that racism is in any event not itself a drive but a symptom of one.

Jacques Lacan may thus be of more use than Sigmund Freud here. That much of the Right can switch its object of fascination, the sublime object of its ideology, effortlessly and swiftly from the Negro who wants to have sex with your daughter to the homosexual who wants to recruit your son is possible, in such an account, because the pleasure one derives from hating and fearing each derives not from either object of hate and fear but from the repetitive movement of the circuit, from the structure itself. While anxiety might seem unpleasant, as both Lacan and Žižek argue elsewhere, people actually enjoy it because it is infinitely preferable to what they really fear, which is feeling nothing at all, the cessation of their circling. Why else would anyone have watched Glenn Beck, whose own credo seems almost eerily Lacanian: "Believe in something—even if it's wrong, believe in it!"? The fantasy that drives the two secessions is the particularly common one of what Lacanians call "the Other who has stolen my enjoyment"—here, the Negro or the homosexual or the federal government or, in other places and times, the Jew, the Roma, Woman. Such a fantasy is hardly limited to the Right: one thinks of Dos Passos's "strangers who have stolen the old words and made them slimy and foul," for example, and one danger of my own approach (as for that of many on the left) is a potential construction of the Christian Right as itself just such a thieving Other.[5] But some fantasies are a great deal more pathological than others, and there are two main problems with the secessionist fantasy that are a great deal more serious than the fantastic elements of left claims about that fantasy may be. First is the secessionists' pathological narcissism. Oppression in this supremacist logic consists not in my being forced to do the will of another, but in not being permitted to impose my will on another, in my being compelled to recognize and respect the boundary between us. Once the logic was—if I cannot hold slaves (or even, more precisely, if I cannot extend slavery into the territories north of 36°30'), I am being oppressed. Then it was—if I cannot discriminate against African Americans, I am being oppressed. Today, it is—if I cannot force women to carry their fetuses to term, regardless of their own beliefs; if I cannot force others to listen to my prayers, regardless of their own beliefs; if I cannot deny gays and lesbians the right to marry that I possess; if I cannot celebrate my own religion on courtroom walls, regardless of (and, not infrequently, to the explicit exclusion of) others' beliefs—I am being oppressed! The second problem lies in the nature of the drive itself: if many conservatives' pleasure derives from the circling, they are going to need a new goal because given the advances of the past twenty years, the dying off of older homophobes, and the much greater acceptance among the young, gay rights are well on the way to becoming an issue nearly as legally settled in the United States as African

American civil rights are now—and as gay rights are in several other countries.[6]

I am hardly the first to suggest that the narcissism of white Christian conservatives structurally duplicates, and in many cases evolves from, the narcissism of white supremacists—and not simply because an older generation of such conservatives, most obviously Jerry Falwell and Pat Robertson, once advocated white supremacy. In 1998, the inaugural issue of the *Journal of Southern Religion* featured a jeremiad by Sam Hill, at the time the dean of southern religious history. Hill missed the point I am trying to make, but not, perhaps, by all that much. He argued that with the fundamentalist ascendancy of the 1970s, "the old base on which [southern] unity and identity rested that was social-cultural-historical has given way to a new base that is ideological, theological, and ethical," and he was not happy about the development. His account was, of course, yet another version of the story of the Other who has stolen our enjoyment; the problem, as he seems to have been at least partly aware, was that the lamented lost order had been profoundly racist. Hill's way around this difficulty was to claim—rather precipitously!—that by the 1970s, the civil rights movement had "succeeded in large degree." Thus the usurped order could be refigured as something inclusive.

It is Joel Martin's thoughtful response to Hill's article that more concerns the present argument. Instead of positing a simple usurpation or succession, Martin suggested a tight *causal* link between the successes of the civil rights movement and the embrace of Christian fundamentalism by white southerners:

> fundamentalism also appealed to white Southerners for region-specific reasons. White Southerners' self-image had suffered terrifically as a result of the outcome of the civil rights movement. Judged by history and the nation as corrupt and bigoted, they longed to restore a sense of themselves as a moral people. Fundamentalism provided the answer with its appeal to a higher authority: the inerrant Bible. In it, white Southerners found "family values" and restored their sense of their own moral propriety. Fundamentalism further appealed to white Southerners by appropriating the rhetoric and tactics of the civil rights movement itself. As Elvis appropriated Black music, fundamentalism encouraged whites to think of themselves as the true heirs of King!

Martin's account closely resembles at key points Alexander and Margarete Mitscherlich's classic analysis of German psychology after the fall of the Third Reich:

> the Germans . . . had received a blow to the very core of their self-esteem, and the most urgent task for their psychic apparatus was to ward off the experience of a melancholy impoverishment of the self. . . . An epoch of maximum self-glorification now proved to be inexorably connected with the greatest crimes. The motivation for its de-realization was not only fear of punishment and defense

against guilt, but also defense against the admission that one was now powerless and worthless and thus had to renounce primitive mechanisms of gratification—the pleasure, namely, of acting out infantile fantasies of omnipotence. (It would probably be no error to connect the ever-recurrent cult of stainless national honor with primary narcissism, that is to say, with very early infantile self-love.) (24–25)

The Mitscherlichs chart several ways in which postwar Germans avoided dealing with the past, but the most important one for us (as for Eric Santner, who builds on the Mitscherlichs' arguments in his book *Stranded Objects*) is identification with the victim—by which is meant not empathy with actual victims, but imagining oneself *as* victim:

> Identification with the innocent victim is very frequently substituted for mourning; this is above all a logical defense against guilt. . . . To the conscious mind the past then appears as follows: We made many sacrifices, suffered the war, and were discriminated against for a long time afterward; yet we were innocent, since everything that is now held against us we did under orders. This strengthens the feeling of being oneself the victim of evil forces; first the evil Jews, then the evil Nazis, and finally the evil Russians. In each instance the evil is externalized. It is sought for on the outside, and it strikes one from the outside. (Mitscherlichs 45–46)

White southerners did not offer a Nuremberg defense per se (even the doctrine of biblical inerrancy—"we are," as it were, "only following orders"—is used to justify present practices, not to excuse apartheid), but the remainder of the Mitscherlichs' critique applies to the fundamentalist turn as Martin describes it. "Acting out infantile fantasies of omnipotence" precisely characterizes *all* forms of white supremacy, for example (not to mention torture, which seeks to recapture a magical lost omnipotence, and which Pew Research tells us is disproportionately supported by fundamentalists), and the discussion of honor as narcissistic maps quite well onto historian Bertram Wyatt-Brown's analyses of southern honor. Moreover, whites in the wake of the civil rights movement, precisely like the Mitscherlichs' Germans, experienced the massive loss of a narcissistic ego-ideal that they were never able to admit, and hence never able to mourn.[7] Instead, they identified as victims of externalized evil forces: of the federal government, and, most famously in the South, of "outside agitators."[8] (Dr. Martin Luther King's refutation in the *Letter from Birmingham Jail* of such charges is worth rereading in this light.) As Santner sums it up in the German context, "This globally deployed narcissism project[s] difference and otherness as something that intervenes from the outside, something that could and should be purged from an otherwise pure system seamlessly continuous with itself" (5).

The work of more recent historians who "challeng[e] southern exceptionalism . . . not to absolve the south but to implicate the nation" (Lassiter and Crespino 7) strongly suggests that, just as the civil rights movement was not limited to the South (see virtually all the essays in Lassiter and Crespino's collection *The Myth of Southern Exceptionalism*), "the post-civil rights moral crisis of whites" was hardly limited to *southern* whites, even if it was strongest in the South. As literary critic Pamela Barnett puts it in a recent reading of white male anxieties in James Dickey's *Deliverance*, "the South was a microcosm of the nation's most anxious responses to civil rights, black nationalism, and feminism. While the entire nation's social structure was in upheaval, white southerners perceived an attack to 'their way of life,' and the rest of the country willingly located the problem below the Mason-Dixon line" (146). Yet even the perception of attack—seemingly the most extreme of reactions—was far from limited to white southerners. Conservative theologian Richard John Neuhaus—who can hardly be called hostile to fundamentalism—argued more than a quarter century ago in *The Naked Public Square* that while liberals imagine "the faults of a conservative government [to be] more passive than active," conservatives think "the sins of liberal government are sins of commission: government does many things they think it should not do and forbids them to do things they think they should be free to do. They are notably outraged by governments that, they believe, advance changes in sexual and family mores—areas that could hardly be more value-laden. . . . On a broad range of issues conservatives react to *a high level of experienced assault*" (31, 34, Neuhaus's italics). Neuhaus's description—he does not intend it as a critique—applies every bit as much to religiously inclined conservative intellectuals as to more "grassroots" conservatives. In a recent festschrift marking the twenty-fifth anniversary of Neuhaus's book, Mary Ann Glendon, the Learned Hand Professor of Law at Harvard University, worries for example that, if the Supreme Court—which since the 1980s has not exactly been the most liberal branch of government—stays on its present course, "it is not fanciful to imagine a Supreme Court majority following a course that could well end by reducing followers of many religions to something like *dhimmitude*—the status of non-Muslims in a number of Islamic countries. The *dhimmi* is tolerated so long as his religion is kept private and his public acts do not offend the state religion. Key positions in society are of course reserved for those who adhere to the official creed" (36). Glendon experiences her high level of assault—her *jouissance*—from rulings "where the Court has sustained efforts to ban religious expression in public school settings" such as a "moment of silence," "prayer at graduation ceremony," and "student-led, student-initiated prayer before football games" (199n2). The counterargument is so obvious—particularly to those of us who have marked several thousand freshman compositions written by students from sheltered backgrounds—that one feels silly rehearsing it in a scholarly book. How would Glendon feel if public schools engaged in formal assertions of atheism at graduations, student-led, student-initiated statements of atheism before football games, and so on? The condition of

assaulted *dhimmitude* she fears is, in fact, precisely the condition of virtually every atheist in the United States under the system of religion-endorsing
state practices the Supreme Court has been rather slowly dismantling.

Much of Neuhaus's own thinking is founded on an argument equally spe-
cious and equally eager to consign the nonreligious to the second-class status
Glendon fears will befall "followers of many religions": "A public ethic cannot be reestablished unless it is informed by religiously grounded values.
That is, without such an engagement of religion, it cannot be reestablished
in a way that would be viewed as democratically legitimate. The reason for
this is that, in sociological fact, the values of the American people are deeply
rooted in religion" (*Naked Public Square* 21). A few years later in an essay
entitled "Can Atheists Be Good Citizens?" Neuhaus explained one corol-
lary of this argument: "In times of testing—and every time is a time of testing for this American experiment in ordered liberty—a morally convincing
account must be given. You may well ask. Convincing to whom? One obvious answer in a democracy, although not the only answer, is this: convincing to a majority of their fellow citizens. Giving such an account is required
of good citizens. And that is why, I reluctantly conclude, atheists cannot be
good citizens." Neuhaus's allegedly "reluctant" claim seems to be advanced
in less than full good faith. (Like Glendon, he happily knows not what he
does.) If Neuhaus truly believed the majoritarian argument (based in "sociological fact") he advances, he would presumably have to concede that Christians cannot be "good citizens" in places like most of Europe, where religious
people are in the minority. The actual grounding for his claim, however, has
little to do with majoritarianism, or with democracy at all. "Can a person
who does not acknowledge that he is accountable to a truth higher than the
self, external to the self, really be trusted?" he asks rhetorically earlier in the
argument, as if forgetting the Blaise Pascal he had approvingly quoted in
The Naked Public Square: "Men never do evil so completely and cheerfully
as when they do it from religious conviction" (qtd. in *Naked Public Square*
8). (Indeed, Pascal's observation is one root of Lacan's argument that to the
atheist *nothing* is permitted because only the atheist cannot generate an exception to the Law by imagining she or he is doing God's will by breaking it.
To put it in a more Southern Baptist context, the atheist is the one who cannot believe she or he will be forgiven—or not "left behind"—because of faith
or a "personal relationship with Jesus.") In such a logic, European democra-
cies, if they function at all, must do so as dystopian Machiavellian hellholes
or at best Hobbesian wars of all against all. Instead, of course, they function
as some of the most stable polities on the planet.

Like white supremacists before them, what Glendon and Neuhaus betray
is, to put it mildly, an inability to deal with difference, with the relatively
minor sacrifices associated with losing a position of legally sanctioned supremacy. As Jeffrey Stout deftly argues in *Democracy and Tradition*, secu-

larization properly defined "just means that the age of theocracy is over, not that the anti-Christ has taken control of the political sphere" (93). This is far from a merely academic point, as Stout himself reminds us: "Theological resentment of the secular deserves attention from theorists of democracy not only because it gives voice to an animus felt by many religiously oriented citizens, but also because it reinforces that animus and encourages its spread. Radical orthodoxy is currently the hottest topic being debated in seminaries and divinity schools in the United States, and thus a significant part of the subculture within which future pastors are being educated" (92). Stout also addresses the profound pragmatic problem with the abhorrence of difference such theology reveals:

> Some theologians hold that the citizenry's common discourse on ethical and political topics suffers from incoherence in the absence of commonly held theological assumptions. They conclude that we should all therefore accept a common stock of theological assumptions in order to restore our shared discourse to coherence. But whose assumptions shall we adopt? And by what means shall we secure agreement on them? The crux of the issue is that nobody currently knows how to bring about by acceptable means what the theological opponents of secularized discourse are suggesting. Their proposals are unrealistic if pursued without resort to coercion and morally harmful if pursued coercively. (99–100)

Of course, from the perspective of a Lacanian drive, theirs is the very "best" sort of resentment because it allows for endless circling. Like John Shelton Reed's Confederate spoons, the putatively "lost" theological groundings are never coming back, so the theological groundings are always present.

If anything, the arguments of those few conservative intellectuals who are not interested in endless circling only place in sharper relief the dispositions of those who are. In a widely circulated May 2009 blog post, conservative legal and economic scholar Richard Posner admitted the satisfaction of his desire "by the end of the Clinton administration":

> I was content to celebrate the triumph of conservatism as I understood it, and had no desire for other than incremental changes in the economic and social structure of the United States. I saw no need for the estate tax to be abolished, marginal personal-income tax rates further reduced, the government shrunk, pragmatism in constitutional law jettisoned in favor of "originalism," the rights of gun owners enlarged, our military posture strengthened, the rise of homosexual rights resisted, or the role of religion in the public sphere expanded. All these became causes embraced by the new conservatism that crested with the reelection of Bush in 2004.

Posner's conservatism, which (whether one agrees with it or not) strives for rationality, has reached its "goal," while mainstream conservatism, in this logic, has shown itself chiefly interested in endless circling—in what, for example, Posner calls "the inanity of trying to substitute will for intellect, as in the denial of global warming, the use of religious criteria in the selection of public officials, [and] the neglect of management and expertise in government." Yet, as we have seen, to large segments of the U.S. Right, any criticism of such inanity—*most of all when rational*—is received with "*a high level of experienced assault.*" (For evidence, the reader is invited to scroll through the comments section of Posner's post.) How do you—how dare you—argue with such narcissism, with subjects who seem so profoundly to be enjoying their symptoms?

Critical Theory, the Religious Right, and the Public Sphere

For all its leftist posturing, American studies has, of course, rarely deigned to engage with them at all; one reason this chapter has cited such conservatives at length is my sense that few in American or southern studies are familiar with the tenor of contemporary conservative or theological arguments. However, the range of critical theory's *possible* responses to the religious Right, and to its southern connections, might usefully be delimited by the approaches of Jeffrey Stout and of Jonathan Culler. So far, scholars have certainly been reluctant either to acknowledge Culler's 1989 warning about evangelical Christianity, or to follow up on his remarkable recommendations. The former prefigures Stout's, but Culler advocates a very different set of tactics: "Literary studies may bear some responsibility for socially and politically dangerous conditions, in which an uncriticized religious discourse helps to legitimate a variety of repressive and reactionary movements. If that is so, then a political criticism ought to promote the critique of religion, not through systematic theory but through diverse challenges, including satire and mockery, in its dealing with literature and with cultural issues" (71). Stout, on the other hand, has proposed a near-blanket prohibition against using critical theory to discuss fundamentalism except under very extreme— one might say life or death—circumstances. Using the remarkable metaphor of ideology critique as a "hermeneutical ambulance," he suggests that "calling upon it too often bankrupts the same democratic process it seeks to serve": critical theorists "end by explaining away, instead of entering into conversation with, nearly everything that real people think, say, and feel" (178). Such critique, he believes, "exacts from the reservoir of substantive respect on which democratic discourse among neighbors can draw" (177). (In general, this has been the response of other scholars in religious studies as well; see, for example, R. Marie Griffith and Melani McAlister's 2007 special issue of *American Quarterly* on "Religion and Politics in the Contemporary United States.")

Our options for dealing with the religious Right thus seem bounded by precisely the generally metropolitan fantasies about "the South" already delineated in this book: on the one hand, its Othering as "an outland where 'we' know they all live: all the guilty, white yahoos" (Baker and Nelson 235); on the other, its construction as a populist world whose inhabitants—"real" people—are possessed of a mythic authenticity and homespun wisdom "we" intellectuals lack.[9] What would it mean to consider religious fundamentalism—which, even on seemingly secular matters, now powers so much contemporary U.S. conservatism, both in its dogma and in its structures of feeling—"in its senseless actuality" instead?

At the risk of stating the obvious, it means to respond rationally—indeed, to measure fundamentalist utterances against a high, not a low, standard of rationality. I want to illustrate this point by arguing first with literary critic Lauren Berlant and then, less fundamentally, with Stout himself. In the climactic section of *The Queen of America Goes to Washington City*, Berlant, who earlier argues flatly that "there is no public sphere in the contemporary United States" (3), advocates a mode of citizenship that operates more performatively than rationally:

> Diva Citizenship occurs when a person stages a dramatic coup in a public sphere in which she does not have privilege. Flashing up and startling the public, she puts the dominant story into suspended animation; as though recording an estranging voice-over to a film we have all already seen, she renarrates the dominant history as one that the abjected people have once lived sotto voce, but no more; and she challenges her audience to identify with the enormity of the suffering she has narrated and the courage she has had to produce, calling on people to change the social and institutional practices of citizenship to which they currently consent. (223)

Berlant seems to believe she has imagined a bold new (even capitalization-worthy) form of leftist intervention, but irrationalist discourse today chiefly enables the circling of the fundamentalist Right, and from a twenty-first-century perspective, what she really seems to have invented is the recipe for Sarah Palin. That the "abjection" of what Palin calls "real Americans"—small-town Christian white people, "sotto voce, but no more"!—exists (objectively speaking) entirely in their heads as a narcissistic response to their diminished superiority—that they are not "the true heirs of King," as Martin puts it—is beside the point. After 2008, what in 1998 may have looked like daring and emancipatory queer practice looks more like yet another iteration of attention-demanding boomer narcissism. (To her credit, by 2008's *The Female Complaint*, Berlant had grown more ambivalent about public melodrama.) Operating in the registers of performance and affect rather than of *logos*, in the real world, Diva Citizenship, perhaps inevitably, goes rogue; it holds tea parties in period drag; it stands athwart history like that old drama queen William F. Buckley, histrionically shrieking "stop."

Stout's resistance to rationality, on the other hand, is grounded in philosophical pragmatism and is more complex. On the one hand, he cautions against critical theory such as Seyla Benhabib's, which "employs the notion of 'rationality deficit'" and hence addresses traditionalists "as something more like patients than as fellow citizens." "The standard of proof," he writes, "for justifying such suspicions [of irrationality] is much higher than most critical theorists imagine. Democratic hopes would often be better served if we used more respectful modes of interpretation as our means of first resort" (178). For people of faith, however, Stout quite literally wants to *lower* the standard of proof. In a crucial footnote, he explains that he "did once argue for a negative conclusion on the rationality of modern religious belief," but that he no longer does so because, first, the argument "wrongly posited modernity as a more or less uniform megacontext in which all modern persons should be assessed epistemically," and, second, it "employed an implausibly rigorist standard of justification" (317n8).

While I am all for acknowledging the presence of multiple modernities in North America, the problem with the first part of Stout's recantation is that it echoes too closely the ideological functioning of a "premodern" South vis-à-vis backward U.S. *racial* beliefs and practices identified by Leigh Anne Duck in *The Nation's Region*: a *Plessy v. Ferguson*-esque deference to "the potential intractability of local circumstances" (213), to the "established usages, customs and traditions of the [southern white] people" (qtd. in Duck 213). Particularly given the structural and genealogical relationships between white supremacy and Christian supremacy, we would do well not to excuse the latter in the same way the nation so long excused the former. The problem with the second part is that, once one has pragmatically conceded degrees of truth and falsehood rather than an absolute difference, it becomes very difficult to identify a "plausibly rigorist" (which sometimes seems simply to mean "mutually agreeable") standard at all. If it is "implausibly rigorist" to reject a belief in God, is it also "implausibly rigorist" to reject a belief in "the efficacy of prayer"?[10] If it is "implausibly rigorist" to reject a belief in the efficacy of prayer, then is it "implausibly rigorist" to reject young Earth creationism? At what point may one start to suspect that someone's ignorance is less the product of his or her particular modernity than of his or her particular enjoyment?

The irony here is that to some degree I agree with Stout: *of course* it is necessary to speak respectfully to those who feel a "*high level of experienced assault*" (Neuhaus, *Naked Public Square* 34)! (One might also do well to avoid sudden movements.) But narcissism, from the milder sort all the way up to narcissistic personality disorder, is singularly resistant to treatment, in large part because the narcissist is, by definition, singularly resistant to the idea that treatment is needed. Moreover, the narcissists' need for affirmation is literally bottomless; one can never concede enough to their imagined superiority and sense of entitlement. In the public sphere as in the private, attempts to conciliate narcissists, or to achieve compromises with them, generally do not fare well. Sooner or later, the narcissists tend to secede anyway.

Yet this seemingly impossible—impassable—situation is precisely where Jürgen Habermas found Germany after the collapse of Nazism. Indeed, as Eric Santner persuasively argues,

> Habermas's interventions in these controversies are directed precisely against this tendency to return to narcissistic patterns of (group) identity formation, patterns that reinscribe, as I have argued, a refusal or inability to mourn. Habermas has, of course, been criticized by just about every postmodern theorist for his refusal to relinquish his commitment to an Enlightenment faith in rationality and the perfectibility of man, and to Western liberal notions of consensus, in short, to the project of modernity. This is not the place to repeat those debates; I would simply like to suggest that Habermas's rigorous adherence to the notions of the shared life-world and communicative rationality is grounded, at least in part, in an understanding of the process of mourning which is necessary for the working-through of the burdens signified by the double "post" of the post-Holocaust and the postmodern.
>
> Mourning requires the availability of a "good-enough environmental provision," a dependable interpersonal rapport that first provides a space in which the work of mourning can unfold. (53)

More recently, in a rare autobiographical moment, Habermas himself has confirmed that his most famous concept, *Öffentlichkeit*, almost universally rendered in English as "the public sphere," arises precisely out of the collapse of German narcissistic supremacism: "It was the caesura of 1945 that first led to the eye-opening experience for my generation without which I would hardly have ended up in philosophy and social theory. Overnight, as it were, the society in which we had led what had seemed to be a halfway normal everyday life and the regime governing it were exposed as pathological and criminal" ("Public Space" 17). If Habermas is not himself beset by the inability to mourn, it seems to be because "I had, in the German phrase, '*die Gnade der späten Geburt*,' the 'good fortune to be born late.' I was old enough to have witnessed the fundamental changes at the end of the Third Reich at a morally impressionable age, yet young enough not to have been incriminated by its criminal practices" (18). Instead, he writes,

> The confrontation with the legacy of the Nazi past became a fundamental theme of my adult political life. My interest in political progress, spurred by this concern with the past, became focused on conditions of life that escape the false alternative between *Gemeinschaft* and *Gesellschaft*, "community" and "society." What I have in mind are, as [Bertolt] Brecht puts it, "friendly" forms of social interaction

that neither surrender the gains in differentiation of modern societies nor deny the dependence of upright individuals on one another—and their reciprocal reliance upon one another. (17–18)

Thus, well before Scott Romine observed that "insofar as it is cohesive, a community will tend to be coercive" (*Narrative Forms* 2), and well before the naïve praise of southern *Gemeinschaft* by Cleanth Brooks (339) that provoked Romine's observation, Habermas was deeply engaged with formulating a way to get beyond the false dichotomy that underlies both conservative and liberal identitarian fantasies in the United States. The narcissistic fans of "community," at least from the agrarians through the current crop of Christian conservative theologians, sing the praises of "a commonly held view of reality": "The common values that bind a community may be defective, even wrongheaded. . . . But a sense of community is in itself good," writes Brooks (339), and Judith Butler (see chapter 1) seems to nod in agreement. Unfortunately, Habermas reminds us (and he is responding *directly* here to precisely the Nazi/Heideggerian celebrations of *Gemeinschaft* of which Brooks should have been aware), such communities "surrender the gains in differentiation of modern societies." Conversely, the free play of much postmodern identity politics tends to "deny the dependence of upright individuals on one another"—even, perhaps especially, when such individuals depend on each other in a polity too large for them to know each other personally.

Neo-agrarians will perhaps not be comforted that the apparent tension in these accounts between generational change (in which the pathological narcissists must die off) and therapeutic change (in which they begin, having been provided an appropriate space, to mourn) is merely a paradox. And here it is worth noting that Berlant does at least recognize something Stout does not. Stout seems genuinely interested in persuading anxious conservatives through "respectful" modes of address. (Good luck with that.) But we might draw on Berlant to remember that rationality itself has a profoundly performative dimension, as the phrase "staging a debate" of course acknowledges. Though I would delight in being proven wrong, I have little hope that the arguments in chapter 1, for example, will cause certain boomer southernists to stop bringing themselves to pleasant tears over long-dead civil rights martyrs, or a certain sort of Gen Xer to stop investing narcissistically in the "authenticity" of Johnny Cash. The chief intent of such a chapter is, obviously, to help dissuade *other* scholars from drifting into what Santner calls "narcissistic patterns of (group) identity formation." (A decade ago, better scholars than I—most obviously Patricia Yaeger, Houston Baker, and Dana Nelson—"dynamited the rails" of old southern studies, and for the most part the field went on just as if they knew not what they did.) The therapy of the gesture is intended not for the old (nor for their most intransigent former graduate students) but for present and future scholars, for those who had *die Gnade der späten Geburt*.[11] This is how the confluence of generational change and therapy in the public sphere is, I believe, supposed to work.

But the preceding is a colossally parochial argument. Out in the real world, the suffering caused by centuries of racism, sexism, and so on will likely pale beside the probable outcome of the challenges of the coming decades, and how (or whether) we address those challenges—I refer preeminently to global warming and only secondarily to the globalization of capital that has operated for three decades as the *objet petit a* of some on the postmodern Left—depends entirely on our ability, as a nation and as a global public sphere, to address them rationally. At present, for reasons I have tried to elucidate in this chapter, a substantial proportion of the U.S. population seethes with resentment at their unmourned lost supremacy—and derives tremendous compensatory enjoyment from that seething. This seething has powerfully influenced the course of national and even world events, very much for the worse. The answer, I suspect, is not to try to get the angry Right to seethe instead at the Other who has stolen the Left's enjoyment, nor is it to attack the very foundations of Western rationality—that has done little except empower Western irrationality—but to act like grownups, and that means to act rationally. (As I write, where Barack Obama, who seems largely to understand this dynamic, has failed, he has generally failed to *act* rationally, not failed to act *rationally*.) In just half a century, whatever its lingering problems, Germany transformed itself from one of the most narcissistic, antirationalist cultures the world had ever seen to one of the sanest. That happened in large part because the postwar generation took it on themselves, as best they could, to be the reality-based, non-narcissistic, non-"know not what they do" grownups the previous generation had failed to be.

It's our turn.

THREE

OUR TURN
On Gen X, Wearing Vintage, and Neko Case

In our final year of high school, my best friend, Lan Ying, and I passed the time with morbid discussions about the meaninglessness of life when everything had already been done. The world stretched out before us not as a slate of possibility, but as a maze of well-worn grooves like the ridges burrowed by insects in hardwood. Step off the straight and narrow career-and-materialism groove and you just ended up in another one—the groove for people who step off the main groove. And that groove was worn indeed (some of the grooving done by our own parents). Want to go traveling? Be a modern day Kerouac? Hop on the Let's Go Europe groove. How about a rebel? An avant-garde artist? Go buy your alterna-groove at the secondhand bookstore, dusty and moth-eaten and done to death. . . . To us it seemed as though the archetypes were all hackneyed by the time our turn came to graduate, including that of the black-clad deflated intellectual, which we were trying on at that very moment. Crowded by the ideas and styles of the past, we felt there was no open space anywhere.
—Naomi Klein, "Alt.Everything" (2000)

Can't seem to fathom the dark of my history,
I invented my own in Tacoma.
—Neko Case, "Thrice All-American" (2000)

People who aren't of Naomi Klein's generation and class may feel little sympathy or even patience toward the bourgeois anomie she chronicles at the opening of "Alt.Everything," the third chapter of her popular book *No Logo*. "After college, should I travel in Europe? But it's *so* been *done*!" Particularly troubling, perhaps, are the elevation of styles to the level of ideas (or the reduction of ideas to the level of styles) and the apparent absence in these girls of any idea that a good, worthwhile, happy, ethical life might be lived regardless of its stylistic novelty. The idea that becoming a teacher has been "done to death" or that being an intellectual bears some necessary connection to wearing black will strike many older or younger and/or less privileged readers as false, beside the point, and shallow. It might seem thus even to the figurative older siblings of Klein and Ying, the hundreds of my own college classmates from the 1980s who dove headfirst into investment banking.

It is no accident, however, that "false, beside the point, and shallow" is also how alt-country fans and performers, heavily Gen X, have sometimes appeared to fans and performers of more traditional country music. Again, as Johnny Cash put it,

> when music people today, performers and fans alike, talk about being "country," they don't mean they know or even care about the land and the life it sustains and regulates. They're talking more about choices—a way to look, a group to belong to, a kind of music to call their own. Which begs a question: Is there anything behind the symbols of modern "country," or are the symbols themselves the whole story? Are the hats, the boots, the pickup trucks, and the honky-tonking poses all that's left of a disintegrating culture? Back in Arkansas, a way of life produced a certain kind of music. Does a certain kind of music now produce a way of life? (12–13)

As he worried about the apparent devolution of country into a vacuous kind of stylistic commodity consumption, Cash was, in fact, talking about "the 'country' music establishment," but his musings, redolent of class—"I wonder how many of those people ever filled a cotton sack" (13)—apply at least as well to the alt-country music establishment—and, I think, to the bourgeois ennui of Naomi Klein. What Klein's adolescent dilemma has to do with branding, the subject of her book, might seem obscure, but the connection may undergird a large portion of the appeal of alt.country. Two pages later, Klein explains, "my frustrated craving for space wasn't simply a result of the inevitable march of history, but of the fact that commercial co-optation was proceeding at a speed that would have been unimaginable to previous generations" (65). She goes on to argue that earlier "scenes were only half-heartedly sought after as markets. In part this was because seventies punk was at its peak at the same time as the infinitely more mass-marketable disco and heavy metal, and the gold mine of high-end preppy style" (67). However, Klein and Ying's anomie may have resulted from the fact not so much that various alt.identities had already been branded as that the pervasive cultural logic of branding had led Klein and Ying by their teens to confuse, as it were, hats and boots with the land and the life it sustains and regulates. Ironically, punk itself may also have contributed, both as a style politics with a depressingly minimal real-world political effect and as the nevertheless dominant bourgeois post- (and anti-) hippie mode of "rebellion."

The present chapter, however, does not to attempt to distinguish, yet again, between "authentic" country and "inauthentic" alt-country—or vice versa. Indeed, Cash himself seems to signal that by the 1990s, neither was "authentic" in the traditional sense, something like "validated by its association with the performance of extremely difficult physical, chiefly agricultural, labor." Cotton sacks get filled by machines these days, and across the South (as has long been the case around the Bakersfield of Merle Haggard and Buck Owens), the most difficult, most unpleasant, lowest-paying work, especially in agriculture (e.g., peach picking in Alabama, tobacco picking in North Carolina, chicken processing in Arkansas [see Byrd, Smith-Nonini, Striffler]), is performed overwhelmingly by migrant Hispanic laborers—not exactly an image lionized on CMT or in the pages of *No Depression*, though it should be.

Instead, this chapter attempts to unpack the (implicitly white) generational rhetoric and fantasies that underlie the authentic/inauthentic, deep/shallow distinction. This rhetoric, I believe, draws on two questionable temporal conceits. The first, which has recently been exploded by new southern studies scholars such as Leigh Anne Duck and Jennifer Greeson, concerns the relationship between the nation and "the South." It partakes, that is, in what Duck calls "the paradoxically frenetic production of southern backwardness . . . placed in dialogue with equally assertive accounts of national progressiveness" (9). By associating the South with the authentic, cotton-pickin' past and "the nation" (including Canada as the ultimate progressive "North" and source of much alt-country) with youth culture and the future, country/alt-country rhetoric tends to lend country music an aura of maturity it does not especially deserve, while simultaneously both valorizing and infantilizing alt-country in terms necessarily similar to those used, as we shall see, to valorize and infantilize Gen X. Such valorization and infantilization represent the second temporal conceit, for the oldest Xers are in their forties now. Yet while scholarship on "the South" is finally growing up, scholarship not only on what anthropologist Sherry Ortner has called "the public culture on Generation X" ("Generation X" 434), but also on alt-country as well, may in contrast necessarily be dying before it grows old. In any event, as Ortner herself first noted, we would continue to do well to ask whose interests have been served—whose guilt assuaged, whose narcissisms fueled—by the discourses and fantasies that have circulated about Xers, and about alt-country, in North American public culture for nearly two decades.

To understand alt-country, that is, it helps to understand the peculiar myths circulating around the generation that more than any other has produced it. That means not only acknowledging Ortner's argument that "Generation X" is a cultural construct addressing complex cultural needs (particularly the needs of older demographic groups) but also complicating her primarily monocausal explanation of those needs, that is, her reliance on increasing income inequality, which she figures as an "abyss" opening in the middle class. Particular additional or alternative factors to consider include (1) the cultural logic of branding that Klein so rightly notes became omnipresent in the 1990s and (2) the legacy of punk, in which so many of alt-country's major figures—Ryan Adams, Neko Case, Alejandro Escovedo, Jay Farrar, Jeff Tweedy, and so many others, most of them Gen Xers—began their musical careers. (Though Douglas Coupland claims the link is coincidental, even the term "Generation X," popularized by Coupland's 1991 novel of the same name, appeared first in punk as the name of Billy Idol's old band.) Identity for both punks and Gen X has tended to be highly oppositional, a matter in both overlapping cases of "distinction" (in sociologist Pierre Bourdieu's sense) chiefly from baby boomers, their music, and what is perceived as their culture of narcissism (in Christopher Lasch's famous phrase). When Gen X hipsters "discovered" country music in the late 1980s and early 1990s, they thought they had found an ally, an entire genre that loathed hippies-cum-yuppies as much as punks did. But the situation was more complicated than that, and not simply because in Muskogee folks still don't take ecstasy or sport fauxhawks. Barbara Ching has compellingly argued that much traditional country music—by emphasizing countriness as a choice, not some naïve lack of "cultural capital"—resists middle-class and college-educated people's attempt to distinguish themselves from the masses by the sorts of things one learns in college. By using country music as a way of distinguishing themselves from the boomers, however, post-punk bourgeois alt-country fans and performers actually reintroduced this kind of distinction into the equation. In short, they made country—as a highly idealized form of "southern identity"—into a form of what Sarah Thornton calls "subcultural capital," a marker chiefly of their own hipness and putative authenticity.[1] More than a few of the tensions between traditional and alternative country can thus be traced to the differing ends to which country style got deployed and performed in each. As Gen X aged out of being a youth market, however, alt-country fandom and performance necessarily diminished. At the turn of the century, Trent Hill, writing within the dominant terms of cultural studies, was precisely right to ask, "Why isn't country music youth culture?" but today there is no obvious wave of twentysomethings swelling up to replace the Ryan Adamses and Gillian Welches who at the end of the last century made alt-country look like something made by young hipsters. (Even Conor Oberst, for example, born in 1980 so technically still an Xer, is not so easily classifiable. Bright Eyes' MySpace page just calls the music "indie"; many of my students just call him "emo.") Because Neko Case not only was one of the most talented performers in that now so-last-century hip country music youth culture but also continues, as it were, to grow up in public, a consideration of her career might offer a useful entrée into the Gen X–style politics of alt-country at the precise historical moment Gen X has grown out of needing either.

In using Case's career to chart the course of Gen X's growing up, this chapter, then, functions as a hinge between part I and part II. If, as chapter 1 argued, in the 1990s Xers tended melancholically to circle the *objet a* of their own lost adulthood, by the 2010s that same generation was showing signs of outgrowing such circling, of more rationally facing the world—and their own mortality—"in its senseless actuality": the first North American generation in some time to start to transcend infantile narcissism and fantasies of omnipotence, to start to model—for American cultural studies, among others—reconciliations with modernity.

Generation X

Now a lamentable cliché, even in its 1990s prime the term "Generation X"[2] seems to have appealed most to people who are drawn to oversimple generalizations: in the early 2000s, if you searched Amazon or Barnesandnoble.com for books with the phrase in the title, you'd find that the overwhelming majority concerned how to evangelize the demographic. The second largest category comprised books about how to manage them; next came books about how to market to them. (Tellingly, many from the 1990s are now out of print.) Famously hostile to evangelists, managers, and especially marketers (hence the need for all the books), Gen Xers themselves unsurprisingly seem rarely to embrace the appellation. As Coupland put it in *Wired* as late as 1997, "Regarding Generation X, well, the whole point is that there never was or will be a definition. . . . Nothing could be less X than wearing a T-shirt saying 'Generation X'" ("Picking Brains"). Appropriately enough, then, six chapters in Stephen Craig and Stephen Earl Bennett's 1997 anthology *After the Boom: The Politics of Generation X* define the group five different ways: those born from 1965 on (two chapters), or 1961, 1963, 1964, or 1972 (one each, 18).

It was Sherry Ortner, however, who in 1998 offered the most provocative definition of Gen X. Referencing Louis Althusser and writing self-consciously from the subject position of Gen X's parents—her initial ethnographic sample was her own 1958 high school graduating class—she concluded that

> the idea of Generation X tells us as much about the anxieties of upper-middle-class parents as it does about some set of young people out there in the world. Indeed, we may think of the public culture on Generation X in part as the product of a cultural scouting expedition on behalf of these people, a trip to what to them is the edge of social space, and a set of postcards from that edge. ("Generation X" 434)

If this seemingly somewhat narcissistic interpretation held true, however, we might expect Gen X rhetoric to continue, for the edge of social space—what Ortner calls the "abyss" of income inequality—has only grown in the years since she first published her article. Instead, our business-oriented public culture has moved on quickly (and with seeming indifference to the parental concerns of Ortner's cohort) to discussions of the *next* Next Big Thing: the subsequent (and much larger) "Generation Y" or the "Millennial Generation," who are figured as an optimistic, can-do, even heroic congeries of tech-savvy multicultural multitaskers with no time for whining—a near-perfect set of incoming capitalist employees, although as consumers they too apparently leave some things to be desired.[3] Given this pressure from below, Gen X's time in the sun may have been restricted to the decade or so in which, while their numbers were smaller than those of the baby boomers or the millennials, they nevertheless benefited from being North America's youth market—and, as such, trendsetters rather despite themselves. This period might also be measured as stretching from 1991, when Coupland's novel *Generation X* made being a Gen-X hipster cool, to around 2002, when LCD Soundsystem's single "Losing My Edge" suggested a redirection of Gen X energies from looking angrily back at boomers to looking nervously forward at millennials,[4] or 2003, when Robert Lanham's *The Hipster Handbook*, following on the heels of "Aimee Plumley"'s website www.hipstersareannoying.com, mocked hipsters' consumption patterns as just as shallowly conformist as everybody else's. In alt-country terms, the period might be measured from 1990, the year Uncle Tupelo's *No Depression*, which shares several themes with Coupland's novel, appeared, to around 2006, when the Jayhawks broke up and Jesse Fox Mayshark, drawing on a fairly wide range of other evidence (including the fanzine *No Depression*'s dropping the term from its tagline), eulogized "the twang that was alt-country" in *The New York Times*. When Ortner's article reappeared, essentially unrevised, as a chapter of her 2006 book *Anthropology and Social Theory*, she wisely conceded in an endnote that "there is some question as to whether the idea of Gen X is still alive" (160n3). Not coincidentally, that year the same could have been said—and was—for the idea of alt-country.

Perhaps the single biggest theme running from Coupland through Klein to Lanham and energizing a generational identity politics or sense of "distinction" is a feeling of betrayal and nihilism once pithily expressed by the Sex Pistols: "No future." Coupland's book appeared early enough that one reason for such an attitude in the novel remains a fear of nuclear Armageddon, but the bigger reason is a generational rage at the boomers for having used everything up. As is often noted, for example, U.S. Gen Xers tend to believe there will be no Social Security left for them after the boomers get through with it. More broadly, as boomer Constance Alexander wrote in reviewing Coupland's novel, "Reading the book forced me to acknowledge some uncomfortable truths about my generation, the Baby Boomers. The sheer numbers of us alone create a tyranny of the aging. It's no wonder the young generation, as portrayed in *Generation X*, feels cheated." Coupland's running glossary includes such terms as "bleeding ponytail" ("an elderly sold-out baby boomer who pines for hippie or pre-sellout days") and "boomer envy" ("envy of material wealth and long-range material security accrued by older members of the baby boom generation by virtue of fortunate births") (21). While saving her greatest ire for multinational corporations, Klein (who appears no stranger to fortunate birth) registers a similar resentment of generational tyranny, however "grooving," in the epigraph to this chapter. "Embrace the fact that baby boomer bashing is fun," advises Lanham (159). Bennett and Craig begin their scholarly introduction with an epigraph from a men's room stall at the University of Cincinnati: "The Baby Boomers [mucked] up the entire planet!" (1, Bennett and Craig's brackets). Even scholars do it. In her early article "Subcultural Identity in Alternative Music Culture," Holly Kruse laments that "the lived experiences of the post-baby boom generation seem especially neglected" in cultural studies, identifies herself in 1992 as "a member of the twentysomething generation"—the favored term before "Generation X" appeared—and proceeds to examine how "college music scenes . . . allow their members to define themselves as separate (though not unproblematically so) from mainstream culture" (33).

Kruse's careful reference to "college music scenes" notwithstanding, however, such generational distinctions too often elide class—specifically educational—issues. As early as the late 1960s, Andrew Greeley "observed greater differences of political outlook between college-educated and lesser-schooled baby boomers than between boomers as a whole and older Americans" (qtd. in Craig and Bennett 9). To this day, when one thinks of a baby boomer, one's imagination rarely conjures up the lesser-schooled sort. Similarly, the big Gen X complaint that their fancy college degrees have gotten them nothing but McJobs (another Coupland coinage) and massive student debt is largely lost on working-class Americans who never got the fancy degrees in the first place and who not infrequently see collegians and the so-called "creative classes" as parasites on their "real" working-class labor—a theme of no small number of traditional country songs from the same period like Brooks & Dunn's "Hard Workin' Man" and Aaron Tippin's "Working Man's Ph.D." Such posturing, however, contains more than a little narcissistic defensiveness as well, and Alan Jackson's recent "The Talkin' Song Repair Blues" is unusual in country music in that it stands up a bit for intellectual work. Nevertheless, to most commentators, the whole boomer/Gen X debate appears a profoundly middle-class one, a debate, perhaps, between North America's last upwardly mobile bourgeoisie and its first downwardly mobile one.

Within public culture, then, one might rather sweepingly suggest that those contesting the meanings of "Generation X" and "alt-country" tend to fall into three camps. The first, favoring country over alt, seems narcissistically invested in overstating the value of its semiskilled labor and in distinguishing itself from collegians; this attitude is frequently associated with masculinity issues, as in Toby Keith or Robbie Fulks, though it can take milder forms, as in the acts Barbara Ching analyzes. The second camp, in contrast, seems narcissistically invested in Gen X distinction from the baby boomers. While avoiding the phrase "Generation X," Trent Hill's 2002 discussion of alt-country in "Why Isn't Country Music Youth Culture?" deploys familiar Gen X rhetoric in at least two ways. As noted in chapter 1, Hill argues that "the cultural politics of alternative country are premised less on the possibilities of flight, freedom, and mobility than on immobility or downward mobility" (183), and he claims distinction from hippies-cum-yuppies, thus overstating, I think, the links between alt-country fans and Ching's traditional country fans: alt-country's "musicians are not, unlike the urban, college-graduate hillbillies of the folk revival, interested in recovering an authentic past so much as articulating a set of connections and alliances within a marginalized present" (183). As oxymoronic "urban, college-graduate hillbillies," that is, the boomer folk revivalists are figured as inauthentic; alt-country fans, on the contrary, are figured as authentically grounded in labor. They "imagin[e] an alternative culture, . . . one that might allow new affective and political alliances to understand the experience of 'working man's blues,' regardless of whether that working man is a truck driver or an office temp, a college-town bohemian or a army vet" (183). While this fantasy may not have been totally repudiated by the Bush years, it has certainly been deferred, and in any event, Neko Case—whom Hill cites to bolster his argument—was in her early career nothing if not an urban, art-college-educated hillbilly.

The third camp is represented in the scholarly realm by Sherry Ortner and in the business realm by the media she most often cites, for example, *Business Week*. Like the trad-country gang, both subcamps have little patience with the "whining" of people like Hill, but their arguments are narcissistically invested not in working-class labor but in a kind of paternalism toward Gen X—for what is inadmissible to both is the idea that Xers' complaints might be objectively justified. (If so, then [1] Ortner's generation has failed as parents, and/or [2] neo-liberalism is not a rising tide lifting all boats.) Ortner seems to deflect attention from the former potential failure by examining the latter. The "abyss" on which her analysis depends takes the form of a remarkably neat gap—the sort literary critics, if not anthropologists, deconstruct almost reflexively—between lower-middle-class Xers and upper-middle-class ones. To her credit, she finds the former's *ressentiment* eminently comprehensible: "it makes sense that people who feel that they are slipping economically, despite their best efforts, would be frustrated and angry. It is more of a puzzle to hear Gen X-type noises from the other side of the abyss" (425). Weirdly conflating the cultural capital of a graduate education with actual capital, she continues:

> Yet every time I gave a talk arguing that the real embodiment of Generation X was the children of the lower middle class, and that the children of the upper

middle class had been in effect terrorized by the media, there were howls of pain from the numerous Gen Xers (that is, graduate students) in my audiences. Finally I reminded myself of the cardinal rule of ethnography: the informant is always right. Even if, "objectively," these kids had nothing to worry about, there was something experientially real to them about the doomsaying forecasts of the Gen X literature. (427)

The condescension here—presumably deriving at least in part from Ortner's parental transference issues—is troubling. Graduate students—adults in their twenties and early thirties—are not simply figured as "children" and "kids," but infantilized as ones who "howl" and make "noises." Yet only one-third of them will ever land the tenure-track jobs for which they are ostensibly being trained (they know full well, however, that their TA-ships enable the 2-2 teaching loads of professors like Ortner), so that two-thirds of them will end up entering the nonacademic workforce—and beginning to save for their Social Securityless retirements—eight to ten years later than their college classmates, armed with hypertrophied skills at ethnography and atrophied skills at most everything else. "Objectively," those adults had *plenty* to worry about—and financial security is in any event hardly the only measure of happiness or success. How do you give someone back his or her twenties?

Punk Style

So it is not that surprising that some of those Xers, depressed or angry at capitalism and boomers, might affiliate themselves with musical genres that seemed depressed or angry at the same things. For nearly two decades after its inception in the mid-1970s, critics from what Rupert Weinzierl and David Muggleton have called the heroic school of subcultural studies famously saw punk as a kind of authentic and, yes, heroic working-class resistance to bourgeois capitalism. As Dick Hebdige put it in the landmark *Subculture: The Meaning of Style*, "It is this alienation from the deceptive 'innocence' of appearances which gives the teds, the mods, the punks, and no doubt future groups of as yet unimaginable 'deviants' the impetus to move from man's second 'false nature' . . . to a genuinely expressive artifice; a truly subterranean style" (19). Yet this idea of punk as anti-bourgeois and radical drew fire from the start. As early as the mid-1970s, critics such as Angela McRobbie and Jenny Garber were pointing out that things were more complicated, that, for example, "female participation in youth cultures can best be understood by moving away from the 'classic' subcultural terrain marked out as oppositional and creative by numerous sociologists" (120). McRobbie would go on to argue for the importance of consumption to subcultural identity formation, noting that "sociologists of the time perhaps ignored this social dimension because to them the very idea that style could be purchased over the counter went against the grain of those analyses which saw the adoption of punk style as an act of creative defiance far removed from the act of buying" (192). Sarah Thornton in her 1995 book *Club Cultures* may have put the last nail in the coffin of subcultural heroism, arguing that the dance-oriented youth subcultures she studies "are *taste cultures*" that "embrace their own hierarchies of what is authentic and legitimate in popular culture—embodied understandings of what can make one 'hip'" (3, Thornton's italics). Pierre Bourdieu has argued that intellectuals in France accrued "cultural capital" (knowledge of wine, art, literature, classical music, etc.) to distinguish themselves from the masses since they lacked the old-fashioned kind of capital with which rich people achieved distinction: money. Thornton applies this approach to subcultures by famously redescribing hipsters' embodied understandings as "subcultural capital": the taste decisions by which they attempt to distinguish themselves from an alleged "mainstream." She has little patience for Hebdige and others' ideas about "genuinely expressive [working-class] artifice":

> Authenticity is arguably the most important value ascribed to popular music. It is found in different kinds of music by diverse musicians, critics, and fans, but it is rarely analysed and is persistently mystified. Music is perceived as authentic when it *rings true* or *feels real*, when it has *credibility* and comes across as *genuine*. In an age of endless representations and global mediation, the experience of musical authenticity is perceived as a cure both for alienation (because it offers feelings of community) and dissimulation (because it extends a sense of the really "real"). As such, it is valued as a balm for media fatigue and as an antidote to commercial hype. In sum, authenticity is to music what happy endings are to Hollywood cinema—the reassuring reward for suspending disbelief. (26, Thornton's italics)

Whether in music or in fashion, in other words, one does not get outside inauthenticity or the market simply by buying or associating oneself with items that predate, or appear to predate, the ages of mechanical reproduction or corporate branding. One is still involved in commodity fetishism, what Angela McRobbie calls "the magical exchange of the commodity" (197).

Unfortunately, McRobbie's 1989 article hasn't stopped people from trying. Consider V. Vale's decidedly heroic-phase account of the origins of the swing revival—there but for the grace of God went alt-country—in his 1998 *Swing! The New Retro Renaissance*:

> At first glance this movement seems to be more about nostalgia than social criticism, but a closer look will reveal a different form of rebellion. . . . The swing movement is about cultural rebellion in its most subversive form: one that uses the symbols of the status quo for its own intents and purposes. This is achieved through the simple means of rejecting corporately-dictated consumption and

embracing forgotten and/or ignored aspects of the American experience (e.g., music, dance, manners, clothing). . . . People consciously seek out older forms of music that have not been put through the corporate music industry's sanitized and stilted face-lift. . . . Judging by the number of morose models in the ad campaigns, the nineties have also been a kind of Great Depression *of the spirit.* . . . Depression may be caused by "mental" factors but ultimately resides in the body. So the body must provide the cure. [Hence swing dancing.] . . . The 90s have been described as the "decade of past decades." (4–5)

Apparently, swingers too thought they were going where there's no depression. The genealogy from punk that alt-country shares with swing is clear here, if implicit. The heroic DIY (do-it-yourself) symbolic rebellion of that movement, its focus on style, gets transferred over to "rejecting corporately-dictated consumption and embracing forgotten and/or ignored aspects of the American experience." Vintage "music, dance, manners, clothing" are embraced as both a punk and a post-punk alternative to, well, the Gap. Of course, the swing revival has the curious distinction of also having been, like alt-country, easily commodified in a Gap ad. Despite, or perhaps because of, the swing revival's ephemerality, the Louis Prima "Jump, Jive, 'n' Wail" ad of spring 1998, with its *Matrix*-style graphics, was far more successful than the Dwight Yoakam "Crazy Little Thing Called Love" ad that followed, not to mention the short-lived one featuring Willie Nelson and Ryan Adams covering "Move It on Over." However, one cannot draw too sharp a distinction between the swing and alt-country scenes: at one point these overlapped considerably in the music of, for example, Big Sandy and his Fly-Rite Boys. In both, too, vintage music and vintage clothing come to take on the same aura of being somehow "outside the market," even as Vale notes that "the proliferation of new 'roots' musicians and bands . . . was facilitated by the invention of the compact disc, which brought about the massive re-release of thousands of obscure recordings in every genre which were formerly impossible to locate, or prohibitively expensive. Basically, our American roots music heritage was restored to us" (4). Vale's syntax conceals the fact that the agents of such re-release and restoration were music corporations.

In fact, the political poverty of punk-cum-retro style, once allegedly so transgressive, may lie precisely in its rather art school assumption that stylistic gestures have ipso facto real-world consequences. The logic behind the idea that by buying and displaying something one can cure alienation and dissimulation—no depression indeed—is also precisely the logic of corporate branding, which in the terms of marketing theorist David Aaker offers a "value proposition" about the "emotional benefits" of a commercial relationship with a particular brand (95–102). In such terms, "vintage" operates as a brand every bit as much as, say, Diesel or Fluevog—or Nike. As Ted Polhemus implies, subcultures and their accoutrements had by the 1990s very much taken on the attributes of brands: "Clubland is a Supermarket of Style where every world and every era you ever dreamed of (and these are, of course, all mythologized places and times) is on offer like tins of soup on a supermarket shelf" (91–93).

When Gen X, coming of age in the 1990s with the apparent triumph of "late" capitalism, set out to distinguish itself from baby boomers, it thus initially tended to make its choices not by constructing a "counterculture" or voting or protesting—such actions seemed useless, unoriginal/unhip, and foredoomed to boomeresque sellout—but by using the logic of branding, of commodity fetishism, and of graphic design (the field that makes corporate logos and elevates visual style to or above the level of content).[5] In such a context, it is no wonder that Naomi Klein and Lan Ying seem to imagine career choices as tired brands competing for their attention and commitment. Unsurprisingly, too, the most visible X-voxes uniformly possess exquisite visual senses. Coupland is a sculptor who has won two major Canadian industrial design awards; *Generation X* begins with an epigraph from an Xer that runs, "Her hair was totally 1950s Indiana Woolworth perfume counter. . . . But the dress was early '60s Aeroflot stewardess. . . . *And such make-up!* Perfect '70s Mary Quant, with those little PVC floral appliqué earrings. . . . She really caught the sadness—she was the hippest person there. Totally" (vii). Klein acknowledges "the ever-fabulous Sara who insisted that *No Logo* must have a design that matched the spirit of its content" (x); Lanham's book is about almost nothing *but* style; even Dave Eggers is nearly as respected (or reviled) for his graphic design work at *McSweeney's* as for *A Heartbreaking Work of Staggering Genius*. And in 1998, a different kind of generational voice, Neko Case, would earn her BFA from the Emily Carr Institute of Art and Design in Vancouver, a school whose most famous recent alumnus at the time was Douglas Coupland.[6]

Neko Case

In her teens and early twenties in the Seattle music scene, Neko Case (born, like Naomi Klein, Dave Eggers, and even LCD Soundsystem's James Murphy, in 1970) was such an avid fan that in 1990 the Tacoma band Girl Trouble (which is not a "girl" group, though it has a female drummer) actually recorded a song called "Neko Loves Rock 'n' Roll." It included the lyrics,

> You may think she'll satisfy your soul
> You may think you're gonna reach your goal
> You better listen to what you've been told
> No, my brother, Neko loves rock 'n' roll. (Blackstock 54)

Yet her style politics as fan-cum-performer became more apparent on her recording debut as part of the punk girl group Maow. Writing about the sleeve of the 1979 Buzzcocks album *A Different Kind of Tension*, designed by Malcolm Garrett, Rick Poynor notes of Garrett's borrowing from an El Lissitzky poster,

> What gets overlooked, when the past is treated as a quarry from which useful visual material can be extracted at will, are the changes of meaning—the drainage of meaning—that occurs when visual ideas with specific purposes are applied in new contexts. In Lissitzky's *Red Wedge* poster, the triangle and circle stand for political factions and progressive visual form underscores a progressive political message. The Buzzcocks' sleeve treats similar motifs as super-stylish product packaging that benefits from a historical association with a radical moment, without representing anything of comparable significance, if it represents anything at all. (76)

On the sleeve of Maow's only album, *The Unforgiving Sounds of Maow* (1996), Case sports a large, furry, Russian-looking hat with a big gold hammer and sickle. The band's name had recently been changed from Meow, but there is still nothing Maoist about Maow, whose sound, look, and subject matter recall nothing so much as those of the pre–*Beauty and the Beat* Go-Gos. While the Go-Gos sang punky, transgressive-for-the-times tunes like "Johnny, Are You Queer?" Maow steps into the ring with "Wank" ("I'll tease you till you think you'll explode / You'll have to go home to blow your load") and, like their predecessors, a plethora of other songs about boys and partying. I don't mean to be humorless here, as the Mao motif could be construed as a complicated gendered joke about music and politics, lending the band a faux-seriousness that the merely catty "Meow" does not, only to undercut that seriousness with that oft-cited Gen X irony. But irony only gets you so far, and when all is said and done the Maow name and sleeve, like the Buzzcocks sleeve, remain "super-stylish product packaging that benefits from a historical association with a radical moment, without representing anything of comparable significance." Or as Case put it in a 1999 interview, "I'm not really country. I just like things to be incredibly archaic all the time. Like pinhole cameras and knee high socks" (Travasos). As she observed after winning *Playboy*'s poll for "hottest woman in indie rock" and gently declining to pose for the magazine, if she *did* pose, "a retro pictorial would be the most fun. I don't want it to be campy, though" ("Country Love Song").

The Go-Gos—as their name suggests—themselves made more than a nod to 1960s retro. Where Maow's retro differs from the Go-Gos' may lie chiefly in Case's contribution of a couple of covers from the late 1950s and mid-1960s: Wanda Jackson's rockabilly "Mean Mean Man" and Nancy Sinatra's country pop "How Does That Grab You, Darlin'?" Both artists were gutsy, sexy women who by the 1990s were obscure enough that covering their works advertised a kind of subcultural capital, a connoisseurship of female rock history. (Hipness index: Sinatra's "Bang Bang" would years later serve prominently on the soundtrack to Quentin Tarantino's *Kill Bill, Vol. 2*.) The gender politics here are admirable: as Case puts it on one of her web pages,

> A pivotal moment in my life was when I realized that Poison Ivy, a hot sexy lady, played that dirty, evil, titillating guitar in the Cramps. I had "Songs the Lord Taught Us" and I loved it. One day, poring over the cover as I'd done a million times, it hit me. I was filled with shame. I loved music. How come I didn't think women played it?
>
> From that day on, I was on a mission to find them all. Punk rock didn't have enough voices I could relate to at that time in my life, except X and a few others. That experience opened up a vast world to search through. All genres, all cultures, all eras. Most important to me was gospel and country. (Case)

(Lest this sound too earnest and hence uncool, however, Case begins her narrative with, "People always ask me 'is it hard to be a woman in rock?' and upon much forced reflection I can only site [sic] two things that make it difficult: (1) repeatedly being asked that question; and (2) finding a clean toilet seat in a dirty rock club" [Case].)

In Maow's original tune "Very Missionary," which Case sang and co-wrote, Case's performance of gender is inextricable from a very clear performance of *generation*. The song is structured around a fundamental opposition between two performers not often discussed in the same breath, Eric Clapton and Hank Williams Sr. "Your songwriting is flaccid / Your covers give me fits, / That's why I think Clapton, you're the shits," she writes of one, while the songwriting of the other is "classy, / To heartache you're the host, / That's why I think Hank, you are the most." Admittedly, some of this is itself pretty flaccid songwriting ("to heartache you're the host"?), but the song still offers a surprisingly complex performative fusion involving gender, fandom, generational identity, punk, and country. The desire of fans for (male) performers that R. J. Warren Zanes, drawing on his own appreciation of the Rolling Stones' Brian Jones, has to construct as "queer" isn't exactly queer when the fan is a straight woman, and the song straightforwardly, if metaphorically, rejects a fantasy missionary encounter with Eric Clapton in favor of one with Hank Williams Sr. Female agency is complicated here. To some degree, a fan's relation to a performer is always passive, the missionary "bottom." On the other hand, Case, like any number of other consumers, expresses agency in her choice: in this case, her choice of which male performer she'd like to get missionary with. And in a typical Gen X move, Case dismisses baby boomer icon Clapton (whether or not she intends it, über-boomer Ann Beattie's short story "Eric Clapton's Lover" is a subtext here) in favor of pre-boomer Williams. As noted above, Case's is a post-punk move as well: the turn to Hank, like other 1990s turns to pre-boomer genres like swing, lounge, and surf, ironically enough represents an attempt to get out from under "the ideas and styles of the [boomer] past": the 1990s evolution of 1970s punk's minimalist and retro abhorrence of the pretentious, narcissistic guitar solos of "classic" boomer rock.[7]

In fact, one of the central draws of country for youthful Gen Xers in the 1990s seems to have been simply that it *wasn't* boomer music, that it wasn't yet even "the groove for people who step off the main groove." After all, the terms of contrast offered by Case's lyrics are largely subjective, describing the singer's response much more than they describe the music itself. Though apparently an exercise in name-calling, the song nevertheless seems, almost against itself, to reinforce the arbitrariness of its own contrasts. Though she ultimately more than resolves any ambiguity with "you're the shits" and "you're the most," for much of the verses Case actually employs could-go-either-way phrasing to describe each performer's effect (listening to one, "the hair stands on my neck," while the other's techniques "make tears roll down my face"); complementarily, in the chorus she uses the same word, *missionary*, to suggest both "possessing the attributes of a banal sexual position" in Clapton's case and "righteous" in Williams's. In the absence of objective reasons for differentiation, the turn to country becomes what Johnny Cash called "a way of talking about choices—a way to look, a group to belong to, a kind of music to call [one's] own": an exercise in what Pierre Bourdieu calls "distinction," an attempt to amass what Sarah Thornton calls "subcultural capital." If Case's choice seems to have despite itself a certain Coke-versus-Pepsi arbitrariness, it may be because both Eric Clapton and Hank Williams operate as metonyms, musical logos for brand classic rock and brand hard country. Case's agency, like that of so many music fans, is not just feminized (or in Zanes's terms, "queer"): it is also literally and figuratively that of a consumer. In the context of 1990s consumption-as-protest, professing to want to get missionary with Hank Williams instead of Eric Clapton is much more than a matter of taste: it's a matter of self-definition.[8]

Yet unlike her performance of gender and generation, Case's performance of *country* in Maow, especially on "Very Missionary," retains a decidedly kitschy and ironic, almost yee-haw, aspect even as she proclaims her country fandom. At the end of the song, she repeats the phrase "makes me feel so fine" four times, pronouncing "fine" a bit like "fahn" and interjecting a fairly ludicrous "c'mon, now" after the third. Case is playing a kind of vocal dress-up, and the phrase is the vocal equivalent of a large, furry, Russian-looking hat. Steve Bailey observes of the spate of what he calls "ironic covers" that "the new versions tend to ridicule the originals, often exaggerating particularly dated or embarrassing aspects of a given song, but, at the same time, they tend to celebrate the continued vitality, despite these shortcomings, of the music and its importance to the rock audience. This is not 'making fun' in a monolithic sense, nor is it pure validation, but rather an often uneasy and thoroughly ironic hybrid" (142). After an analysis of 1970s precursors of the present wave of irony, he concludes,

> Much as [Bryan] Ferry's work betrays the heavy influence of his art-school background and fascination with pop art, and [Todd] Rundgren's evokes his anti-pop, elitist sensibility, the recent wave of ironic discourse across a wide variety of media reflects the dissemination of an avant-garde sensibility to the domain of the popular. As a general phenomenon, the process begins with the work of liminal figures who work within popular art forms—rock music, Hollywood cinema, mass market novels—but who situate themselves within a relative elite in these fields. (155)

Case's "Very Missionary" belongs in this ironic tradition.

As noted above, Barbara Ching has rightly argued that *all* country music is "performative" and that much of the best of it is, in fact, campy. While camp and irony bear some similarities, something different from camp—and I think genuinely new—was going on with early Case and with early alt-country more broadly. For Ching, "country music plays in the space of white Americans who are on the whole less educated and hold low status jobs. . . . this is a population that lacks, again in Bourdieu's terminology, 'cultural capital'" (108). Thus, she concludes, "instead of legitimating the cultural choices that create the distinction of the privileged, country music underlines the production and dubiousness of such distinctions" (109). By recasting country as subcultural capital for punky Gen-X hipsters, however, *alt-country reinscribed these distinctions.*

Yet as Gen X individually and collectively ages, the situation is growing more complicated. In 2004 boomer journalist Ann Hulbert observed in the *New York Times Magazine,*

> You may remember all the hard-bitten qualities that once gave young Gen-X'ers a bad name: their disillusioned pragmatism and underachieving fatalism. The tables have turned. Those traits have now metamorphosed into a welcome antidote to the boomers' competitive, perfectionist brand of "hyperparenting."
>
> America's debt-burdened younger parents . . . embrace their prospects of downward mobility with equanimity—even enthusiasm. Unlike their elders, they value family time over money and status.

In many ways, the article is predictably depressing. Hulbert draws most of her evidence from marketing research and, with a familiar if still breathtakingly un-self-aware boomer narcissism, manages in the final paragraphs to make the article really about boomers after all. ("Make room for us, Gen Xers"!) Still, the article draws on a body of research suggesting (in the usual sweeping terms) that while the boomers started out idealistic and veered rapidly toward the shallow and self-indulgent, Gen Xers may be moving in the opposite direction. We might expect factors other than "distinction" to arise in their aesthetic choices; we might expect their creative cultures to be something other—more—than mere "taste cultures." We might expect Gen Xers to become something like post-hip.[9]

Though she seems unlikely to embrace parenting anytime soon—her 2004 live album *The Tigers Have Spoken* closes with a modest proposal about feeding children to tigers—a similar evolution is taking place in the career of Neko Case. Her early post-Maow work remains haunted by a diminishing punky, ironic, narcissistic, look-at-me-I'm-singing-country affect. On *The Other Women*, the live acoustic album she recorded with Carolyn Mark as the Corn Sisters in 1998, the two perform, among other things, a cover of "Long Black Veil." However, while Mark and Case—unlike, say, Emmylou Harris changing the words of Steve Earle's "Guitartown" to create a ramblin', don't-tie-me-down female speaker, thereby inverting some stereotypes—do not change the gender words, the result does not subvert "heteronormativity," as one might expect. In *Performing Rites*, Simon Frith rightly notes that "gay and lesbian singers can subvert pop standards by *not* changing the words: Ian Matthews bubbling that 'I met him on a Monday and my heart stood still'; Mathilde Santing realizing that 'I've grown accustomed to her face'" (195). Mark, the lead vocalist on this number, indeed sings, "The judge said, *son*, what is your alibi," but she does change another word, continuing, "if you were *somewheres* else, then you won't have to die." Performers as diverse as Johnny Cash, the Country Gentlemen, and Jason and the Scorchers all sing "somewhere," which is what Marijohn Wilkens and Danny Dill originally wrote. To have the judge, a presumably educated authority figure, instead say "somewheres" is in a 1998 recording to overdo the countriness, to suggest that the South is a land of just unremitting redneckness. What one hears when two female Pacific Northwest hipsters sing "Long Black Veil" is thus an ironic, almost Brechtian performance of country in which one can't fully suspend disbelief (and a story told by a dead man demands some suspension) not least because the gender terms foreground the fact that a female hipster is singing country. Similar ironies abound on Case's first solo album *The Virginian*. Even the title both claims and ironizes a kind of southern/country authenticity for Case. The title song, though sung in the third person, is clearly autobiographical, but Case is a Virginian in name only: she was born there (in Alexandria, which many Virginians consider to be less Virginia than a deregionalized suburb of the nation's capital), but the family moved soon afterward.

Yet things start to change for Case on *Furnace Room Lullaby*. The album opens with "Set Out Running," which itself sets out with Case singing, "Want to get it all behind me, / You know everything reminds me, / I can't be myself without you." What a listener is presented with first and foremost on the song and hence the album is the sheer spectacle of Case's voice, heavy on the reverb and unaccompanied until the rhythm section kicks in on "get." At least since punk, and perhaps since early Bob Dylan, rock music concerned with "authenticity" has tended (pre-irony) to embrace what Hal Foster dubbed "the anti-aesthetic," presuming that what was pretty was fake and that authenticity lay in the gritty voice of a Bob Dylan or a Joe Strummer. Of Poly Styrene's famous vocal performance on X-Ray Spex's "Oh, Bondage, Up Yours," Simon Frith writes, "it is not 'feminine'; it is not sweet or controlled or restrained. Such rawness also serves to register the track's punk authenticity. . . . its 'unmusicality' is crafted. It is necessary for the song's generic impact" (196). Yet as so many other awed critics have noted, Case has in just a few years matured into what they call a "big" voice; here one luxuriates—on top of the reverberation, the tempo is a slow waltz—in both its depth and force and its *beauty*. Her voice, gorgeous and vaguely Reba-ish in the country context, is rendered even more powerful in the context of punk: its radical "generic impact" lies, paradoxically, in its beautiful old-fashionedness. Instead of "look at me, I'm singing country," her voice is now starting to say, "listen to me, I'm *singing*." In Case's ironic vocal performances, the "dated or embarrassing aspects" tend most often to be played up by the accents and embellishments ("c'mon, y'all," "fahn"), while the "continued vitality" gets carried in large part by the power of her voice. As the accents and embellishments fall progressively away, the irony diminishes, and the performances approach instead an unapologetic vitality.

Such *singing* is, I think, what the later Case means by wanting to be retro without being campy. When Robert Christgau, reviewing the New Pornographers' CD *Electric Version*, remarks, "I wish the sparingly deployed Neko Case would abandon her faux-country career," he misses the point. As Ching argues, "country songs are often about being a hick, about being unable to participate in urban culture even while being bombarded by it. Country music songs are about why hicks—whether they be remote rustics or urban newcomers or perennially alienated city-dwellers—listen to country music" (109). But Case's music offers no winking pact between performer and audience about (their) performed rusticity. To a traditional country audience, Case's adoption of a "country" or southern accent on "Set Out Running"—how she pronounces "me" "muh-ee" or puts a sob in "cry"—will probably still seem "faux," especially if one hears her accent-free singing with the New Pornographers on *Mass Romantic*, released the same year. Yet I suspect the problem here lies less with Case than with the country audience's expecting a performer to flatter their countriness through camp, not mock it through irony. (Like costume—Nudie suit or furry hat—the accents and embellishments seem to be the medium of both camp and irony, as of "country" itself.) Ching also points out that "the only way for a critic to really start thinking about this music is to escape this double-bind of authenticity that can so readily dismiss or celebrate it" (111), but even her argument threatens to let authenticity in by—what else?—the back door: country is, properly, music of "hicks," playing "in the space of white Americans who are on the whole less educated and hold low status jobs" (108); Ching herself is proudly from Dubuque, "the classic hick town" (108). The argument, that is, could replace the perception of country as the music of stupidly un-self-conscious hicks with an image of it as the music of cleverly (and sometimes angrily) self-conscious "hicks."[10]

Case, on the other hand, starts out as a Gen X hipster singing for other Gen X hipsters.[11] Yet if as audience we refuse the discourse of authenticity, as Ching rightly argues we should, then the absence of either kind of authentic countriness must not matter. Frith, citing David Brackett's analysis of how the Bing Crosby version of "I'll Be Seeing You" sounds to Billie Holiday fans and vice versa, points out that "'truth' is a matter of sound conventions, which vary from genre to genre": "it is almost impossible to hear both of them as sincere: the assumptions behind a reading of Holliday's voice as 'witheringly' sad entail our hearing Crosby's voice as 'shallow' . . . while someone hearing Crosby as reassuringly direct and friendly could only hear Holliday as mannered" (197). Such neat binarisms are always suspect, of course: listening groups (what Stanley Fish might call musical "interpretive communities") are rarely as segregated as this obviously race-inflected example from the 1940s imagines, and there are no doubt plenty of hip hicks and hick hipsters.[12] Either way, however, Case makes no bargains with hicks.

The way to approach Case's music from *Furnace Room Lullaby* onward is therefore not—despite the obsessions of *No Depression*—to see it as something that tries to be "authentic" country and largely fails, as Christgau implies, nor as yet more 1990s hipster art-school irony, but as music that tries to expand the generic boundaries of post-punk hipster music—and that succeeds admirably,[13] as *Lullaby*'s hitting #36 on the *Village Voice*'s list of the top 100 albums of 2000 might indicate. Across her career, Case's hipster irony has lessened with each record. Indeed, irony might be seen as among the forms of specifically *youth* "distinction" Sarah Thornton critiques:

> The material conditions of youth's investment in subcultural capital (which is part of the aestheticized resistance to social ageing) results from the fact that youth, from many class backgrounds, enjoy a momentary reprieve from necessity. . . . Without adult overheads like mortgages and insurance policies, youth are free to spend on goods like clothes, music, drink and drugs. (103)

As Case starts to outgrow hipster irony, her authority as a performer must come from more enduring sources. Part of it now comes, of course, from the force, control, and sheer *ambition* of her voice. Part of it comes from the first words of *Furnace Room Lullaby*, "[I] want to," a straightforward act of female self-assertion even, as it will turn out, in the face of apparent self-abnegation. Part of it comes from the fact Case wrote the song, rightly or wrongly suggesting a note of first-person autobiography.[14] Frith notes that "as listeners we assume that we can hear someone's life in their voice—a life that's there despite and not because of the singer's craft, a voice that says who they really are, an art that only exists because of what they've suffered" (185–86). Hipsters tend to be a little less sentimental than this—the whole irony thing again—but in Case's case something similar still goes on. The hickness of "Set Out Running"—by which the song might live or die for traditional country music fans—comes off as largely beside the point. Given the emotional power of that voice portraying the imagined situation of a speaker who realizes she's "nothing in your eyes" (when she is everything in "your" ears)—the country affectations appear to hip and post-hip listeners, I think, as mere examples of "the singer's craft." Perceived authenticity of feeling trumps perceived authenticity of accent. (And, admittedly, when it comes to the latter many hipsters can't tell the difference.)[15] Such perceived authenticity also means Case, and perhaps other graduates of alt-country, are moving beyond hats-and-boots dress-up, beyond the mere stylishness of being "incredibly archaic," or—in Coupland's words—"the hippest person there. Totally." By 2002's *Blacklisted*, which hit #23 on the Pazz and Jop poll, Case was singing with almost no visible or audible stylistic props, and with virtually no diminution of authority.

And that's a good thing. Jesse Fox Mayshark writes of 2006's *Fox Confessor Brings the Flood* that "the twang and two-steps that colored [Case's] early efforts have been subsumed by noirish pop" (B26). Pitchfork calls the album only "shaded" by "finely-tuned, country-noir twang"; the Onion A/V Club gets it just right: "Case has finished paying homage; she's making Neko Case music now." Doing so has been a good career move: *Fox Confessor* landed way up at #8 on that year's Pazz and Jop, and—for better and for worse—three weeks after its release I heard a track from it being played in the Anthropologie store in Atlanta's posh Lenox Square Mall. More than a year later, when on May 15, 2007, I checked Amazon to see what else people who bought *Fox Confessor Brings the Flood* were buying, Case's fan base appeared to have widened well beyond even alt-country: the only alt-country record listed was Lucinda Williams's *West*. Instead, people buying *Fox Confessor* bought other Case albums (*Furnace Room Lullaby* and *Blacklisted*), the New Pornographers' *Twin Cinema*, and albums by the Decemberists, the Shins, Cat Power, and Jenny Lewis. Even people who were buying Case's earlier albums weren't buying other alt-country anymore; they were just buying more Neko Case (including The New Pornographers). By the time *Middle Cyclone* appeared in 2009 (placing #3 on Pazz and Jop for that year), the "customers who bought this item also bought" feature had been expanded to seventeen pages (the whole "long tail"). While a few albums by Steve Earle, Ry Cooder, Gillian Welch, and so on still turned up in that long list, the dominant feature—after other Neko Case and New Pornographers albums—was the eclectic, indie nature of the list, from the Dirty Projectors' *Bitte Orca* to St. Vincent and the Flaming Lips.

It's called growing up. In 2007, revising this chapter for its publication in Barbara Ching and Pamela Fox's collection *Old Roots, New Routes*, I listened again to the 1999 K-tel anthology *Exposed Roots: The Best of Alt. Country* (edited by Grant Alden and Peter Blackstock of *No Depression*), which is full of urban twentysomething hipsters who, usually in the early 1990s, had begun listening to less punk and more "roots music" and then making music of their own that, a decade later, sounded innocuous, even homogeneous, despite the genre's oft-alleged indefinability. It already felt like an artifact, like watching *Pulp Fiction* (remember the surf revival?), and I was compelled to agree with Mayshark: alt-country—as the kind of youth culture phenomenon that both cultural studies scholars and the music industry prefer to validate—was over. Journalists—both mainstream and "indie"—keep using the term, as Ching has reminded me, and no doubt will keep doing so. In the May 8, 2007, *New York Times*, Kelefa Sanneh, covering the Stagecoach country music festival in California, refers casually to one of the four stages, the "Palomino," as the "alt-country" one—the other three being the "Mane" (main) stage, where Sanneh spent most of his time, and which featured Kenny Chesney, Alan Jackson, and so on; a bluegrass stage called the "Appaloosa"; and a sort of western-swing catchall stage, the "Mustang," which featured everything from Asleep at the Wheel to Garrison Keillor. With the exception of the Railbenders, however, not a single act on the "Palomino" stage—where Neko Case headlined and, according to Sanneh, "seemed out of place"—was under thirty; some, like Emmylou Harris, Willie Nelson, and Kris Kristofferson, were twice that.

Of course, much alt-country, like other 1990s retro movements, wanted to be about getting beyond the boomer dead end of a self-proclaimed youth culture aging gracelessly, refusing to admit that youth's window had been slammed shut. Hence the reclamation, back then, not only of Merle Haggard, Loretta Lynn, and Johnny and June Carter Cash, but of Mel Tormé, Tony Bennett, Dick Dale, and on and on. As early as 1992, Lawrence Grossberg observed that "for the baby boomers, youth is something to be held onto by cultural and physical effort" (*We Gotta Get Out of This Place* 183), and the giant Gen X and alt-country reclamation project was a response to that. ("Interestingly enough," bubbled V. Vale, "much of the backbone of the new swing movement is provided by people who are in their 50s–80s. . . . This underground is *de facto* combating society's vile obsession with the cult of perpetual youth" [5].) But in general, Gen X seems to be aging a bit more gracefully, and one nice thing about growing old is that you no longer have to mourn your lack of authenticity by buying some old Johnny Cash record and getting off on *his* melancholy. You *are* old. A 2006 interview suggests Case knows just that:

> PITCHFORK: So you're saying that people shouldn't believe some of the rumors about there being dissension within [the New Pornographers]?
> CASE: I think that those things came from the fact that we're incredibly boring. None of us are drug addicts or alcoholics. All we do is work. I'm sorry that we're not the Rolling Stones getting busted at the border for heroin. People just fill in the blanks. It's not easy to be a rock writer and I don't envy that position because what kind of exciting sex angle are you going to put on a middle-aged rock 'n' roll band that works all the time?

It's comments like that—happily contrasting "boring" adult behavior by people in their late thirties with "exciting" adolescent behavior by boomers a good deal older—that make me think Case has a real shot at not becoming her generation's Eric Clapton—and that her generation, insofar as it shares that sensibility, has a real shot at not repeating the follies, the narcissistic fantasies, of "youth culture." In Slavoj Žižek's words from *Looking Awry*, "instead of running after the impossible"—the old circling their lost youth, the young circling their lost adulthood—Gen X may indeed be on track to "learn to consent to our common lot and to find pleasure in the trivia of our everyday life" (8)—the subject of part II.

RECONCILIATIONS WITH MODERNITY

FOUR

TWO TIES AND A PISTOL
Faulkner, Metropolitan Fashion,
and "the South"

Sometimes the trivia of everyday life can be hard to find pleasure in. One reason my wife and I loved Birmingham so much is that we had moved there from a small town in Mississippi (where my wife had been teaching at a small public liberal arts university) an hour from the nearest interstate. Consumer culture in such places is hard to describe if you haven't lived in one of them. There is no Starbucks to complain about, nor any independent, more "authentic" coffeeshop at which to exert one's consumption-as-protest. Instead, there is, almost invariably, a strip of four-lane highway between half a mile and three miles long. It contains two competing supermarkets, one of them in the Walmart; the abandoned shell of the old Walmart that wasn't big enough for the grocery store; one or two auto parts stores; several fast food restaurants; several gas stations; an Applebee's or Chili's or some such; and honest to God I cannot go on. When my wife's colleagues asked, "Did you get out this weekend?" they meant, "Did you get out *of the state*?" A running joke— also a statement of fact—was that if you lived in Starkville, Mississippi, you did your shopping about twenty miles east in Columbus, Mississippi (where we lived); if you lived in Columbus, you did your shopping another hour east in Tuscaloosa, Alabama; if you lived in Tuscaloosa, you shopped in Birmingham; and if you lived in Birmingham, you shopped in Atlanta—which at the time held, to give a sense of things, the only Ikea between Washington, D.C., and Houston. (Another has since opened in Charlotte.) In the less densely populated parts of the country, how "alternative" your modernity is, is not at all unrelated to the narrowness of your consumer options.

Despite Wal-Mart's being both rooted and headquartered in Arkansas, it has been more or less continuously fashionable, at least since the agrarians, to decry such sprawl as a recent "foreign" imposition upon the South. It isn't: it is the direct result of the small-town South's own anti-government, anti-zoning conservatism. *Community in Alabama*, a beautiful coffee-table book published by the Alabama Architectural Foundation, begins by plugging the American Institute of Architecture's "Ten Principles for Livable Communities." The principles are too lengthy to repeat here (though easily Googled), but the omnipresent strips of highway described above violate all ten. In *Community in Alabama*, then, community itself, along with the good design that fosters it, functions largely as a "foreign" concept imported to Alabama readers: the book aims "to open readers' eyes . . . to the knowledge that what we surround ourselves with matters" (Bowsher 3). Not surprisingly, the book's examples of community-encouraging spaces do not come predominantly from small towns—though one site that does is the campus of the University of Montevallo, laid out a century ago by the nationally known Olmsted Brothers firm. Instead, as editor Alice Meriwether Bowsher concedes, "despite an effort to represent the noteworthy buildings of all regions of the state, there is a disproportionate number of places from the Birmingham area" (xi).

This situation may be worse than it used to be, but it is far from new. Poor design, limited consumer choice, and the narrow horizons and relatively bleak lives that can result from them have long been the story of small-town life—not only in the South, of course, but across North America. When, after a hard day's ethnography, you can just get in your truck and thirty minutes later be back in Austin, it is easy to romanticize such depressing places as "authentic" populist worlds. When you're stuck in them, you might well find yourself romanticizing precisely those hip urban places where your consumer choices, and perhaps the rest of your life, feel more beautiful and more free. Most important, most of us, as I suggested in the introduction, live in places somewhere in between, finding ourselves pulled in both directions.

It is from marketing theory's understanding of this fundamental *similarity* between "the South" and bohemia as "populist worlds," at least in consumerist fantasy, that I wish to approach what I consider one of the trickier novels in the William Faulkner canon, *The Mansion*, and in particular chapter 7 of that novel, sometimes referred to as the "Greenwich Village" chapter. Consumerism is central to *The Mansion* as a whole: even the unnamed Booker T. Washington-quoting principal of the Negro school Linda Snopes Kohl visits tells Gavin Stevens that the only remaining ties between whites and blacks in the South are consumerist: "There is no place for us now in your culture or economy either. We both buy the same installment-plan automobiles to burn up the same gasoline in, and the same radios to listen to the same music and the same iceboxes to keep the same beer in, but that's all" (224).

Moreover, I hope in examining a few elegant examples of this consumerism to address some fundamental issues within southern studies. For at least the sixty-eight years between the Twelve Southerners' *I'll Take My Stand* and Michael Kreyling's *Inventing Southern Literature*, mainstream southern literary studies overwhelmingly and explicitly presented the region as precisely Douglas Holt's sort of populist world, and for nearly as long the field of Faulkner studies—with some notable exceptions—has been about as guilty as anybody else, however paradoxically, of marketing the South, and the works of Faulkner in particular, as an antidote to the anxieties of Yankee capitalism. Perhaps the high-water mark of this sort of sales pitch was Cleanth Brooks's essay on Faulkner for *The History of Southern Literature*, in which Brooks explicitly contrasted northern *Gesellschaft* with the southern *Gemeinschaft* to be found in Faulkner. Those terms from the German sociologist Ferdinand Tönnies are usually translated respectively as "society" and "community," with all the implications I've been sketching above.[1] By the end of the twentieth century, the situation had gotten so bad that critics like Kreyling and Patricia Yaeger were apparently conflating Faulkner himself with his southernist critics, positioning not Faulkner studies but Faulkner himself as the "Dixie Limited" that was getting in the way of a fresh and more honest approach to southern literature; both contemplated "dynamiting the rails" of said Limited.[2]

Yet Faulkner, I hope to show, is a good deal hipper than his critics have been. When I began thinking about this chapter, I meant that term somewhat ironically. *Hip* was originally an African American term deriving from Wolof and meaning, roughly, the state of having one's eyes open; it was popular among jazz musicians but was widely picked up by white Beats in the 1950s. Today, though, *hip* has largely been appropriated by a racially heterogeneous, but chiefly white, semi-subculture living in places like Williamsburg, Brooklyn; Echo Park, Los Angeles; and Prenzlauer Berg, Berlin. In this world, hipness is largely mediated by commodities, defined, in Sarah Thornton's icy term, as a kind of "subcultural capital." In her Bourdieuian reading, hipness is little more than a new way in which one group of people purports to distinguish themselves from an imagined square "mainstream": in this case, by knowing how to dress—usually ironically—and what bands and kinds of drinks are cool.

Yet on the shuttle from the Memphis airport to the 2005 Faulkner and Yoknapatawpha conference, where I first presented a version of this chapter, Don Kartiganer told me a story Albert Murray had once told him, and it got me thinking. Apparently Murray was working at Random House in the 1950s when Ralph Ellison stopped by. Faulkner happened to be in the building, and Murray arranged a meeting. When Ellison returned, Murray asked him how it went. Ellison's comment was about dress. He said he'd always heard Faulkner dressed like a raggedy farmer. Instead, Ellison marveled, "he dresses like we do!" Given that *Invisible Man*, from its title on down, is obsessively about the visual presentation of the black southern male body, this is both a striking compliment and a telling observation. I do not think Faulkner "dresses black" in any simple way, and I don't think that's what Ellison meant. But the need to negotiate between authentic southern yam-eating roots and a shifting cosmopolitan identity is something Faulkner absolutely shared with Ellison and, I would argue, with the whole ethos of bebop, even if his personal musical tastes were more archaic.

Thus if chapter 7 continues to resist interpretation in and by the southernist interpretive community—or society—one reason it has been unreadable may be that for a long time it has been unbearable. A long quotation from a contemporary review of *The Mansion* (by one Louis D. Rubin) should illustrate the point:

> *The Mansion* is a failure as a novel, an unbelievably awkward failure.
>
> All of which goes to prove something about Mr. Faulkner. So long as this great Mississippi novelist deals with rural Southern life, so long as his milieu is primitive and pre-modern, he is matchless. From the earliest Yoknapatawpha tales right down through Mink Snopes in the present novel, Mr. Faulkner is the greatest novelist of his generation.
>
> But when he attempts to deal with a sophisticated, modern milieu, with characters living in the present and requiring the subtle, intellectual characterizations of moderns, his technique fails, his rhetorical gifts emphasize the failure, and our greatest American writer falls flat on his face. It is not his world; as a writer, his universe is bounded by Nineteenth and early Twentieth Century Yoknapatawpha county. Within those boundaries he has no peers. But let him attempt to step outside the time or the place and he is lost. (449)

Lost to whom?

Faulkner seems to play for the wrong team here, to present the South as embodying a kind of lack that can only be filled in the populist world of Greenwich Village. If for agrarians and neo-agrarians the problem with urban life is alienation and anomie, for Faulkner (as for others) the problem with the traditional South is—in *The Mansion*, at least—boredom. If at first glance this seems a comedown from the grander themes of works like *Absalom, Absalom!* it is not, in fact, a trivial matter either theoretically or empirically. In *Boredom: The Literary History of a State of Mind*, Patricia Meyer Spacks notes that "boredom in its verbal renditions usually masks another condition" (x), often aggression, and links the very acts of reading and writing to boredom's avoidance: "as action and as product, writing resists boredom, constituting itself by that resistance. In this sense all writing—at least since 1800 or so—is 'about' boredom, as all physical construction is 'about' entropy" (1). (Her observation seems particularly applicable to modernist writing, especially Faulkner's.) In *The Feminine Mystique*, Betty

Friedan characterized 1950s American women as suffering a kind of epidemic of boredom. And of course, in *The Mansion*, Eula Varner Snopes is agreed to have committed suicide out of boredom and even Flem Snopes is hypothesized to have done so.

Unsurprisingly for a book published in 1959, these issues of modernity and the good life, if I might fairly call them that, get worked out, I wish to argue, in Faulkner's treatment of material culture, of more or less everyday objects: in particular, an abstract sculpture, a piece of wood, two ties, and a pistol. "The fifties," Joanne Jacobson reminds us, perhaps a bit too nostalgically, in a review of Alison Clarke's important book on Tupperware,

> may have been the last great moment when Americans entrusted their dreams of transformation to the material world. In the postwar years rationed hunger was let loose on a whole new world of goods, visible manifestations of the possibilities of upward mobility that were renewed in the boom economy. More even than symbol, the material world became a theater of transformation. On the glowing, capacious stage of *things*—cars, hula hoops, rockets—our destiny of motion was revealed. And our destiny of metamorphosis: as malleable as Silly Putty, Play-Doh and Jell-O.

In this context, Faulkner's lifelong and obvious love of well-designed objects—both in the trilogy and in his own fastidious taste in clothes—should remind us that, for Faulkner at least, there are different kinds of bourgeois consumption and "identity construction." The author's profound distaste for conformist small-town southern peasant-cum-bourgeois consumerism is matched by his admiration for more individualist small town cum big-city bourgeois consumerism. In other words, his disdain for the pursuit of respectability is matched by his admiration of the pursuit of beauty, particularly when that pursuit, that "excessive" consumerism, puts food on the tables of artists and designers. The Snopes trilogy begins with what I would call Flem's proto-punk critique of small-town bourgeois masculine identity—a turn to what art critic Hal Foster once labeled the anti-aesthetic. Richard Godden has already noted that Flem's tiny two-inch black bow ties, with what Faulkner calls their "quality of outrageous overstatement of physical displacement," sitting against Flem's white shirts, tie him, in the eyes of men of small means, to his rebellious peasant barn-burning father ("Earthing *The Hamlet*" 77–79). It is but a small step to characterizing these ties as proto-punk, in their ironic, combative minimalist commentary on the whole notion of bourgeois male business dress, on the whole notion of vanity.[3] (Flem is said to buy these ties by the gross, and in Hell the Prince of Darkness can't buy him with the vanities because he has brought a gross of them along with him, a clear reference to those ties [58, 151].) But in *The Mansion*, the trilogy closes with a kind of dialectical return to the aesthetic.

By the end, then, Faulkner's aesthetic focus on objects *as* objects—as neither symbols nor signs—will also disrupt a cultural studies that would associate fashion, or even art, with the punkish deconstruction of tradition. To both the tweedy neo-agrarian and the black-spectacled communist antecedents of the two fields I work in, Faulkner says, not at all simply, a plague on both your outfits.

In *The Mansion*, Faulkner follows the retold story of Eula Snopes's suicide with what might seem a bit of comic relief: Ratliff and Gavin Stevens making an almost carnivalesque trip to Greenwich Village to attend her daughter Linda's wedding to Jewish communist sculptor Barton Kohl. I'd like to defer the obvious Cold War implications of this for a moment to look at what I take to be a related phenomenon: not only does Linda choose to marry a maker of beautiful things, but the chapter also appears structured by the contrast between two design objects. Flem, who has taken over Major De Spain's bank, has the entire De Spain house done over to look like Mount Vernon because, in Ratliff's words, "the house [Flem's depositors] would see him walk into every evening until time to unlock the money tomorrow morning, would have to be the physical symbol of all them generations of respectability and aristocracy that not only would a been too proud to mishandle other folks' money, but couldn't possible ever needed to" (153). Yet Ratliff makes an interesting distinction:

> it was jest the house that was altered and transmogrified and symbolized: not him. The house [may have changed], but the feller the owners of that custodianed money seen going and coming out of it was the same one they had done got accustomed to for twenty years now: the same little snap-on bow tie he had got outen the Frenchman's Bend mule wagon in and only the hat was new and different. . . . It wasn't that he rebelled at changing Flem Snopes: he done it by deliberate calculation. (154–55)

Faulkner here appears to deploy—unconsciously, I think—two very different, even contradictory, figures for the self. On the one hand, the self seems to be—in good cultural studies fashion—conflated with clothes and hence with performance: as an appositive, for example, "the same little snap-on bow tie" *renames* "the same feller," a function the phrase "only the hat" repeats through its parallel grammatical, or more properly ungrammatical, relation to the phrase about the tie. On the other hand, in *The Mansion*, domestic *interiors*—modeling an old public/private split—repeatedly appear to suggest a more traditional model of a stable, "authentic," and even rather precious private, noumenal self hidden from public gaze.[4] In these private recesses, Flem has done something unusual: on one of the fireplaces "with colonial molding and colyums and cornices," he has had his carpenter cousin nail up what Ratliff calls "not a defiance, not a simple reminder of where he had come from but rather as the feller says a reaffirmation of his-self and maybe a warning to his-self too: a little wood ledge, not even painted, nailed to the front of that hand-carved hand-painted Mount Vernon mantelpiece at the exact height for Flem to prop his feet on it" (156). Here Faulkner appears to reinscribe the notion of the South as an anti-fashion—more on this term in a moment—populist world, for it is hard to miss what is surely an intended contrast between this secret, humble bit of wood, this "reaffirmation" of Flem's authentic self, and the very different object Ratliff buys in New York a few pages later in the same chapter. Ratliff, or Faulkner, appears to set this contrast up as a joke at Ratliff's expense. When Gavin Stevens drives Ratliff to the Jefferson train station, we are told he "stopped and opened the door and looked at me and then done what the moving pictures call a double take and says, 'Oh hell.' 'It's mine,' I says. 'I bought it'" (165). The object referred to is a necktie, which—unlike his shirts—Ratliff pointedly has bought, not made. In curiously class-based terms, we soon learn that the problem is not just that he is wearing a tie, changing his signature "look"—which is a powerful reinforcer, like Flem's, of his professional and personal petit-bourgeois "brand identity"—in a way that, contrasted with Flem's "calculation," seems surprisingly reckless. The problem is also that the tie is ugly: "It was all right as long as just railroad conductors looked at it but you cant face a preacher in it," insists Stevens (167). In fact, not only is the tie ugly in itself, but for reasons known only to Ratliff, he has also chosen to wear with his trademark blue shirt a tie that is "pink and green" (167). Having thus declared this necktie unacceptable on a mix of class and aesthetic grounds, Stevens, adopting a kind of mentor role, takes Ratliff to a particular sort of New York boutique: "a store," as Ratliff describes it, "with a show window, an entire show window with not nothing in it but one necktie" (166). There is nothing inside the store either, "except some gold chairs and two ladies in black dresses and a man dressed like a congressman or at least a preacher, that knowed Lawyer by active name" (167). In a complicated exchange to which I will return, Ratliff ends up paying Myra Allanovna, the designer and boutique owner, 150 1936 dollars—more than 2,400 2012 dollars[5]—and obtains 2 ties. Dressed in one of them at a Greenwich Village party that evening, and in the new white shirt Stevens has had the tie people send out for, Ratliff is presumed to be either an Oklahoma oilman or a Texas cattleman, and two different people recognize his tie admiringly as "an Allanovna" (170, 172).

At first glance, then, Faulkner seems to be taking a stab, perhaps even a cheap shot, at the absurdities of New York commodity culture. "Seventy-five dollars for a necktie?" exclaims Ratliff to Stevens at one point. "I cant! I wont!" (169). Indeed, later in the novel Faulkner will make Mink Snopes's trip to Memphis to purchase his own design object—a rusty, snub-nosed pistol[6] of questionable functionality that "looks like a cooter" (291)—echo this trip to the city that never sleeps: "Now [Mink] was in what he knew was the city. For a moment it merely stood glittering and serried and taller than stars. Then it engulfed him: it stooped soaring down, bearing down upon him like breathing and the vast concrete mass and weight until he himself was breathless, having to pant for air. Then he knew what it was. It's un-sleeping, he thought. It ain't slept in so long now it's done forgot how to sleep" (285). "The city had never slept," Faulkner repeats of Memphis four pages later, just as Stevens had earlier teased Ratliff in Manhattan that at 7:00 a.m. "They haven't even gone to bed yet. This is New York, not Yoknapataw-pha County" (166).[7] Yet the trip to purchase the pistol puts Mink in mind of an earlier trip to Memphis to visit the brothel "which he had entered with his mentor that night forty-seven years ago" (290). And just as Mink is led to meditate on the pistol in terms of its appearance and "function" (when Flem is shot, Stevens reports grimly of the pistol that "it functioned" [395]), so too does he think of the prostitutes as design objects, literally and quite oddly de-fined by shape and color and function: "women not only shaped like Helen and Eve and Lilith, not only functional like Helen and Eve and Lilith, but col-ored white like them too" (290).[8] In a particularly grim bit of irony, Faulkner carefully notes—from the point of view of a necessarily omniscient narra-tor—that while the New York trip successfully reunites Linda with Hoake McCarron, her biological father, and she recognizes him, Mink's last Mem-phis trip takes him past the same brothel he'd visited in 1899, where "he didn't know it of course and probably wouldn't have recognized her either, but his younger daughter was now the madam of it" (290). In this context, coupled with Allanovna's insistence during their bargaining that Ratliff kiss her, New York designer boutiques and commodity culture come to look like little more than the rich man's bawdy house.

Yet Faulkner, I would like to believe, is rarely given to cheap shots, and what looks like stark contrast (or parodic comparison) may well be some-thing more complex. Fashion theory can offer us a provisional way in here. While Mink's pistol is crucial to my argument, Faulkner appears to juxta-pose most closely—in the same chapter—Ratliff's ties and Flem's footrest as embodying the two poles of what almost thirty years ago Ted Polhemus and Lynn Procter identified as fashion and anti-fashion. (Despite some notable problems, their book remains powerful in fashion circles, still serving, for ex-ample, as the theoretical starting point of the 2002 second edition of *Fash-ion as Communication*, Malcolm Barnard's popular introductory textbook.) Writing in the heyday of Birmingham school cultural studies, Polhemus and Procter observed that "anti-fashion is composed of numerous and unrelated body and clothing symbols. Fashion, on the other hand, is a unified system of arbitrary body and clothing signs" (18). In their now-famous example, a prostitute dressed like a prostitute is saying "I am sexually available"; an art student dressed like a prostitute "does not in her style mean 'I am sexually available.' Her message is simply 'I am fashionable.' Three months ago she may have looked like Chairman Mao, and in six months' time she may look like an innocent adolescent schoolgirl" (19). This difference between symbols and signs is, in their argument, profoundly political in all the ways we associate with Birmingham school cultural studies, which arose as the youth of post-imperial England, like those of the post–civil rights South, struggled to slough off a hierarchical culture overdetermined by the importance of knowing one's place: "Traditional societies are by definition conservative: they seek to preserve their culture despite the threat of change and instability. Anti-fashion, especially when the body is permanently customized, is perhaps the most powerful weapon with which a society can protect itself. Anti-fashion is a time capsule which one generation leaves for the next, a machine designed to symbolically defy and destroy change" (22).

Fashion, on the other hand, is "the natural, appropriate language of the socially mobile, those between rather than within social groups. While symbolizing social mobility and change, fashion also symbolizes the social rootlessness, anomie, alienation, and atomization which are the requisite and the result of this social change. Fashion's function is to represent and identify the social and cultural limbo of modern urban society" (20).

Ratliff's Allanovna ties seem to be the epitome of fashion in just these terms: not unlike the Invisible Man's zoot suit and dark glasses in Ralph Ellison's novel of eight years earlier (in which, of course, another southerner comes north to New York City) they lead to a comic case of mistaken identity, of unexpected social mobility in a destabilizing urban setting. This social mobility is heightened by contrast, and doubly complicated, because Ratliff's initial tie purchase results from his quest to reclaim his own social roots. One purpose of this trip for Ratliff is a "sentimental pilgrimage" (175): a visit to Saratoga, where Ratliff's first American ancestor, "that-ere first immigrant Vladimir Kyrilitch," served with the Hessians in the English General Burgoyne's defeated army (164). In preparation for that trip, back in Jefferson he buys his first tie "to let all them V.K. Ratliff beginnings look at me for the first time. Maybe it's them I'm trying to suit. Or leastways not to shame" (165).[9]

Conversely, Flem's unpainted footrest seems to be the epitome of anti-fashion: seemingly tucked away from public gaze "like a secret chapel or a shrine" (159) in a house to which "he hadn't never invited nobody in" (155), nailed on a fancy mantelpiece not only in disregard of but as an assault on the fake colonial décor, and described in terms of pure function, as complete absence of ornament, it seems to operate not as a sign but as one true symbol among the faux-colonial many. More than anything else except perhaps his patiently waiting for Mink to pull the trigger a second time, it is this little wooden ledge, this organic residuum of authentic Flem-self hinting (perhaps) at crucifixion, which has generated a fair amount of critical sympathy for Flem at the end of the trilogy.

Yet given the salted-mine trick by which Flem in *The Hamlet* has conned Ratliff and Henry Armstid into buying a worthless old mansion by digging in the garden as if for buried treasure and as if no one were watching him, and given Ratliff's suggestion Flem himself had more recently chalked the anti-Semitic graffiti outside his own house to generate sympathy in the community, the authenticity of the ledge-gesture is hard to, well, authenticate. Ratliff himself notes Flem has put it up "like one of them framed mottoes you keep hanging on the wall where you work or think, saying *Remember Death* or *Keep Smiling* or—*Working* or *God is Love* to remind not jest you but the strangers that see it too, that you got at least a speaking acquaintance with the fact that it might be barely possible it taken a little something more than jest you to get you where you're at" (157). Ratliff's simile suggests the footrest is only partly about humility and partly about advertising that humility to "the strangers that see it too." Moreover, while "Remember Death" and "God is Love" might point to humility, "Keep Smiling" and "Keep Working" make the overall list less redolent of private reflection than of technologies of disciplining employees, forms of Taylorist manipulation. Ratliff metaphorically figures the "little wooden additional ledge" as both private residuum of Flem's peasant roots and public bourgeois supplement to his success. As Ratliff also shrewdly notes, that ledge exists not in simple contradiction to the hand-carved, hand-painted mantelpiece (here denoting less craft than consumption) but in "unpainted paradox" to it, implying that any contradiction is only apparent (157).

If Faulkner carefully subverts our admiration for Flem's ledge, so too does he undercut our rather petit-bourgeois—or is it peasant?—disdain for those excessive ties. Initially, Ratliff is conveyed as understanding the importance of anti-fashion to his status in the conservative southern business community every bit as much as Flem does: "I jest cant," he explains to Myra Allanovna. "I sells sewing machines in Missippi. I cant have it knowed back there that I paid seventy-five dollars apiece for neckties. But," he continues, "if I'm in the Missippi sewing-machine business and cant wear seventy-five dollar neckties, so are you in the New York necktie business and cant afford to have folks wear or order neckties and not pay for them. So here" (176).

But the situation is a good deal more complicated than this. At an early age Faulkner himself forcibly rejected the conservative, provincial white southern businessman as a masculine role model. This is not at all to say he was opposed to more urbane sorts of consumption. While Faulkner was no Elvis, throughout his life the novelist was neither blind nor immune to spectacular dress. His letters are peppered with references to clothes; he would sometimes draw them for his reader. In 1925, traveling in England, he gushed about finding "the best-looking sport jacket you ever saw" (*Selected Letters* 30); in 1960, upon his admission to the Farmington Hunt Club outside Charlottesville, he wrote Albert Erskine, "I have been awarded a pink coat, a splendor worthy of being photographed in" (*Selected Letters* 450), an observation Joseph Blotner felt important enough to include in his highly selective chronology of Faulkner's life for the Library of America volumes (*Novels 1936–1940* 1104). And, in fact, Faulkner *did* have himself famously photographed in that very coat, though we should also note that, as a uniform Faulkner had for once actually earned, the coat chiefly operated at least among the Albemarle County cognoscenti as anti-fashion: as symbol, not sign.[10] Yet in this letter, Faulkner seems at least as enthusiastic about the more purely aesthetic "splendor" of the coat,[11] and photographs and letters attest that throughout his life Faulkner was, at least when he chose to be, impeccably dressed. In his younger years, the attire was often a kind of costume: the RAF uniform he had no right to wear; his bearded Parisian artiste getup of the early 1920s. As he grew older, costume generally matured into style (with certain exceptions for posing theatrically as decayed gentry or mustachioed horseman). But even early on, he was remembered as a "fashion plate" at Ole Miss dances, perhaps, Joel Williamson suggests, because even back then he bought his clothes in Memphis (173).

Most important, I don't think I have ever seen a photograph of Faulkner wearing an ugly necktie. In *William Faulkner and Southern History*, Williamson captions the 1942 J. R. Cofield photograph of Faulkner "A Worried Man, 1942." With no small degree of melodramatic projection, he intones, "Summer, 1942, age forty-four. The years of genius have passed. He will never again write a great novel. He is broke, and he had difficulty staying sober for an interview. . . . In a sense, he is dying, an uncounted casualty in the Hollywood War" (n.p.). Me, I'm admiring Faulkner's tie, its knot held in place under the starched collar by a perfectly placed tie pin. The tie, so far as I can see, is of an elegantly minimalist yet varied design: a pattern of small dots and small horizontal and vertical line segments, a clean mix of order and variety. Nobody who dresses like that (or whose taste in wine is as expensive as a speaker at the 2004 conference showed Faulkner's to be) is likely to write about designer ties merely as satire.

Certainly Faulkner's language points us in other directions. Through Ratliff, he sets up the shop-window scene in language that is, at best, straining for effect: "at least some weather was jest made for New York. In which case, this was sholy some of it: one of them soft blue drowsy days in the early fall when the sky itself seems like it was resting on the earth like a soft blue mist, with the tall buildings rushing up into it and then stopping, the sharp edges fading like the sunshine wasn't just shining on them but kind of humming, like wires singing" (166). This neither sounds much like Ratliff ("the sky itself seems like it was resting on the earth"?) nor even very good writing (the too-close repetition of the phrase "soft blue"). But unlike the prose of so many writers bent on describing urbanity's alienation from nature, here sky and earth are in harmony with each other and with the skyline, whose "sharp edges" fade like Ratliff's shirts into a "soft blue," and where sun and buildings combine to make "singing," quite unapologetically the peculiarly high-tech variety made by power lines. And it is at this moment of exquisite urban harmony between nature and culture that Ratliff sees his first Allanovna tie.

A page later, in the shop, Ratliff fantasizes to Allanovna as follows: "I was jest thinking that if you could jest imagine a necktie and then pick it right up and put it on, I would imagine one made outen red with a bunch or maybe jest one single sunflower in the middle of it" (167). Stevens has already described Greenwich Village as "a little place without physical boundaries . . . where young people of all ages below ninety go in search of dreams" (151), so the idea of the place as a magical one where fantasies materialize has already been established. In his fantasy, Ratliff prefers primary colors—he wishes his pink and green tie were yellow and red, and he favors blue shirts—but Allanovna first brings out one much subtler than that: "it looked like the outside of a peach, that you know that in a minute . . . you will see the first beginning of when it starts to turn peach. Except that it dont do that. It's still jest dusted over with gold, like the back of a sunburned gal" (167, 168). "This one for now," explains the designer. "Tomorrow, the other one, red with sonnenblume" (168).

It seems clear the man writing this rather *likes* the *Gesellschaft* of the modern metropolis, which appears here as a magical playground, not—as for the Nashville agrarians or for Cleanth Brooks (or T. S. Eliot, or, for that matter, Theodore Dreiser[12] or the Birmingham school)—a hotbed of alienation and spiritual emptiness. Indeed, immediately after Ratliff pays Allanovna and refuses to take the ties, she brandishes another design object whose form belies its use—as Ratliff describes it, "a thing on the desk that looked like a cream pitcher until she snapped it open and it was a cigarette lighter" (176)—and threatens to burn the money, which is what he himself has in effect already done by refusing to accept what he has paid for, by writing the money off as a loss. Ratliff balks, of course, and instead of getting out-capitalisted by Flem, gets out-sacrificed by Allanovna. After soliloquizing that "only the gauche, the illiterate, the frightened and the pastless destroy money," she continues, "You will keep it then," but she means not the money but the one tie he pays for:

> You will take it back to . . . Mississippi. Where is one who, not needs: who cares about so base as needs? Who wants something that costs one hundred fifty dollar—a hat, a picture, a book, a jewel for the ear; something never never never anyhow just to eat—but believes he—she—will never have it, has even long ago given up, not the dream but the hope—This time do you know what I mean? (177)

And Ratliff replies, "I know exactly what you mean because you jest said it" (177). (Notably, "Missippi" is figured here precisely as a drab place where dreams *don't* materialize unless you bring them back from New York.) In their compromise, then, Ratliff buys one tie for $150 and Allanovna gives him the second. This second tie, he explains to Chick Mallison years later, "is a private matter"; Mallison has never seen it and, says Ratliff, "I doubt if you will" (232). If Flem's ostensibly private wooden ledge seems to operate as symbol, however questionably, Faulkner makes it difficult to assign a single meaning to "the tie" at all because we have two ties vibrating unstably, Heisenberg fashion, between purchase and gift.

What Allanovna conveys in her homage to expensive beauty is a desire that Faulkner does not describe as representative of a scandalously excessive capitalism, a horrific *Gesellschaft*, but rather a desire that in itself *Gemeinschaft*—here, the *Gemeinschaft* of the southern peasantry and petit-bourgeoisie—can never fulfill. If it is Ratliff's bourgeois standing that prevents his accepting the ties, Faulkner has Allanovna show us, his ultimately doing so represents a dawning understanding of life beyond the petit-bourgeoisie who amass surplus items solely as symbols of their status, their anti-fashion respectability.

But if the ties are not anti-fashion, it also seems clear that neither Myra Allanovna nor Faulkner sees them entirely as fashion in the Birmingham school sense either, for despite Ratliff's experiences at the party, they do not see fashion primarily as communication. Instead, their artistic vision appears closer to what Herbert Blau describes in his iconoclastic 1999 book *Nothing in Itself: Complexions of Fashion*. After discussing a black Koran-embroidered evening dress by Karl Lagerfeld as modeled by Claudia Schiffer in 1994, Blau concludes that book as follows:

> While it can make a dissident statement, or work for identity politics, at the level of its deepest motives there is no justice in fashion. Which augments the perpetual blush.
>
> We may, as we look in the mirror, be mortified for the moment, but dressing up or dressing down, there's a certain expectancy in clothes, as if woven into the fabric, even technofabrics, with something of the sensuousity of sewing or weaving itself. . . . If there's no last word in fashion, despite all the exquisite, ravishing, undeniably elegant things, that's because even what we think of as timeless is suffused with anticipation. Even before the garment is worn there's something erotic in the prospect of wearing, unsubdued by evanescence, the thing half understood, what makes fashion fashion, if sinister, threatening, even aroused by that. (252)

Blau's central project is to redirect our gaze toward the fashion object as aesthetic, even of course erotic, object; he wants to acknowledge the designer's exquisite craft even in the most "political" seeming garb. An Allanovna tie is, perhaps above all else, an "exquisite, ravishing, undeniably elegant thing," and her list of items—"a hat, a picture, a book, a jewel for the ear"—deliberately blurs the boundary between design and art.[13] This is an important step for Faulkner, whose characters up to this point have generally, in their progress from peasantry to respectability, amassed design objects solely as markers of their status: what Shreve McCannon in *Absalom, Absalom!* mercilessly calls Thomas Sutpen's "crystal tapestries and . . . Wedgwood chairs" (148). To put it perhaps a bit too cynically, after his New York visit, Ratliff seems to graduate from reading *Southern Living* to reading *Wallpaper**.[14]

Faulkner's mocking characterization of Sutpen's status-bestowing design objects as made of ludicrously fragile china and crystal is more than echoed, though with an overtly erotic twist, two decades later in *The Mansion* in Ratliff's strangely fearful approach to the second tie: "I hadn't even teched [it] yet because I was afraid to. It was red jest a little under what you see in a black-gum leaf in the fall, with not no single sunflower nor even a bunch of them but little yellow sunflowers all over it in a kind of diamond pattern, each one with a little blue center almost the exact blue my shirts get to after a while. I didn't dare touch it" (176). What are we to make of Ratliff's fear in the face of Allanovna's object, "red jest a little under" and packed with *jouissance*? Why the strange disjunction between seeing and touching? We seem to be back in the rich man's bawdy house, Ratliff's fear like that of Clyde Griffiths visiting his first prostitute in Dreiser's *An American Tragedy*: "She might charge him more than he could afford. He was afraid of her—himself—everything, really—quite nervous and almost dumb with his several fears and qualms" (67). Yet ultimately, it will be this tie that Ratliff chooses to display in his home "on a rack under a glass bell" next to one of Barton Kohl's sculptures (231); the peach-colored tie, even more sensual as it recalls the back of a sunburned girl, which he keeps genuinely private. Perhaps from time to time he even touches it. All Mink has to play with, on the other hand, is a pistol. Firearms are phallic enough without embellishment, but Faulkner embellishes: "snub-nosed, short-barreled, swollen of cylinder and rusted over, with its curved butt and flat reptilian hammer it did resemble the fossil relic of some small antediluvian terrapin" (291). "Hit's dirty inside," complains Mink (292).

Yet even though these objects appear to stand in for eroticized body parts, I am still not convinced this is fetishism, exactly, at least not on Faulkner's part. For one thing, as Victoria de Grazia reminds us on the opening page of the essay collection *The Sex of Things*, "In Western societies, acts of exchange and consumption have long been obsessively gendered, usually as female" (1), and some recent work by Bill Brown suggests that psychoanalysis has made objects inexorably symbolize body parts—breasts, genitals, etc.—only because it has underestimated the appeal for humans of things in themselves ("Object Relations").

For another thing, the association of big city objects with forbidden human sexuality extends in the novel even to Barton Kohl's sculpture. Admittedly, here the sexuality is chiefly a matter of Chick Mallison's insinuation to Ratliff: "It's that sculpture you liked: the Italian boy doing whatever it was you liked that Gavin himself who has not only seen Italian boys before but maybe even one doing whatever this one is doing, didn't even know where first base was. But it's all right. You don't have a female wife nor any innocent female daughters either. So you can probably keep it right there in the house" (203–4). Mallison later confesses to the reader that "if Gavin was still looking for first base, I had already struck out because I didn't even know what it was, let alone what it was doing" (232). Chick insinuates a double sexuality: that the boy is doing something with his genitals, and, via the baseball analogy, that understanding abstract sculpture is somehow like sex. (If this line of thinking seems adolescent, well, that's Chick Mallison, who keeps joking about how "once you get the clothes off those tall up-and-down women you find out they aint all that up-and-down at all" [205]. Hubba hubba.) Here Ratliff succeeds where the two Harvard graduates fail. To view his sculptures, Kohl leads him away from the party to the private section of the house—"a room not jest where folks used but where somebody come off by his-self and worked" (172). (Functionally if not aesthetically, this is of course just the sort of space where Flem will keep his ledge and Ratliff his peach tie.) In the loft, Ratliff gazes

> at some I did recognise and some I almost could recognise and maybe if I had time enough I would, and some I knowed I wouldn't never quite recognise, until all of a sudden I knowed that wouldn't matter neither, not jest to him but to me too. Because anybody can see and hear and smell and feel and taste what he expected to hear and see and feel and smell and taste, and wont nothing much notice your presence nor miss your lack. So maybe when you can see and feel and smell and hear and taste what you never expected to and hadn't never even imagined until that moment, maybe that's why Old Moster picked you out to be the one of the ones to be alive. (173)

Ratliff's artistic education is proceeding apace. If Mallison and Stevens, Harvard aesthetes though they may imagine themselves to be, still imagine art to be fundamentally representational, Ratliff—in only his first experience of abstract sculpture—almost immediately, "all of a sudden," comes to realize the essence of art is, instead, formal innovation: experiencing "what you never expected to and hadn't never even imagined until that moment" (173). This modernist emphasis on experiential newness is virtually indistinguishable from Faulkner's description, in his Nobel Prize speech, of his own attempts "not for glory and least of all for profit . . . to create out of the materials of the human spirit something which did not exist before." None of this is how

Kohl expects Ratliff to react. "Shocked? Mad?" he asks after giving Ratliff "time and room both to look" (173). "Do I have to be shocked and mad at something just because I never seen it before?" asks Ratliff. Kohl's answer is curious: "At your age, yes. . . . Only children can stand surprise for the pleasure of surprise. Grown people cant bear surprise unless they are promised in advance they will want to own it" (173).

In its celebration of childhood and its rejection of getting and spending, it's an oddly romantic attitude for a modernist sculptor, certainly a more "innocent" vision than Chick Mallison's. Kohl's attitude nevertheless recalls Stevens's description of Greenwich Village as a place "where young people of all ages below ninety go in search of dreams" (151). And youth in this chapter is pitted, to make matters still more complicated, against totalitarianism: "Young people today don't have any [time] left because only fools under twenty-five can believe, let alone hope, that there's any left at all," declares Stevens, going on to declaim against totalitarians in Italy and Germany and Spain and at home, whom he describes partly in terms still appropriate today as "the fine names confederated in unison in the name of God against the impure in morals and politics" (160, 161). Of the domestic totalitarians listed, none are associated with Greenwich Village, but the South has plenty: "Long in Louisiana and our own Bilbo in Mississippi, not to mention our very own Senator Clarence Egglestone Snopes," plus its fair share of the Klansmen and Silver Shirts Stevens also mentions. Ratliff adds Russia to the list, of course, but Stevens goes on again: "when you are young enough and brave enough at the same time, you can hate intolerance and believe in hope, and, if you are sho enough brave, act on it" (161). And Ratliff adds, with a hint of corrective parody suggesting he's a bit skeptical about dividing the world up so easily into hopeful youth and intolerant elders, "I wish I was either one of them. To believe in intolerance and hope and act on it" (161).

Thus chapter 7, seemingly a light jaunt to Greenwich Village, comes on the heels of a beautiful woman's suicide from boredom and ends with apocalypse: "and now we watched the lights go out in Spain and Ethiopia, the darkness that was going to creep eastward across all Europe and Asia too, until the shadow of it would fall across the Pacific islands until it reached even America" (178). Kohl dies, and Linda, they predict, will return to Yoknapatawpha because "it's doom" (178). Yet the enemy here is not capitalism, patriarchal or otherwise, but rather what Faulkner labels "intolerance," a remarkably mild word for National Socialism, fascism, Stalinism, and so on, but one aptly suited to the reception of startling, difficult art in the South. It's that intolerance that leads to boredom by expelling the surprising, the creative.

I don't want to suggest that Faulkner plays down the murderousness of totalitarianism. But if Priscilla Wald's "Atomic Faulkner" essay has reminded us all of the complex relations between big fears and small fears, I think *The Mansion* reminds us of the complex relations between big acts of resistance and dignity and small ones. For various kinds of oppressed men—gay men and African American men in particular, but in much fashion theory working-class white Britons as well—snappy dressing has derived from an insistence on dignity, an assertion of a kind of sophistication readable only to others in the know, sometimes even "a black thing you wouldn't understand." Ellison's Invisible Man uses fashion as a kind of flashy invisibility: he becomes flashy to those who get it, invisible to those who don't. In such a context, a one thousand-dollar necktie is not some decadent bourgeois excess. It is a celebration of beauty, an assertion of personal dignity, and, most of all, an affirmation of selfhood.[15] Faulkner was not, of course, oppressed in the ways gay and black men have been. But for much of his life he was miserable for other reasons, reasons that often did have to do with mainstream America's "intolerance," its hatred of surprise, its drive, especially in the 1950s, toward a world—and not just a world of Wal-Marts—that any artist would find boring.

The morning after that ride from the Memphis airport, an early-morning run took me by Faulkner's grave. Left there was the usual assortment of whiskey bottles. Myself the child of an alcoholic, I find such "tribute" tremendously depressing. In my own ideal world, in St. Peter's Cemetery people would not leave empty flasks of alcohol. Faulkner's grave would be festooned with beautiful neckties.

FIVE

FLYING WITHOUT WINGS
Race, Civic Branding, and Identity Politics in Two Twenty-first-century American Cities

On March 2, 2003, when readers of the *Boston Globe* opened their Sunday papers and turned to the *Parade* magazine inside, they may have noticed, with St. Patrick's Day fast approaching, the full-page Franklin Mint advertisement on the back cover for the "Irish Blessing Charm Bracelet" featuring "the treasured symbols of Ireland captured in stunning 24 karat gold accents, and steeped in the traditions of Irish history and design." However, readers of papers throughout the South—the *Greensboro News & Record*, *Atlanta Journal-Constitution*, *Birmingham News*, *Mobile Register*, and *Orlando Sentinel*, for example—found quite a different Franklin Mint ad reigning in their *Parade*. "Lee. Jackson. Stuart," it read. "Honor the spirit of the South's favorite sons by wearing the . . . Pride of the South Civil War Ring." The blurb on the lower left corner of the page read in full,

> Presented by The Civil War Library & Museum and The Franklin Mint, this powerful tribute is masterfully crafted in *solid sterling silver*. Its compelling design is based on the Battle Flag of the South [sic], artfully enhanced by an intricately sculptured rendering of a Bald Eagle. The unique shield design recalls the uniform buttons worn by Southern troops, and is complemented by the familiar crossed sabres of the cavalry. Richly accented with *24 carat gold*, and featuring the famed "Southern Cross."
>
> A compelling tribute to the heroes of the South! Order now! The Franklin Mint / Sharing Your Passion for Collecting. (24)

The timing of the ads is notable, particularly in the Atlanta paper. Georgia Governor Sonny Perdue had recently won office by appealing to small-town and rural white Georgians who resented his predecessor's having shrunk the presence of the battle flag of the Confederacy—first introduced in 1956 in response to the civil rights movement—on the state flag. Though some observers expected him not to follow through on his campaign pledge, Perdue had in early February proposed a two-part nonbinding referendum on the flag. Voters were to be first presented with an up-or-down vote on the present flag. Then, if their vote was "no," they would be asked to choose between two earlier flags, the pre-1956 flag or the 1956–2001 one. The Sunday before the ads appeared, the *Atlanta Journal-Constitution* had reported on a growing divide on this issue between Atlanta and much of "the other Georgia." By Friday, February 28, newspapers around the world were reporting that Perdue, a Republican, had enlisted former Democratic Governor and U.S. President Jimmy Carter to help Georgians resolve their differences.

It should not take a Nobel Peace Prize winner to solve what is essentially a graphic design problem. Clearly, however, it does, and this chapter is largely about *why* it does. In using not Slavoj Žižek but marketing theory—not hitherto a field known for its theoretical profundity—I do not mean in what follows to belittle issues of U.S. southern iconography, nor to trivialize by literalizing what George Lipsitz names the possessive investment in whiteness. Southern civic brand identities are a great deal more in flux than the old static, red-state "Mississippi" model allows. Second, it suggests that Birmingham and Georgia, while less glamorous than L.A., may nonetheless, in their negotiations of sharp internal conflicts between liberals and conservatives, better indicate at least some of the key issues that should be defining contemporary American studies as the nation emerges from one of the most bitterly divided, and spatially inflected, partisan eras in its history. Third and perhaps most crucially, a phenomenon like *American Idol*—based in Los Angeles but deriving much of its power, in several senses, from a rebranded southernness—points toward the complicated political, economic, and cultural relays that define twenty-first-century U.S. culture as much more than the (merely) coastal. Finally, the very act of analyzing civic brand identities within the field imaginary of American studies implies that this imaginary itself cannot claim to stand outside the branding process. What we have been schooled to call the field's paradigm dramas may also be described—and critiqued—using the terms of marketing theory.

Naomi Klein indicates the global political and economic power of design and branding in both the title of *No Logo* and its opening sentence: "The astronomical growth in the wealth and cultural influence of multinational corporations over the last fifteen years can arguably be traced back to a single, seemingly innocuous idea developed by management theorists in the mid-1980s: that successful corporations must primarily produce brands, as opposed to products" (3). The impact of branding can be seen, for example, in every Franklin Mint ad—whether for a Confederate ring or an Irish charm bracelet or "the official John Deere pocket watch" (which appeared that Sunday in the *Chicago Tribune*'s *Parade*) or "the Vietnam Veterans Service Ring"

(*San Francisco Chronicle*) or "the Power of the Emerald Isle Celtic Cross Ring" (*Washington Post*)—for each contains the phrase "sharing your passion for collecting." With that phrase, the Franklin Mint is trying to move away from its stodgy, quasi-governmental "brand image" as, well, a Mint, toward a more warm and fuzzy perception of it as a friend who "shares your passion." In the terms offered by leading brand management professor David A. Aaker, the Franklin Mint is offering a "value proposition" about the "emotional benefits" of a commercial relationship with the company. More precisely, it is doing just what another brand expert, Lynn Upshaw, advises, "humanizing the identity": "When the personality extends seamlessly from the brand's positioning and captures the most exciting human qualities ["sharing your passion"] of the brand, the result can be an unstoppable brand identity" (vi).

The implications of branding theory for what we call "the South," the nation, and the field of American studies are sizeable not least because although for Klein multinational corporate branding "is waging a war on public and individual space" (5), corporations are not the only entities being branded. In a recent *Foreign Affairs* article, Peter van Ham argues that branding— "giving products and services an emotional dimension with which people can identify"—has meant that "Singapore and Ireland are no longer merely countries one finds in an atlas. They have become 'brand states,' with geographical and political settings that seem trivial compared to their emotional resonance among an increasingly global audience of consumers" (2). Daryl Travis, noting that the phenomenon occurs not only with nation-states but with cities and other political units, refers to these units as "Civic Brands" (252).

Moreover, like branding in general, civic branding links iconography with capital via the notion of "brand equity." Aaker defines the latter as

> a set of assets (and liabilities) linked to a brand's name and symbol that adds to (or subtracts from) the value provided by a product or service to a firm and/or that firm's customers. The major asset categories are:
>
> 1. Brand name awareness
> 2. Brand loyalty
> 3. Perceived quality
> 4. Brand associations. (7–8)

The classic example of brand equity is Atlanta-based Coca-Cola. As Travis notes, "Coke's fixed assets are worth something like $7 billion, but according to one consulting firm, its brand value is worth $84 billion." Take away Coke's fixed assets, and it could rebuild. Take away its brand equity, and the company is sunk. Asks Travis, "How's that for an intangible?" (4).

To consider the nation and the region as civic brands represents, I think, one next logical step in American studies' ongoing post-essentialist examination of North American identity politics, because, as Patricia Yaeger puts it in the southern context, "older models . . . are no longer generative" (xv). At first, for example, that one version of white southernness should occupy the same space as Irishness in *Parade* might appear to support John Shelton Reed's old model of (white) southernness as a kind of ethnicity. Yet when we look at Franklin Mint *Parade* advertisements nationwide on the same day, the picture grows more complicated: all that cheap jewelry is about identity politics, but it would be very unusual to characterize service in Vietnam or an affinity for green tractors as an "ethnicity." To characterize them as nationalities, another model that Michael Kreyling, Richard Gray, and Michael O'Brien have all more recently used to characterize southernness, would be even odder.

A broader advantage to discussing southernness, for example, as a brand as opposed to an ethnicity or a nation is that, rather than forcing a false binarism between national and postnational identitarian models or between nationalist and cosmopolitan affiliations, a brand offers a more inclusive and hybrid range of participation in "imagined communities" ranging from nations to veterans' groups to tractor fans to whatever sort of community consumers of a product imagine themselves participating in by buying into it. Indeed, nations, states, and cities are explicitly rethinking themselves as civic brands precisely because it is *already* getting harder and harder to distinguish imagined civic identities and communities from imagined noncivic ones. Such leveling, however, is not necessarily always and everywhere bad. If you are Canadian, as Klein is, it probably *is* a bad thing that "global" brands—nearly all of them U.S. in origin—are edging out your "concept of nationality," and even worse if they are "waging a war" on it and on your "unmarked space" (5). But if you are southern, the issue is more complicated because that region's public sphere much more conspicuously has never consisted of pure, unbranded space.[1] For most of the past century, much of the white South has repeatedly embraced the civic brand called Dixie and its logo the Confederate battle flag. Rarely did this embrace entail literally *buying* the civic brand, despite the considerable availability of kitsch, but it nonetheless demanded a sometimes militant *subsidizing* of it, and such subsidies required, and derived from, a substantial emotional and identitarian investment in that particular red, white, and blue object of cathexis, a belief that those dead rebels "share your passion." Icons, logos, and brands, in short, do not carry pernicious economic and identitarian force only when they are merely corporate.

Conversely, in some cases branding can also direct identity, civic and otherwise, away from a melancholic fetishization of the dead and toward the realm of ethical aspiration and the embrace of "the other." As David Aaker puts it in describing the "self-expression" model of branding, "some brands become vehicles to express a part of [consumers'] self-identity. This self-identity can be their actual identity or an ideal self to which they might aspire. People express their own or idealized identity in a variety of ways, such as job choice, friends, attitudes, opinions, activities, and lifestyles" (153).

Here brand management and cultural studies coalesce. Aaker goes on to quote consumer anthropologist Grant McCracken to the effect that consumers "use these brand meanings to construct and sustain their social self" (153)—much the same point cultural studies scholar Stuart Ewen makes in *All Consuming Images*, for example.

Seen from this angle, branding emerges as, among other things, a neutral tool for the making and unmaking of southern civic feeling in ways that advance the projects of such new southern studies works as Patricia Yaeger's *Dirt and Desire*, Tara McPherson's *Reconstructing Dixie*, and Houston Baker's *Turning South Again*. Of course those projects, like the argument that southern affiliation operates as a kind of brand, reject the bizarre idea fostered by the agrarians that a society that enslaved humans—a system whose regional, national, and global economic legacy persists into the twenty-first century—ever *was*, much less *is*, outside the market, "a needed corrective," as Louis D. Rubin admiringly put it at the height of the civil rights movement in 1962, "to America's head-long materialism" (xxv).[2] However, other advantages are more specific and, I hope, less obvious. Yaeger doesn't just argue that "older models of Southern writing are no longer generative" (xv); she specifically looks "at black and white women writers using similar rubrics to map out the regional geographies that they do and do not share" and seeks "a sense of the ways race functions in the nonepic everyday" (xv). This question of sharing and not sharing everyday identity is central to McPherson's project as well: "In a culture that has all too often revolved around policing purity and guarding against miscegenation," she writes,

> it is crucial to divorce identity from sameness. We need to think of the South as a dialectic between tradition and change, a relationship in process, in flux, in movement. We need models of southern mixedness less rooted in the abstractions of poststructuralism and the politics of difference and more rooted in the learned lessons of everyday life in the South, a life that is not finally reducible to the iconic status of certain southern symbols but is instead fluid and changeable. I want tales from the South where white supremacy and racism are not inevitable and impenetrable, though these tales may not be easy ones to find; we need a creative imagining that brings different people together to move the country's political center. The history of black activism and agency in the South offers one vibrant counterhistory. (31)

Finally, Baker also draws on that counterhistory of agency, fluidity, and mobility and calls for a "black-majority, politically participatory, bodily secure GOOD LIFE" (83). Building on Malcolm X's claim that Mississippi is anywhere in the United States south of the Canadian border, he closes *Turning South Again* as follows:

> Black-south blues traditions . . . empower us to alter the sign "Mississippi" to read "Alabama." Staying in "Alabama" for days too long carries us beyond Tuskegee zones of discipline and confinement and through time to the righteous civil rights motions of the black-South body. We find ourselves in the extraordinary company of Mrs. Rosa Parks and the Reverend Dr. Martin Luther King . . . just one hour down the road from Mr. Washington's *plantation*. Black modernism has bright birth in Montgomery. Breaking the frame. In 2000, such modernism waits to be academically and politically shaped into a black-South, black-majority public-sphere mobility for a new century. (98)

By 2003, rebranding—"altering the sign"—in the service of such shaping was again underway in Alabama.

By way of contrast, however, we first need to look closer at the debate that year over the Confederate battle flag in Georgia. It is too simple to say the debate simply divided the state between those who wished to affiliate themselves with Brand Confederacy (conservative whites) and those who did not (everybody else). Rather, as in similar recent conflicts in Mississippi and South Carolina, the conflict might also be said to have divided the state between those who see themselves chiefly as producers of Georgia's brand identity—the businesspeople, chiefly in greater Atlanta, who see the return of Confederate associations as bad for civic brand equity (especially in terms of attracting tourists and business)—and those who not entirely consciously position themselves as the consumers of the Confederate facet of that brand identity—people who in fact *derive* a significant portion of their identity from it, chiefly poorer whites in "the other Georgia." What makes this issue unique and important for much cultural studies is that the traditional (and often facile) dichotomy between "good" consumer-citizen and "bad" capitalist producer underlying work like Klein's or *Adbusters'*, for example, is forcefully reversed. Consider the following rural white responses to the new Georgia flag, as reported in the *Atlanta Journal-Constitution*: "I'm not prejudiced. I just like flags the way they are. I don't want them changed"; "I don't like [the new flag] and I'll never fly it. It just doesn't look right"; "The Confederate flag has nothing to do with slavery. If you take away the flag because it's offensive to somebody, where are you going to stop?" and, amazingly, "There ain't nobody but [racial epithet] and dumb folks that think that flag is racist" (McWhirter C1, C7; last brackets are McWhirter's). What Charlie

Frenette, a high-ranking Coca-Cola executive, says about the famous New Coke debacle is instructive here: "What we learned from that is that we don't own this brand, the consumer does. . . . The product is not just about [the taste test]. It's an idea" (qtd. in Drawbaugh 30).

In the South as elsewhere, official civic branding generally goes on at the levels of the state and the city: we all know "Virginia is for Lovers." Mississippi and Alabama, for example, now routinely compete for auto plants, and the brand image of each state plays a large role—though not perhaps so large a role as tax incentives—in the location decisions not just of Mercedes, Honda, and Nissan, but of other kinds of companies as well.[3] These things tend to snowball; the status-brand Mercedes plant between Birmingham and Tuscaloosa is generally held to have improved Alabama's brand equity significantly, particularly in differentiating it from "Mississippi." Yet if Alabama is now somewhat tenuously considered a higher-status brand than its western neighbor, the eastern contrast—in particular, that between the cities of Birmingham and Atlanta—is at least as illustrative. In 1948, the two metropolises were about the same size; fifty years later, Atlanta was three times bigger. According to Sam Masell, mayor of Atlanta in the early 1970s, "You'd see them on TV over there [in Birmingham], and it was good ol' boys talking. We decided when the cameras were on Atlanta we wanted to see the brightest, most progressive leadership talking" (qtd. in Wyatt). Mercedes plant or not, to this day Birmingham remains known chiefly as "the city that turned firehoses and dogs on civil rights marchers" (Wyatt; see also Witt).

At least since the heyday of the New South in the early twentieth century, this sort of concern with public relations has most often been referred to not as branding but as boosterism. What most distinguishes the newer form of public relations from the older, other than the newer kind's greater systemization, is its concern with the visual image, its concern with how it looked "when the cameras were on." For branding purposes, Birmingham is perhaps less the city that turned firehoses and police dogs on its citizens than the city that let itself be photographed doing so. Diane McWhorter drily summarizes the point of view of upper-class Birmingham whites in 1963 thus: "It might have all gone away but for that news photograph of a colored boy who had stepped into the jaws of one of the German police dogs. As Eric Sevareid had said on the *CBS Evening News*, 'A snarling police dog set upon a human being is recorded in the permanent photoelectric file of every human being's brain'" (22). Civil rights agitation would not have gone away, of course, but the blow to the city's brand image would certainly have been lessened. After all, while news of lynchings had been coming out of Mississippi for decades, it took the photographs of Emmett Till's open casket to galvanize public outrage. The videotape of police beating Rodney King had a similar effect on the image of the Los Angeles Police Department—and, arguably, on that of predominantly white urban police forces throughout the country. It is not enough that things have really changed in Birmingham: as the city moves to alter its brand image, it must seek out a new set of visuals.

To the surprise of many, in 2003 that process began to take shape—the round shape of Ruben Studdard, the 6'4", 350-pound black man from Birmingham who in May of that year won the second season of *American Idol* before 34 million viewers, more than had watched that year's Oscars. Precisely because of his exceptional body, which he used literally as a billboard for Birmingham, Studdard's ascendancy was packed with symbolism as no other candidate's could be, and it involved—and, as I write, continues to involve—at least five different levels of brand management: Brand Ruben, Brand Birmingham/Brand South, Brand Blackness, Brand *American Idol*, and Brand America.

Particularly in the early phases of the competition, Studdard wore brightly colored 5XL jerseys emblazoned with "205," the Birmingham telephone area code. By thus "representing" Birmingham, Studdard immediately moved the electoral issue away from the question of "idol" status—vocal ability, bland boy-band good looks—toward a question of voting for the home team. On February 28, 2003—the same day papers reported Jimmy Carter's riding to the rescue of Brand Georgia—the *Birmingham News* reported on a survey of civic pride in the city. Eighty-five percent of residents were proud to live in Birmingham; 46 percent of blacks and 47 percent of whites were "very proud." Yet only 24 percent of people believed that people outside the state viewed Birmingham positively, citing "racial history" as the most prominent reason. David Adkisson, president of the regional Chamber of Commerce, summarized the results as follows: "I think you see a lot of people kind of wringing their hands about how the community is perceived. I think this survey proves that we who live in the community are very positive about it" (Abrams 1B). As the flag controversy unfolded in Georgia, bringing out the vote for Studdard would in Birmingham become an exercise in identity politics and civic rebranding. Unlike the Confederate flag, "205" numerically located Birmingham not in history, but in space, on a global communications network. Everybody in North America has an area code, and everybody in the same area has the same code. In a paradox that might send the Nashville agrarians spinning, the system—precisely *because* of its abstraction—generates a sense of place crucially untainted by notions of "knowing one's place."

During the months of Ruben mania, a Huffman High School yearbook photograph circulated widely in the Birmingham media, though not much in other parts of the country. It showed the 1996 senior class's two "most talented" individuals: Studdard and Kristie Morgan Frazier, a white girl who had herself gone on to record a gospel album. Gazing at the camera, they are smiling. Their hands are clasped on the table. It looks a little like an engagement photograph. Virtually no one who lived in the Birmingham metropolitan area could miss what this photo meant. Citizens, black and white, most of them too young now to remember the Bull Connor era but well aware of its legacy for the city's image, got out the vote in droves. "Go Ruben!" signs went up in shop windows in the posher suburbs south of the mountain. (Red Mountain, running from southwest to northeast, divides downtown Birmingham from the leafy neighborhoods to the south. The previous year Diane McWhorter, a native of Mountain Brook, had won a Pulitzer for *Carry Me Home: Birmingham, Alabama, The Climactic Battle of the Civil Rights Revolution*, which detailed those suburbs' role forty years earlier in backing Connor and his ilk.) A church on Valleydale Road, which runs through the enclaves of Hoover and Pelham, "organized a voting challenge with other churches in Birmingham to turn out the vote for Ruben" (Sepsas 143). Dennis Leonard, general manager of Fox 6 television in Birmingham, reported that ratings for *American Idol* ran 67 percent higher in the greater Birmingham viewing area than nationwide (Sepsas 144).

Studdard continued to market himself as the candidate of racial reconciliation. "I love everybody," he replied to one question about what he wanted the viewers to know about him. And on March 25, 2003, on the competition's "country night," he sang "Sweet Home Alabama," omitting verses about Neil Young and the Muscle Shoals swampers. Thus abbreviated and in a new context, the song took on new significations. "In Birmingham they love the governor" means something quite different when the governor is Bob Riley than when it is George Wallace. Moreover, Studdard changed a key lyric from "Watergate does not bother me" to "Watergate does not concern me," again emphasizing historical distance. Lynyrd Skynyrd, singing in 1974, sought to deploy an ancient white southern trick of deflecting attention from their failures onto those of northern white liberals, but Studdard deflects attention away from a narcissistic gaze at *any* past. "Watergate does not concern me" not because it was not a heinous episode in the nation's history but because it had happened thirty years earlier, literally before Studdard was born. At issue is not past trauma but simply the present: "Does your conscience bother you?"

Lyrics notwithstanding, Studdard's body signified on the national level as well. While the CEO of a marketing firm dubbed Studdard "the round mound of sound," the slogan that stuck came from Gladys Knight: "the velvet teddy bear." Knight's term offers a cross-racial tribute in its allusion to Mel Tormé, the Velvet Fog, but it also alludes, obviously, to the softness of Studdard's large body. (One female *Washington Post* critic, apparently interpreting that fat as feminine, referred to Studdard's 205 jerseys as "muumuus" [de Moraes C01].) In *Hoop Roots*, John Edgar Wideman has written of how Michael Jordan transformed one kind of large black male body from an object of fear to one of desire and emulation in white U.S. culture. But the *Post* notwithstanding, Studdard became a sex symbol precisely by being more cuddly than phallic, his fat working in much the same way the Beatles' unmasculine hairdos once did. Yet, as with Barry White and Luciano Pavarotti, his size also connotes literal and figurative substance: bulk here connotes mature, "authentic" masculine talent, and to that degree Clay Aiken, Studdard's boyish, mop-topped, rail-thin final competitor, comes off as the androgyne. Indeed, Lisa de Moraes suggests that judge Simon Cowell "worked . . . hard to send 'hello, might be gay' messages to the hordes of smitten young women who have formed the Claymates fan club" (co1). (Aiken finally came out five years later on the cover of *People* magazine.)

Nationally, of course, Studdard's candidacy raised exactly the same issues as it had in Birmingham. Could a large black man be an "American idol"? (After all, four of the top five of the 2003 finalists—two black, two white—had thought Tamyra Gray, who is black, would win the first competition, and she hadn't even made the final three.) The often political comic strip *The Boondocks* weighed in with a "Go Ruben!" Salon.com opined near the end that a black man had a better chance of surviving a slasher movie than Studdard had of winning. The *American Idol* contest was never designed to be simply about vocal ability; judge Simon Cowell had made cruel comments about several other candidates' weight, for example—including that of Hispanic Atlantan Vanessa Olivares—but he never attacked Studdard's (de Moraes co1). Was black beautiful? On April 30, Studdard and Trenyce, the two darkest-skinned candidates out of five remaining (four southerners and a rather oafish white active-duty Marine from Oceanside, California, who had served as the competition's "country music" and "we support the troops in Iraq" candidate, making him at the time effectively a fifth southerner), found themselves—despite being lauded by the judges as among the best of the remaining group—the bottom two. Trenyce was voted off. Pundits came up with all sorts of explanations—that voters for the two had been so sure of their candidates' success they hadn't bothered to vote that week, for example—but the implication was obvious: the voters (whom Fox kept—and keeps—calling "America")—were racist.[4] It didn't help that *Idol*, even more than most reality television, represented itself as a kind of American democracy in miniature, in which "the people" choose the winner; many African Americans were still feeling disenfranchised, still stinging from the Florida election fiasco.

Yet after Studdard won—initial reports were that he'd done so by 1,335 votes, off by a factor of 100—and love seemingly defeated love and theft, the opposite question was raised, again reflecting the 2000 presidential election. Had the contest been rigged? Or, as the cover of *Us* magazine blared,

"Did the best man win?" As noted above, a number of sources, including de Moraes in the *Washington Post*, suggested the judges had slanted the contest toward Studdard, featuring him unduly, particularly in the Ford-sponsored skit portion of the show. When by July 1 Clay Aiken's single had outsold Ruben's 393,000 to 286,000, some of these felt vindicated, apparently believing the market's voice to be truer than the voters'. And all this took place, with exquisite historical irony, not simply as the Georgia flag debate reached an eleventh-hour resolution but as the Supreme Court deliberated on the Michigan affirmative action cases.

But even as his 205 jerseys seemed to lift Birmingham out of its history, Studdard's first video, "Flying without Wings"—filmed in Birmingham a week after his victory and released barely a month later—placed it squarely back in. Directed by Erik White, the video consciously revisits a single paragraph of Dr. Martin Luther King Jr.'s "I Have a Dream" speech: "I have a dream that one day, down in Alabama, with its vicious racists, with its governor having his lips dripping with the words of interposition and nullification, that one day, right there in Alabama, little black boys and black girls will be able to join hands with little white boys and white girls as sisters and brothers. I have a dream today!" (82). The video opens with Studdard crooning, "Long ago and oh so far away." There is a shot of a group of black children; two of them share on their laps a portable stereo, as though the singing is coming from the giant boombox. We cut to another shot of a group of kids—establishing children as the major theme of the video—with Studdard sitting among them, smiling. As he sings "oh so far away," we cut to a shot looking east on Birmingham's Third Avenue to one of the city's landmarks, the Alabama Theatre. Its façade dates from 1927, and viewers not recognizing the landmark simply see the word "Alabama" running vertically down a building's front in an old-looking downtown. In the lower left foreground of the frame, in heightened contrast with the dark foliage of a street planting and balancing the dark Alabama sign in the upper right, a black girl slowly walks from left to right in a bright white dress, white socks, and black shoes, a costume reminiscent of an early 1960s black girl's Sunday getup—which we'll see again in this video. Because the two most powerful images are deliberately retro, the viewer crucially, if momentarily, has difficulty placing the shot in time. Even though if one pauses the video one can see recent-make cars on the street, in real time it's not until a 1990s-model car moves from the right foreground into the background that we realize for sure we're in the present. The shot, which lasts about a second, powerfully establishes the old southern theme of "the presence of the past" (the second most important theme of the video). For Birmingham residents, however, the image carries additional meanings. The Alabama Theatre (which only connotes the "long ago" and "far away," standing as it still does only a few blocks from Linn

Park, where the opening shots of children were filmed) is a major symbol of Birmingham architectural preservation, of a positive relationship between past and present, of the value of the city's better urban history. Of course that symbolism remains racially inflected. To many, perhaps most, whites, the preservation of the theater represents a commitment primarily to Birmingham's architectural heritage. To many blacks, its preservation represents a commitment chiefly to the largely black urban core of Birmingham. Still, both groups well know the theater was built to be "The Showplace of the South." With this shot, the video announces itself and Birmingham— at least *to* Birmingham—as another such showplace. More important, because of Studdard's insistence on where his video be filmed, the video resists offering some "outside" video director's view of what would constitute a symbol, a set of clichéd images of the city.

We cut again to Studdard in a crowd of children, talking to one and pointing to something in the distance near the camera. Perhaps it *is* the camera: look, child, the whole world is watching *you*. The cameras are on Birmingham again. The song proper then begins as we cut to the first of one of the many crowd shots taken during the filming of the video by the fountain in Linn Park, which I attended. We fade to a shot of Studdard's back as he faces a very large crowd of people, then see him from the front, with the fountain and courthouse (which notably contains the very Birmingham Jail that held Dr. King) behind him. These shots were actually done at two different times of day, and the crowd was asked to move around from in front of him to in back when the camera angle moved, so that the crowd looks somewhat bigger than it actually was. The remainder of the video cuts between shots of Studdard singing in Linn Park, shots of the biracial Linn Park audience, clips from him singing on *Idol* (and of the announcement he'd won, and his family's reaction), clips of him singing as a boy, and clips of children and families at play.

The shots of Studdard singing are fairly standard, full of sweeping arm motions. Much more interesting are the shots of the audience and the signs they hold up. The first one we see, held by a blond white couple as he sings "Everybody's looking for that something," reads "Roll Tide Ruben!!" We cut back to Ruben by the fountain, then Ruben in a black outfit on *Idol*, then Ruben—once this cutting-across-time convention has been established—as a boy of about eleven with a (Birmingham native) Carl Lewis fade haircut singing in what is probably Zion Star Missionary Baptist Church in Birmingham since the podium to his left reads "Zion Star." The shot is edited so that the young Studdard appears to be singing along with "Flying without Wings." As the opening sequence promised us, past and present are merging in this video. Back to *Idol*, back to the fountain. Then, as Studdard sings "Some find it in the faces of their children," we see, predictably, a black dad pitching to his son, who smacks the ball over the father's shoulder. A white dad stands in the background; the game is interracial. Back to the fountain. "Some find it in their lover's eyes" shows, equally predictably, a pretty young black woman, a young black man just to her left, looking up at the camera. Back to *Idol*. As Studdard sings "you're flying without wings," yet another predictably literal shot shows a white boy launching a balsa wood glider. (He appears also to be in Linn Park, minus the crowds.) Back to Studdard singing in the park, back to *Idol*.

But here the video takes an unusual turn. As Studdard sings "You find it in the works of others"—for about a second, actually less time than he takes to sing the line—we cut to a color still (the whole video is in color, actually, a choice that tends to keep us focused on the present) of four smiling black girls, about age twelve, standing in white Sunday dresses in front of a building.

It's the Sixteenth Street Baptist Church.

I find it hard to describe why the shot works since it could have come off as ghoulish, like something out of *The Shining*. It's not that these manifestly *present* girls have replaced the famous Four Little Girls murdered on September 15, 1963; nor is those first four girls', and the community's, suffering diminished. Nobody is forgetting the past that looms so large in the background, but nobody is stuck in it, either. The image, it seems to me, achieves what Houston Baker demands of black modernism: "finding a black voice that if it did not *transcend* the past would at least ameliorate, accommodate, and critique the past in ways confidently articulate with what the majority of black people require (especially *racially*) for the present and future" (*Turning South Again* 15). Baker's emphasis on the voice might usefully be extended here to the image: for better and for worse, the latter may now be more important for mass purposes of amelioration, accommodation, and critique—and for the purposes of civic rebranding.

Back to *Idol*, to a still photo of Studdard as a teenager, to a crowd shot, back to *Idol*. "You find it in the deepest friendship," sings Studdard, and on the word "friendship" we cut to two boys, each smiling with his arm around the other. The black one musses the white one's hair, and the shot would be just so much ebony-'n'-ivory cliché if it weren't for one thing. The boys are in Kelly Ingram Park (also in downtown Birmingham, it adjoins the Sixteenth Street Baptist Church and the Birmingham Civil Rights Institute), and behind them is the statue of a white police officer siccing his dog on a black civil rights marcher. The racial positions have been reversed: the white boy stands beneath the protester, the black boy underneath the police officer. What in turn keeps even that juxtaposition from heavyhandedness, I think, are two things. First, although the longer duration of this shot, about three and a half seconds, pushes us toward spectacle, the moving children in the foreground keep us focused on the nonepic everyday, so that the history in the background is kept from being overdetermining, and second—as is the case with characters throughout the whole video—the children seem obviously not actors. This kind of "home movie" quality—accentuated by the inclusion of actual Studdard home movies—gives the video a sense of "reality" almost equal to that of the photographs of dogs and firehoses it so self-consciously sets out to replace. While the photographs by Charles Moore, Spider Martin, and others were striking in part because they showed living, moving scenes of barbarism against the static, gray backdrop of a "modern," skyscrapered downtown, "Flying without Wings" positions its running, mussing, playing, smiling children against the static background of what now represents the past: the Sixteenth Street Baptist Church, the statue in Kelly Ingram Park with its bronze German shepherd forever frozen in mid-lunge. Instead of real trauma against a static background, we have real friendship against a static background of sculpted, memorialized, and, crucially, *mediated* trauma.

Cut to *Idol*. Cut to a middle-aged white lady holding a sign saying, "Go 205! We ♥ R ♥ ♥-♥ ♥-ben!" Then cut to an odd juxtaposition: more white people in Linn Park holding signs. They read, from left to right, "I WANT A RUBEN SANDWICH," "Let Freedom Ring," and "You're money!" Cut to Studdard in front of fountain. Cut to multiple childhood photos of Studdard, culminating with someone in the crowd holding up a nicely framed picture of the adult Ruben. Several shots of Studdard singing. Shot of five white kids flying a kite. They're in Kelly Ingram Park, and for half a second that statue is in the background again, almost subliminal, almost impossible to notice if you don't pause the video. Cut to fountain, cut to *Idol*, cut to host Ryan Seacrest (a hiply styled and beautiful young white Atlantan) announcing Studdard's victory (as Aiken struggles to mold his face into an I'm-happy-for-you smile). Cut to Studdard singing in the park, to his family's reaction to the announcement back in the *Idol* audience, to a shot of the *Idol* stage. Cuts back and forth between the park and the confetti-drenched *Idol* finale. Final shot from camera "flying" up and away from Ruben and the park.

Beyond the glass-is-half-full idea that Studdard's victory represents a kind of culmination of King's dream—Southern Black Man Wins National Election—a viewer can take two things away from this video. First, the video enables, in the Freudian terms Eric Santner has applied to Germans' struggle to work through trauma, the work of mourning, a "process of translating, troping, and figuring loss." Instead of investing in what Santner calls "narrative fetishism" ("the construction and deployment of a narrative consciously or unconsciously designed to expunge the traces of the trauma or loss that called that narrative into being in the first place" (144), that is, a form of melancholy associated with the Confederate battle flag and with much of white Birmingham's initial resistance to commemorating the marches with statuary and a Civil Rights Institute), the video repeatedly alludes to (memorials of) Birmingham's violent past in order, like Kelly Ingram Park itself, to transcend that past. It's no coincidence that the Westlife song "Flying without Wings" opens with the prospect of the narcissistic self-seeking to fulfill its lack: "Everybody's looking for that something, / One thing that makes it all complete." Nor is it coincidence that the next two lines are "You'll find it in the strangest places / Places you never knew it could be." Narcissistic fulfillment—the good life—the video implies to its several audiences, is to be found, of all places, in present-day Birmingham, Alabama, in area code 205. One implication here, a perspective forcefully advanced in 1963 and 1964 by such figures as King and Ralph Ellison, is that living black and white Birminghamians/Southerners/Americans affectively provide "completion" for each other—not least "in the deepest friendships"—in ways dead rebels cannot.[5] Of course, most people in the national audience will not recognize the Alabama Theatre or the statue in Kelly Ingram Park *as* allusions. (The four little girls perhaps stand a better chance of registering.) Rather, such images represent Studdard's understated commitment, at the local level, to such transcendence, such "flying." The very act of recognizing the landmarks, recognizing a local history whose interpretation they share, binds black and white citizens together. Should that message comes through at the national level, fine.

Still, I remain fascinated by those three signs, which in their mix of desire, idealism, and commerce seem to summarize Brand Ruben better than anything else. Held by a young white woman, "I want a Ruben sandwich" seems a straightforward acknowledgment of Studdard's sex appeal, a version of the many "Marry me, Ruben" signs we saw on *Idol* (and there is one of those in the Linn Park audience, too). "Let Freedom Ring" is more complicated. As the climactic phrase of the "I Have a Dream" speech, it's so appropriate for the video that one has to wonder whether the producers planted it. Still, the video differs from, say, the NuSouth emblem (a commercial clothing logo depicting the Confederate flag in the colors of African American liberation)[6] because Studdard is not actually selling a racial-reconciliation commodity-fetish; as of this writing, the *video*, in fact, is not for sale even on iTunes. Indeed, the paradox of Studdard's nascent career is that while he, his body, his victory, and his video symbolize something to the nation (and more emphatically to Birmingham), his music—well-sung generic R&B pop—may not, and so far it's the only thing of his that *is* for sale. This may be one reason why Aiken's work, though arguably no less generic, has been outselling his.[7] Brand Ruben "shares your passion." So far, relatively speaking, his actual product doesn't.

All of which is not to say Studdard isn't "money." In July 2003, very shortly after the video was released, the *Birmingham News* reported—in the

Money section—that "The Greater Birmingham Convention & Visitors Bureau has launched an advertising push in key Southeastern markets to build on what could be called the 'Ruben effect'" (Williams 2D). The video is credited with "showcasing the idea of a 'new Birmingham,'" and even before the video Studdard's victory had prompted considerable interest in Birmingham from tourists and meeting planners. Bureau President Jim Smither said of the video, "When you see little black and white kids playing together, it reminds you of the dream Martin Luther King Jr. had in his famous speech. People from out of town may be surprised at how blacks and whites rallied behind Ruben, but those of us who live here aren't" (Williams 1D). This is spin, of course. By my estimate, the crowd at the video shoot was about 80 percent black, not a perfect representation of the Birmingham area's racial mix, and to its credit the video doesn't try to alter that percentage through clever cutting. Still, nobody, neither Studdard nor Smither, is rebranding Birmingham as some kind of racial utopia. But if Atlanta is the "city too busy to hate," Birmingham in this video is having too much fun interracially playing with its kids to hate. Relatively small-town leisure opposes Atlanta's big-city busy-ness. Neither label offers the whole truth, but each is true enough, in at least an aspirational sense, to sell its city. "Flying without Wings" offers branding in the service of civics, fetishizing neither the dead logo of Dixie nor the fashionable commodities of the moment. (In a dispute over money, Studdard suspended his relationship with the 205 Flava company shortly before shooting the video, which is itself devoid of bling.) Repeatedly emphasizing icons of a shared past and present, it is about acknowledging a new regional identity, a new kind of Birmingham (and southern) social self.

None of this is to suggest that substantial obstacles do not remain to black mobility and modernism in Birmingham. The mobility of the black majority remains restricted in big ways and small, from a woefully inadequate public transportation system (were Rosa Parks alive today and in Birmingham, her first challenge might be *finding* a bus) to the lack of a sidewalk on the central thoroughfare running over the mountain from Birmingham's Southside to the majority-white suburb of Homewood (a street named, ironically enough, Richard Arrington Boulevard, after Birmingham's first black mayor). While the present mayor and a majority of the city council are African American, their ability to improve basic social services is sharply curtailed by the outdated and racist Alabama Constitution, which sharply limits cities' and counties' "home rule," especially on matters of taxation. The "rule" instead lies chiefly in Montgomery, and "the other Alabama" affects Alabama politics at least as much as "the other Georgia" affects its neighbor's. And the image of the "plantation"—Baker's model for limits on black mobility—is not dead even in Birmingham, a city built well after the Civil War. In early 2006, as a private-public partnership to build a Railroad Reservation Park downtown nearly broke down over the white private backers' insistence on too much control over the project, Mayor Bernard Kincaid forcefully described theirs as a "plantation mentality." The two sides came to a mutually acceptable resolution shortly thereafter.

So, too, did Atlanta and "the other Georgia" in 2003, though it required the state's longest legislative session in more than a century. At first, it looked as though voters would get to choose between the Barnes flag and the 1956 one. Then a third design (by Bobby Franklin, state representative from Marietta, in Newt Gingrich's old congressional district) entered the discussion. It was modeled on the Confederate Stars and Bars (not the same thing as the battle flag, and hence not as inflammatory) and would have the words "In God We Trust" prominently displayed in the upper left corner. Then it looked as though there would be two referenda: one an up-or-down vote on this Franklin flag and, if that flag failed, an immediate referendum to choose between the 1956 flag and a late nineteenth-century one. In the Georgia House of Representatives, all but 2 of the 71 Republicans who voted—all of them white—voted in favor of this pairing. Democrats split badly: all 39 black representatives voted no, and of the 67 white Democrats who voted, 26 voted no—"virtually all of them from metro Atlanta." The remaining 41, "almost all from small towns or rural Georgia"—voted yes. But Ed Jackson, the state's flag expert, noted that Franklin's design, as passed by the House, called for a 3'x6' flag instead of the standard 3'x5' size. Jackson told the Senate Rules Committee, who chose not to act on the information, but on the floor, Senator Kasim Reed proposed that the bill be amended to correct the size. Reed also proposed that the second referendum, which offered the possibility of bringing back the 1956 flag, be dropped from the bill. That amendment failed, but not by as much as people had expected. However, the size amendment caused the bill to go back to the House. There, seeing the relative support in the Senate for dropping the second referendum, and negotiating with the governor on a tobacco tax, the House ultimately, on its second-chance vote, voted 91–86 to drop the second referendum from the bill. That bill then passed the Senate 33–23. Governor Perdue chose not to veto it. As reporter Jim Galloway put it, the deal allowed both sides to "dodge the Confederate Minié ball." And despite a great deal of talk from the "flaggers" about throwing various "turncoats" out of office, by June it appeared that House speaker Terry Coleman, who cast the deciding vote, would retain his seat come November, as he did.[8]

In a nation emerging from (or, for pessimists, entrenched in) a period of partisan red-blue division at least as sharp as Georgia's, lessons from Ruben Studdard's Birmingham, liminally positioned between "Atlanta" and "Mississippi" ("the other Georgia"), arguably offer insights of national relevance. In both the regional and national contexts, the aspirational possibilities of branding suggest that, rather than insisting civic branding reflect reality—as the celebration of the Confederate battle flag has certainly never done—we might all do better to work to find a better brand identity, and strive to reach the aspiration it defines. This was Dr. King's strategy by another name, and American studies might take its cue from Studdard's reworking of King's speech. The field might be said already to engage in rebranding: after Gene Wise, we call such shifts "paradigm dramas." When one says, with Stanley Bailis in the first epigraph to Wise's oft-cited essay "'Paradigm Dramas' in American Studies: A Cultural and Institutional History of the Movement," that American studies "embraces America in a Whitmanish hug, excluding nothing and always beginning" (166), "the personality" quite explicitly, in Lynn Upshaw's terms, "extends seamlessly from the brand's positioning and captures the most exciting human qualities of the brand." Like the Franklin Mint, this Walt Whitman of a field "shares your passion." When Wise, in Donald Pease and Robyn Wiegman's words, himself "put into service terms that advanced the dynamic aspects of the emergent field while recasting the entire history of American studies as the outcome of the monumental actions performed by exemplary figures" (2), he performed the same task, this time dramatically associating dynamism with the (somewhat less) charismatic but nevertheless Hegelian figures of Vernon Parrington and Perry Miller to capture "the most exciting human qualities of the brand." Pease and Wiegman, not least in titling their book *The Futures of American Studies* and their introduction "Futures," attempt to rebrand the field yet again. Wise, it turns out, "regulated the temporal dynamics of both social and disciplinary change" because of his "generational identifications" (15). Pease and Wiegman again deploy the language of dynamism and youth, citing "irresolvable tensions between social movements and the already instituted field" and enthusing that "future-oriented and linked to the emergence of unanticipated transformations and unpredicted rearrangements of the institutional order, the radical imaginary announces the possibility of a break from previous historical determinations" (22). Futurity, in fact, "erupts" despite Wise's best efforts at generational control—and that futurity, we learn, erupts in ways variously "counterhegemonic" and "posthegemonic" (23).

Surprisingly in 2002, this dynamic, radical futurity—as noted in the introduction—turns out to offer only the continuation of miscellaneous *1960s* countercultural projects, but to note my disappointment, as a scholar barely *born* in that decade, might well be to begin the rebranding process all over again. Here I would make a more modest appeal. From Miller's famous parenthetical claim in *Errand into the Wilderness* that "I recognize . . . the priority of Virginia; but what I wanted was a coherence with which I could coherently begin" (viii)—everybody's looking for that something—through the 2004 celebration of *American Quarterly*'s move from one blue-state coastal metropolis to another and of Los Angeles as a site "indicative of the key issues that define contemporary American Studies" (499)—and the editors do not appear to be talking about George Lipsitz's claim in *The Possessive Investment in Whiteness* that Los Angeles is part of "the Mississippi of the 1990s"—the South, for a long time with the collusion of the old southern studies, has steadily remained the staid, backward Other to a nation and a field continually rebranded as energetic, future-oriented, young, and passionate.[9] Yet an American studies that continues to rely on such a convenient southern exceptionalism is, surely, no American studies at all.

At present, American studies needs to acknowledge more than it has that dynamism and flux exist both within "the South" and, perhaps more important, between the South and the very blue-state metropolises from Boston to Los Angeles around which the field historically has centered itself. The first process might be seen in Studdard's rebranding of Birmingham and, more broadly, in the intrastate conservative/liberal tensions in several southern states, dynamics that may be at least as "representative" of national political divisions as those centered in the field's currently preferred sites. The second appears in the phenomenon of *American Idol* itself, based in L.A. but repeatedly, by the finals, drawing much of its appeal from a South it is helping rebrand and that, in turn, is rebranding the show and—given the show's claims, beginning with Studdard's victory, to a kind of idealized or aspirational American democracy—perhaps rebranding the nation itself. Critical as its approaches to these identificatory processes must be, American studies as a field or even a "radical imaginary"[10] has never been and cannot be positioned entirely outside them. Still, it would be unfortunate if we found ourselves behind them, the Mississippi of the 2010s.

Postscript

In a much more meaningful partial fulfillment of Dr. King's dream, on November 4, 2008, Barack Hussein Obama was elected president of the United States. He did not carry Alabama. In the north-central part of the state, he carried Birmingham but not the white-flight suburbs that had rallied behind Studdard. He garnered around 20 percent of the white vote in those suburbs, roughly double the state average of 10 percent (the lowest in the nation—even Mississippi mustered 11 percent). In Georgia, he carried 23 percent of the white vote. In North Carolina, which he won (thanks in part to television ads featuring Andy Griffith), he carried 35 percent of the white vote, and in Virginia, which he won more handily, 39 percent of white voters cast their ballots for him. Nationwide, Obama carried 43 percent of the white vote in 2008. Four years later, 37 percent of whites nationwide voted for Obama, including 16 percent in Alabama, 10 percent in Mississippi, 31 percent in North Carolina, and 37 percent in Virginia (2012 figures for Georgia remained unavailable as this book went to press).

In 2008, Ruben Studdard, who as of 2012 remains the only black man to win *American Idol*, raised funds for Obama and co-wrote the song "Footprints in the Sand," which was inspired by Obama's campaign.

The gap between symbolic politics and real politics, between how we like to feel and what we like to do, remains rather wide—a useful reminder for American cultural studies.

SIX

IN THE GARDEN

I think having land and not ruining it is the most beautiful art that anybody could ever own.
—Andy Warhol

In May 2003 I was walking through Kew Gardens—the horticultural equivalent of the British Museum—with my English half-sister when we came upon a small ornamental tree. Though a gardener—like seemingly everybody else in England—she was unfamiliar with it. I wasn't, but we read the label to be sure: *Lagerstroemia indica*. Crepe myrtle. It was a postcolonial moment for me, because crepe myrtle, though native to China and Korea, is one of the most widely used flowering trees in the yards and gardens of the southeastern United States. It wasn't just that I saw something with which I was if anything overfamiliar framed as rare and exotic in a garden laid out in part to render the British Empire incarnate in plant tissue—the shock of seeing an aspect of myself or my local culture through post-imperial eyes.[1] Nor was it simply a smugly sympathetic "authentic" awareness that crepe myrtle usually requires at least a couple of weeks of temperatures in the nineties (Fahrenheit) before it can bloom properly in late summer; given global warming, that London specimen may well produce a real bloom or two, if it hasn't already. (Recently, famed University of Georgia horticulturalist Michael Dirr reports seeing crepe myrtles blooming as far north as Martha's Vineyard [162].) After all, it is a cliché of postcolonial literature, at least from William Faulkner's wistaria-Quentin on, to describe a global southerner's experience in some global-northern metropole as that of a flamboyant tropical or subtropical species disastrously transplanted to some sort of literal and cultural northern winter and struggling to acclimate lest she/he/it die amongst the, you know, ice people.

Rather, my experience was broader than that. Many of the key terms of postcolonial theory derive from botany: Srinivas Aravamudan's tropicopolitans, Homi Bhabha's hybridity, the roots and rhizomes of Gilles Deleuze and Félix Guattari that underlie Edouard Glissant's idea of root versus relational identity, even the very notion of culture itself. In this final chapter I want both to literalize and to personalize several of the ideas that have run through this book by tentatively setting out my garden as a metaphor for the kind of post-hip ontology I have been pointing toward. In her recent retheorization of site-specific art *One Place After Another*, Miwon Kwon calls for "imagining a new model of belonging-in-transience" that would counter "both the nostalgic desire for a retrieval of rooted, place-bound identities on the one hand, and the antinostalgic embrace of a nomadic fluidity of subjectivity, identity, and spatiality on the other" (8). "It is not," she concludes, "a matter of choosing sides—between models of nomadism and sedentariness, between space and place, between digital interfaces and the handshake. Rather, we need to be able to think the range of the seeming contradictions and our contradictory desires for them together; to understand, in other words, seeming oppositions as *sustaining* relations" (166). Echoing Anne Boultwood and Robert Jerrard's notion of ambivalence, here Kwon goes well beyond Martha Schwartz, the landscape architect whose work draws most heavily on the traditions of (first wave) site-specific and installation art. In her autobiographical essay and mission statement in *The Vanguard Landscapes and Gardens of Martha Schwartz*, edited by Tim Richardson, Schwartz details the influences on her work of, among other things, Robert Smithson's *Spiral Jetty*, minimalism, and pop art (80–87, 120–27). Noting "the sense of deliberate artificiality" resulting from Schwartz's use of bright colors, artificial materials, and absurd scale and repetition, Richardson explains that Schwartz "is also aware of the close relationship between comedy and anger, and she utilizes a kind of visual sarcasm as a way of venting frustration at, for example, society's sentimental attitude to nature" (10–11). (In short, she's punk.) Schwartz's breakthrough first piece *Bagel Garden* (1980) did just that: in Back Bay, Boston, Schwartz transformed a small, rectangular, very WASPy garden of trimmed boxwoods through what in hindsight seems an irreverent eruption of gender, ethnicity, and transient nomadism, only thinly veiled by the high/low pomo discourse most often used to describe it. What distinguished her installation was not so much the loudly purple gravel she spread between the rows (it matched the foliage of the overarching Japanese maple) but the eighty-two lacquered salt and pumpernickel bagels she laid out at regular intervals on the gravel, their curvy Jewishness radically disrupting the very "squareness"—in a double sense—of this traditional garden hemmed in by wrought iron. Indeed, shot as it is through the iron fence surrounding the parterre, the Alan Wald photograph of the garden that ultimately appeared on the cover of *Landscape Architecture* makes the bagels seem caged by their own hardscaping—an apt metaphor for Schwartz's frustration with the grumpy WASP masculinist pieties of her field. In retrospect, as Schwartz admits, *Bagel Garden* "established me as a presence in the profession and created a mark in the sand that eventually defined the beginning of the postmodern era in landscape architecture" (21).

For Schwartz, then, it *is*, or was, "a matter of choosing sides," as her "mark in the sand" comment shows. And who can blame her? What thoughtful southerner has not felt that frustration with the tedious ubiquity of a very, very small range of square WASPy icons presented uncritically across multiple media as "inherent" or "natural"? Indeed, what thoughtful southern gardener did not grate her teeth when in *The Southern Living Garden Book*, Steve Bender declared,

> True Southernness grows from a fervent quest for continuity. . . . [The] isolation and self-reliance [of the agrarian southern past] produced a conservative outlook, not only in politics and religion, but also in gardening. . . . Southerners go with what works. We prefer the plants our parents grew, whether these be natives or long-established exotics. . . . Oh, from time to time we flavor the stew, but we never forsake the old family recipe. Our garden designs are conservative, too. (8)

(The magazine practices what it preaches: the *Southern Living* demonstration garden at the Birmingham Botanical Gardens is one giant overstuffed floral-print sofa of a design.) Yet Bender's telling description of southernness as a "fervent quest" for continuity reveals yet again, as does the entire *Southern Living* enterprise, that traditional, and very white, southern "identity" of this sort constitutes not an identity at all but a narcissistic lack of it, a lack to be filled—yet again—through fetishes, fetishes not so different from those Schwartz has effectively disrupted.

Bender's work is, in fact, typical of mainstream southern gardening literature, which through the 1990s remained dazzlingly white in its focus and perspective. "The South is inherently agrarian," proclaims the first page of *Taylor's Guide to Gardening in the South*. "The region was farming long before settlement pushed into the heartland of this country" (Buchanan and Holmes 1). Especially for those who, like gardeners, work with nature, this is an astonishingly short history of the region, and the utter absence of Indians from the virgin-land narrative of pushing settlement completely elides, despite all the recent espousal of "native" species and condemnation of "invasive" ones, the fact that such "pushing" constituted the most literal and complete invasion this land has ever seen. Southern garden writers tend to speak of the invasive horrors of kudzu (which is Japanese in origin), Japanese honeysuckle, and Chinese privet a great deal more than they do those of even more invasive English ivy, not to speak of the English. "In the 400 years since settlement began," laments the introduction, "people have cleaned the Southern landscape of all but vestiges of its original soil layer and forest cover" (2). Yet the author, Glenn Morris (a former landscape design editor for *Southern Living*) still asserts that (white) southerners possess an "inherent feeling for growing things" (1). On the one hand, for Morris the "inherent" nature of the place begins with the European invasion; he defines out of the story not only native Americans but also the environmental destruction associated with that invasion (which "people" devastated the soils and forests?). On the other hand, somehow the groups most responsible for this devastation, in a region still characterized by some of the nation's weakest environmental enforcement, possess for Morris an "inherent feeling for growing things." Among other prominent southern garden writers, Michael Dirr (a midwestern transplant) seems not to indulge in this sort of invasive nativism, but Felder Rushing feels compelled to begin his back-of-the-book biography proclaiming his status as a "10th-generation Southern gardener" (see, e.g., the *Alabama and Mississippi Gardener's Guide*). Indeed, only with the 2004 second edition of *The Southern Living Garden Book* did African American southern gardening practices—often a willful repudiation of conservative "white" styles—garner mention. I don't mean to downplay this shift, merely to note that it is overdue.

But three decades after Schwartz's debut, does a rejection of *Southern Living* southernness (as a figure, throughout this book, for a bankrupt, bad-faith, and oxymoronic white nativism) necessarily require an eruption of bagels? Or, as Kwon puts it, "What would it mean now to sustain the historical and cultural specificity of a place (and self) that is neither a simulacral pacifier nor a willful invention" (166)?

My backyard garden is sited on the steep north slope of Red Mountain in Birmingham, Alabama, about 60 vertical feet down from the ridgeline and about 250 feet above downtown.[2] In front of our home extends a suburban landscape of half-century-old houses. There is not a front porch in my entire neighborhood; whether despite or because of this, the homes—which I might generously describe as "midcentury modern"—exude a remarkable kind of 1950s optimism not ordinarily associated with the South, and from every window in the front of our house we can see, on a clear fall day, between five and fifteen miles. (Even in the post-bubble Los Angeles real estate market, this would be a multimillion-dollar view. We bought the place in 2003 for $137,000.) In the winter, when the leaves have finally fallen from the white oaks, the view includes the modern downtown skyline. Behind and above us, however, Red Mountain is too steep to build on, so there's nothing but second-growth hardwood forest and a few limestone outcrops between us and the condominiums at the top of the ridge. Through the woods just behind our lot, about twenty feet above the house, runs the old grade for the Birmingham Mineral Branch of the Louisville and Nashville Railroad, which carried iron ore from the mines that still angle down into the narrow seam of ore-bearing sandstone that runs along the ridge. Today, it's a footpath that intersects, three-tenths of a mile to the east, a paved section called the Vulcan Trail, which itself runs, closed to motor vehicles, exactly a mile to the base of the Vulcan statue. In 1924, when America's leading landscape architecture firm, Olmsted Brothers, put together their proposal *A System of Parks and Playgrounds for Birmingham*, they recommended this area be part of a "radical expansion" of Green Springs Park (now George Ward Park) at the base of the mountain (12). "It is worth while," they wrote, "also to provide parks of the mountain type—places where people can climb, can enjoy the wild woods, and can enjoy that sense of freedom and expansion, in contrast to the restrictions of a city, which comes with the contemplation of distant and spacious views, even though in detail these views may be largely over urban districts. Because of its height and its nearness to the city, the Red Mountain ridge is particularly fitted to this purpose" (20). Because the iron mines were still running at full tilt, Olmsted Brothers realistically anticipated the land would be difficult to obtain. They were right. Our neighborhood, initially Lebanese, was built shortly after the mines shut down; the city purchased the steepest section, a strip about two hundred feet wide, less because of civic foresight than because real estate developers couldn't use it. Fortuitously, that strip is today poised to become part of an extensive network of linear parks across the metropolitan region.

The site is thus classically liminal, on the threshold between city and forest, automobile grid and curving mountainside. Deranged by the mountain, parallel grid lines converge here: below our house, Twenty-second Avenue intersects Twenty-first. We float on red Alabama clay between service and industry, between Birmingham's present skyline of banks and hospitals and its past mine railroad, between midcentury modern house and neighborhood and second-growth woods that seem much older. More: Red Mountain is almost the last ridge of the great Appalachians running nearly the length of the eastern United States. Topographically if not quite culturally, Birmingham sits where the post-plantation Deep South in which I lived and worked from 1995 to 2010 meets the Appalachian South near which I grew up. When in *Absalom, Absalom!* Faulkner's Thomas Sutpen falls Miltonically from the (West) Virginia mountains into the Virginia tidewater, "descending perpendicularly through temperature and climate" (111), the landscape he plummets through on his way down—the Piedmont Virginia of Thomas Jefferson, James Madison, and James Monroe, all of whom would have been alive as he passed through—looks surprisingly like Birmingham's.

Edward O. Wilson claims we are hardwired to want to live in places like this one. Across cultures, he argues, "people prefer to look out over their ideal terrain from a secure position framed by the semienclosure of a domicile. Their choice of home and environs, if made freely, combines a balance of refuge for safety and a wide visual prospect for exploration and foraging" (135). Yi-fu Tuan phrases the balance more elegantly: "Place is security, space is freedom: we are attached to the one and long for the other" (3).

From the start, and quite unavoidably (given the glory of the site), I imagined my garden as site-specific art, a celebration of both place and space. What I wanted—my wife, far the more experienced gardener, ceded the yard to me, as I was obviously obsessed with it—was a seamless transition from the retro-modern ambience of the house to the woodlands above: a garden that would understand and embody "seeming oppositions as sustaining relations." The hardscape of the yard made achieving this goal much easier: near the house rose a series of whitewashed terraces, their walls still in good condition, with a set of concrete steps heading up toward the gate in the chain-link fence. But the steps stopped about two-thirds of the way up; here there were still terraces, but separated by slopes rather than walls, and the path curved around to the right before angling back up the slope to the gate. Outside the gate, the natural curves of the hillside had remained, and we discovered a lush, level area with a limestone outcrop just below the footpath. When we moved in, all of this was overgrown with vines and all the invasive (sometimes botany employs political discourse, too) non-native species mentioned above—mercifully minus kudzu but plus mimosa. Our discovery that the fence even *had* a gate was the result of an almost archaeological investigation.

Unlike my midwestern in-laws, my parents (a North Carolinian and a New Yorker) were not gardeners; to follow my "family recipe" would have been to plant a few flowering dogwoods (classic understory plants) in full Virginia sun, fail to water them enough, and watch them "mysteriously" die.[3] Instead, I spent hours and hours online and poring over books checked out from the Birmingham Botanical Gardens library. When I started, I had four or five general ideas, each of which stayed with me through the process, and which I hoped to weave into a seamless whole. I wanted some plants that were native to this area, chiefly to blur the boundary between the public park behind the house and our yard, but also to begin to diversify the ecosystem in the woodland park since even the native species that had recolonized that area over the past half century were still far less diverse than what had once been there. (I also wanted plausible deniability since I was, in a few places, planting on city property, practicing what David Tracey and Richard Reynolds, among others, call "guerrilla gardening.") I wanted to attract and sustain birds, butterflies, and other wildlife, and I had a certain fantasy, drawing on German *Schrebergärten* and English garden allotments, of the kind of public European footpath that people garden right up to. Second, I wanted plants that reminded me of Appalachian and Piedmont Virginia as much as the site itself did: the classic exile's garden.[4] Third, since the house, with its wide eaves and long, low midcentury-modern form, drew on a vaguely East Asian stylistic language, near it I wanted plants with a Chinese or Japanese provenance—daphnes, gardenias, camellias, lacecap hydrangeas. (While there were several evergreen azaleas already on the property, however, I was not tempted to add to their number.) Fourth, somewhere under the power-line easement out back where I could see it from my study window, I wanted a small, tropical-looking area full of huge leaves and bright color all summer. Part of this was my nod to the more irreverent and ebullient traditions of African American southern gardening and yard art; part, too, was my nod to global warming, since, defying stereotypical notions of unchanging "place," Birmingham has rather firmly moved in the past fifteen years from USDA Zone 7 to Zone 8.[5] I have invested a significant part of my career arguing for certain shared features of the U.S. and global Souths, and in addition I did want a small eruption of Martha Schwartz-y "artificiality," even if only in the form of decidedly "out of place" shrubs and perennials, since, for example, the bright-orange plastic garden bench in the Design Within Reach catalog was, for two Alabama college professors, not within reach at all. Hence cannas, Formosa lilies, ginger lilies, hydrangea aspera, a bougainvillea experiment, lobelias, a deciduous Ashe's magnolia—the latter two, native but tropical-looking, to tie the tropical and native areas together. I even put in a couple of Sabal "Birmingham," a hardy cultivar one of whose ancestors is almost surely the cabbage palm (Sabal palmetto), the state tree of Florida and South Carolina. (Since I could only afford young plants, they simply look, even now, like large gladiolas.) In the drought that ran from 2006 to the end of 2008, the worst in recorded history, when plants native to central Alabama themselves struggled, I learned to overcome my resistance to yuccas, several of which—some native to Alabama, others introduced from Mexico, whose climate we may have begun to borrow—now lend their strikingly sculptural presence to key focal points of the garden. In the late summer of 2007, I installed by my downspouts six rain barrels. Half an inch of rain yields 330 gallons, which, hand-carried up the slope, can keep my ornamental shrubs alive from two to four weeks.

Insofar as the garden abutted a public pedestrian thoroughfare, what I wanted, too, was a sense of surprise for those pedestrians who happened upon it. Though polemical, Lucy Lippard's definition of public art as "accessible art of any species that cares about, challenges, involves, and consults the audience for or with whom it is made, respecting community and environment" (264) is helpful here.[6] My garden—small-scale art for the long haul, as Lippard would say—is inevitably about motion too. For now, the footpath behind it serves as an unmarked spur off the paved Vulcan Trail. Precisely because at present the trail doesn't "go" anywhere, many of the people on it are first-timers. Six hundred yards from the paved section, after a shady stretch through invasive English ivy behind our neighbors', the curious come across the spray of native rhododendrons that is slowly forming a flowering evergreen screen between the trail and our property. A break in the row reveals three stone steps (edged in spring with Virginia bluebells) descending into a small garden with mountain laurel, deciduous native azaleas, bottlebrush buckeyes, Alabama snowwreath, smooth and oakleaf hydrangeas, American beautyberry, a sourwood and a silverbell tree, atamasco lilies defining the curve of a limestone outcrop, Stokes' aster, foamflower, Indian pinks, a few trilliums (*T. cuneatum*) that were already on the site, and a host of other small native flowers gleaned from Jefferson County's annual landfill digs. Closer to the terraces are my wife's rosebushes (increasingly shaded out as the woods behind continue to grow) and a pair of fastigiate Graham Blandy boxwoods mock-pretentiously guarding the gate in the chain-link fence. In future years, I'd hoped to make the footpath truly pass through, instead of just alongside, a subtly landscaped area, with redbuds, dogwoods, red buckeyes, and, someday, American chestnuts all brightening the woods above the trail. Ideally, people would not realize the area is landscaped at all.[7]

Two steps inside the gate in the fence, just where the natural curves of the mountainside give way to the terraced slopes planted with hydrangeas and brugmansia, hellebores and ginger lilies and crested iris, a previous owner— I could never have done this—had bolted through the trunks of two young pine trees to create a frame for an outdoor swing, though when we moved in no swing hung from the 4x4s fixed there. We purchased by mail and assembled one made of—globalization strikes again—sustainably harvested teak. And it is here at night, especially in winter when the mosquitoes are gone and the view is unobstructed by oak leaves, that we will sit and look out over the city of a million people in which we live. Often I can see the glow of my computer monitor through the study window; from the roof above it, the DSL connection over which most of the plants in this garden were researched and ordered runs up the telephone line to the row of poles behind us. This is where I most want to sit, the most liminal place in the whole liminal site. My physical pleasure—visual, auditory, and tactile—in the urban space is inseparable from my pleasure in the place from which I view it. And this latter pleasure is complex.[8] Like the bodily pleasure of swing dancing noted by V. Vale, it's been partly the pleasure, after hours each week in front of that monitor (and of students!), of hauling eighty-pound chunks of sandstone to make steps, of spreading compost, of planting and tending mountain laurel and silky stewartia (the latter, I confess, unsuccessfully). Yet it is not and, unlike swing dancing, has never been, hip, and while I tend to buy my plants not from big-box chains but from smaller local nurseries or places like Woodlanders in South Carolina (for southeastern native plants), or Greer Gardens in the Pacific Northwest (for rhodies), or several of the edgier nurseries run by globetrotting "plant hunters" (Plant Delights, Yucca Do, or Heronswood when it was run by Dan Hinkley), it isn't consumption as protest. In fact, despite a significant cash outlay, it's not really reducible to consumption, any more than the pleasure of running is reducible to the pleasure (or hassle) of buying running shoes. And though I have consulted gardening books from the 1940s, 1950s, and early 1960s, even laying out a garden incorporating plant combinations and design philosophies favored in those decades does not feel like wearing vintage. As separate, living organisms (i.e., as the Real), all but the most ancient individual plants resist the artifactuality, perhaps even the implicit narcissism, of a skinny tie or, for that matter, a postwar Danish credenza.[9]

Even ten years ago, most critics of southern culture—ignoring the DSL connection and the urban setting—would have discussed my garden labors, if pressed, as evidence of my southern "sense of place," my "attachment to the land," and so on. Confusing me, perhaps, with Walker Percy, others might alternately have read all this as tragically "post-southern": removed from the land of my ancestors, thrust into a world of postmodern space, I desperately attempt to reestablish connection, to re-create place. Conversely, many postmodern geographers, still under the spell of what Edward Soja happily calls "the Edge City maxim, that every American city is growing in the fashion of Los Angeles" (401), would have simply ignored the site, and potentially all Birmingham's parks as well, considering Birmingham, if at all, as a kind of poor man's or proto-Atlanta, itself a kind of poor man's or proto-Los Angeles of simulacra and abstract capitalist space.[10] Neither approach suffices.

In this book, I've criticized both hipsters and hicks, both *The Face* and now—I probably should have done it sooner—*Southern Living*. I've argued that the current spatializations of time—blue states for the future, red states for the past—and of ethics and authenticity are symptomatic of a national and transnational process of Othering and self-definition—and of seeming contradictions and contradictory desires for them, in Kwon's terms—which goes back a very long time. I've argued that works such as the alt-country of Neko Case are brilliant in part because they disrupt these spatializations of a divided American and global jihad-versus-McWorld psyche. Indeed, one of the most useful books for me in coming to understand the South has been Mike Davis's *City of Quartz: Excavating the Future in Los Angeles* because the book deals with the South's mirror-myth. The U.S. South and Southern California actually share a lot: both regions are now called "sunbelt"; both have a remarkable history of disciplining black bodies (Davis wrote before Rodney King, but he quotes Langston Hughes to good effect on this history), of white supremacy, and of bombastic fundamentalisms; Southern California rather weirdly (at least to my Skynyrd-trained ear) calls itself "the Southland"; and both are powerfully invested in myth.[11] Yet the myths propagated about each represent mutually constitutive polar opposites. As I noted near the start of this book, Davis lays out the L.A. pole as follows:

> [B]y hyping Los Angeles as the paradigm of the future (even in a dystopian vein), [the "L.A. school" tends] to collapse history into teleology and glamorize the very

reality they would deconstruct. [Edward] Soja and [Fredric] Jameson, particularly, in the very eloquence of their different "postmodern mappings" of Los Angeles, become celebrants of the myth. The city is a place where everything is possible, nothing is safe and durable enough to believe in, where constant synchronicity prevails, and the automatic ingenuity of capital ceaselessly throws up new forms and spectacles—a rhetoric, in other words, that recalls the hyperbole of [Herbert] Marcuse's *One-Dimensional Man*. (86)

In versions like Steve Bender's, the South, by contrast, is a place where nothing is possible, everything is safe and durable enough to believe in, where history prevails, and the capitalist parade of new forms and spectacles never trickles in.

It's astonishing, in this age of simultaneous pre- and postmodern geographies, how resolutely we cling to these bogus divisions. Yet rocking up here in the dirty South of my backyard garden above my modern, affordable, integrated Hispanic-South Asian-Lebanese-black-white neighborhood, I take in a view much like that from the Getty Center, much like (though less sinister than) that which Oedipa Maas takes in of Los Angeles laid out like a transistor—and I do it swaying gently in what both is and is not a southern—global southern—porch swing. I am not unique. This is how a lot of us live. It is not a matter of choosing sides.

NOTES

Introduction. What Does an American Studies Scholar Want?

1. I am making this example up, but—at the risk of stating the obvious—the old CCCS-derived formula oppressed and/or colonized group + medium = resistance (a formula of whose limits the Birmingham school was more aware than its latter-day adherents) maintains a certain hegemony within American studies. The essay portion of the June 2011 issue of *American Quarterly* (the latest as I write this) is composed, for example, of three articles: one on Asian Americans offering a "subjectless" critique through theater; one on Sauk Indians using photography "to generate meanings and histories more compatible with their own experiences"; and one on the ways a U.S.-sponsored Guatemalan reality TV show succeeded in its aims—ways that clearly *ought* to have been resisted.

2. I am using the phrase "structure of feeling" as a hinge between Raymond Williams, who coined it, and Jacques Lacan, a hinge made possible by the structuralist underpinnings of the thought of each. Lawrence Grossberg has recently suggested that Williams's idea of a "structure of feeling" should be taken as his (missing) theory of modernity. For Grossberg, the usual ("Euromodern") way of understanding temporality is as follows: "History is constructed through difference and negativity: the past and the future are the not-now, the not-present" ("Raymond Williams" 31) but this isn't the only way to see it. "Recognizing that other ways of being modern are real (even if as yet unactualized), might offer us a different way forward, one that makes other pasts and futures—and hence, other presents—possible" (32). I'll use Lacan as the best analyst of those who conceive of past or future as lacks ("the not-now, the not-present"), and then pursue examples of living in modernity that don't see things this way.

3. It's true but too easy to point out that the ideological alienation felt by many in my generation is hardly comparable to the sorts of raw bigotry experienced thirty years ago by second-wave feminists and people of color as they first entered the academy in large numbers. Rather than reminding younger scholars of their own early difficulties and triumphs, boomers—if they are to be true to their own youthful

ideals—might pause to consider instead what difficulties their own residual struc-tures of feeling engender thirty years later. What I am saying of American academe Barack Obama has said better of American politics: "In the back-and-forth between Clinton and Gingrich, and in the elections of 2000 and 2004, I sometimes felt as if I were watching the psychodrama of the Baby Boom generation—a tale rooted in old grudges and revenge plots hatched on a handful of college campuses long ago—played out on the national stage" (*Audacity* 36).

4. My paradigm here is actually not a presidential address—what I found impres-sive about Ruth Gilmore's most recent one was precisely its insistence that we were NOT doing enough activism—but a recent "Editor's Note" in *American Quarterly* in which said editor used the Gabrielle Giffords shooting as evidence to support the fol-lowing: "It is thus imperative, as much as ever before, for American studies scholars and activists to engage these questions [of "borders, both literal and metaphorical"] through careful explorations of the intersections of histories, economies, identities, and institutions. The field of American studies must resist constructing impermeable boundaries between and within different areas and forms of scholarship, as well as maintain the field's commitment to social justice" (Banet-Weiser ix). Thus the shoot-ing of a congresswoman becomes a pretext for urging American studies scholars to keep doing what they've always done, "as much as ever before."

5. The problem was not so much that so many panels were on such traditional cul-tural studies topics as "The Worlding of Hip-Hop I and II." The problem was that, even though the conference was set in Atlanta, the perennial wannabe global city for whom hip-hop is, ironically, one of the most viable media for achieving that dream, the papers on the panels were, predictably, on things like "Hip-hop, Masculinity, and the Politics of Queerness" rather than on, say, the relations between the global and the black southern in Goodie Mob, Cee-lo Green, OutKast—even Ludacris. Riché Richardson's brilliant paper on "Gangstas and Playas in the Dirty South" was segregated off on the seemingly less trendy "Representin(g) the Black South" panel.

6. For similar callings-out within queer American studies, see the work of John Howard, Patrick Johnson, and Karen Leigh Tongson.

7. "Tweedy, out-of-touch mandarins" is Felski's wonderful description of the old guard that claimed to resist cultural studies in the name of aesthetics (503).

8. Also peculiar is the editors' inattention to William McClung's *Landscapes of Desire: Anglo Mythologies of Los Angeles*, whose more nuanced argument that "imagining Los Angeles has been . . . a process of aligning a model of a hoped-for Utopian future with one of an allegedly Arcadian past that cries out to be redeemed" (12) in some ways prefigures my own argument about much of the rest of the nation, particularly the contemporary South.

9. The strong demurrals by Betsy Erkkila and Barry Shank to the Michael Hardt essay on Jefferson that inspired the March 2007 cover—as well as the fact that the cover was slyly taken from the White House homepage's section for children—strongly suggest we may read it as the exception that proves the rule. In general, how-ever, this sort of widespread scholarship-as-consumption maps closely onto early Jür-gen Habermas's concern about the decline of the public sphere: "When the laws of the market governing the sphere of commodity exchange and of social labor also per-vaded the sphere reserved for private people as a public, rational-critical debate had

a tendency to be replaced by consumption, and the web of public communication unraveled into acts of individuated reception, however uniform in mode" (*Structural Transformation* 161). Like Russ Castronovo and Susan Gillman, who are as hesitant about "inclusion" as I am about "consumption," I want to mark my "difference from prevailing feel-good methods, which, too often, operate according to principles that are merely additive, a sort of scholarly liberal pluralism that fails to address how interdisciplinary practice might actually throw into question the disciplinary assumptions of history, textual analysis, and cultural studies from which they draw" (3). Or, as Walter Benn Michaels memorably puts it in *The Trouble with Diversity*, "There is nothing politically radical about insisting on or even celebrating diversity . . . ; on the contrary, celebrating diversity is now our way of accepting inequality. This is why it's a mistake to believe that the humanities departments of our universities are hotbeds of leftism. . . . In fact, they're more like the research and development division of neoliberalism" (199–200).

10. Although Mexican American neighborhoods are, obviously, not necessarily "immigrant," they function as equally "authentic" and hence compelling populist worlds.

11. This anxiety may be best expressed in the entry of white Parisian artist "JR," as described by the Tate: "JR's paste-up image shows a black man holding what, on first glance, appears to be a gun. On closer inspection it is in fact revealed to be a video camera. The deliberately aggressive and confrontational image forces us to reassess our assumptions, both exposing and counteracting negative media stereotypes" (Tate Modern). Whose assumptions are we talking about, exactly?

12. However, I would emphatically reject the false either/or choice underlying Slavoj Žižek's analysis of postmodernity, his assertion in *Did Somebody Say Totalitarianism?* that *"today's (late capitalist global market) social reality itself is dominated by what [Karl] Marx referred to as the power of 'real abstraction'*: the circulation of Capital is the force of radical 'deterritorialization' (to use [Gilles] Deleuze's term) which, in its very functioning, actively ignores specific conditions and cannot be 'rooted' in them" (2, Žižek's italics). The circulation of abstract Capital does not, for one thing, always ignore specific conditions, and in any event it is quite possible, again, to participate *both* in mass, capitalistic culture and in "the local." I would concede Žižek's claim in "A Plea for a Return to Différance (with a Minor Pro Domo Sua)" that "it is easy to conceive such a multiplication of modernities as a form of fetishistic disavowal" (241), but I would also note it is even easier to conceive claims for "a singular modernity" as precisely the same thing.

13. However antiheroic, such a modernity necessarily operates as part of a symbolic order and hence as a fantasy space in its own right. Still, I largely mean "real" here in Žižek's Lacanian sense: a Real of which both cultural studies and southern studies, as constructors of fantasy spaces, have tended to serve as strategies of avoidance; a Real that, if it cannot be symbolized, is still worth gesturing toward. Besides, the fantasy of being a bourgeois grownup (in the wake of the patently false, and ever falser, academic boomer fantasy of being a perpetual radical youth) is at least worth traversing.

14. For a full discussion of Vancouver's "grounded globalism," as James Peacock might put it, see Berelowitz, *Dream City*.

15. For the classic postmodern-geography treatment of Atlanta, see Charles Rutheiser. Jay Watson's essay "Mapping out a Postsouthern Cinema: Three Contemporary Films" usefully links John Portman's Westin Bonaventure in Los Angeles with his Peachtree Plaza in Atlanta (as portrayed in *Sharky's Machine*) in just the ways I imply here.

16. See Riché Richardson, "A House Set Off From the Rest" for a sustained engagement with Hazel Carby on this point.

Chapter One. Songs that Move Hipsters to Tears

1. For an excellent and appropriately skeptical analysis of the quasi-religious treatment of "memory" in recent scholarly discourse, see Klein, "On the Emergence of *Memory*."

2. In his introduction, Scott Romine argues with my formulation, in a review of Martyn Bone's *The Postsouthern Sense of Place in Contemporary Fiction*, of "the South absent essentialism," suggesting there can be no such thing (*Real South* 7, 13–14); I might have been clearer had I referred to the South "in its senseless actuality." On this point I continue to differ with Romine's postmodern approach. Although Romine deploys Žižek as a kind of updated Hayden White disputing the validity of all historical narratives (*Real South* 6–7), Žižek is deeply critical not only of the melancholy turn but also, as the phrase "only proper attitude" suggests, of postmodern relativism. The Real may be inaccessible, but the fantasies that deflect that access vary greatly in pathology. This theme runs consistently through his work at least from *Tarrying with the Negative* (1993) through *The Monstrosity of Christ* (2009): "This is how," he writes in the latter, "we should subvert the standard self-enclosed linear narrative: not by means of a postmodern dispersal into a multitude of local narratives, but by means of its redoubling in a hidden counter-narrative" (65).

3. Susan Donaldson's introduction to the 2006 reissue of *I'll Take My Stand* performs such an analysis admirably.

4. Alone among this chapter's epigraphists, Fred Hobson answers his own question with a "Perhaps, but . . .," suggesting a degree of healthy skepticism toward this line of questioning.

5. For the full context of Reed's penning the song, see Reed's chapter "My Tears Spoiled My Aim: Violence in Country Music" in *My Tears Spoiled My Aim*. I would note that Reed's pithy merging of sorrow and anger exactly embodies melancholy as described by Giorgio Agamben, whose account underlies Žižek's: "In melancholia, love and hate—engaged in pitched battle around the object, 'one to separate the libido from it, the other to defend from attack this position of the libido'—coexist and reconcile in one of those compromises possible only under the laws of the unconscious" (21), a.k.a. the laws of country music.

6. For the classic analysis of this melancholy, see Richard Godden's 1997 *Fictions of Labor: William Faulkner and the South's Long Revolution* and 2007 *William Faulkner: An Economy of Complex Words*.

7. Karla F. C. Holloway's *Passed On: African American Mourning Stories* (2002), on the other hand, is very much a "southern" project, yet one suffused with healthy mourning, not pathological melancholy. In invoking Holloway, I am not attempting to

imply some tendentious opposition between "authentic" African American mourning and "inauthentic" white boomer melancholy; I do, however, admire what I take to be Holloway's hard-earned adulthood. In any event, as a pathological response liberal white southern studies' kind of melancholy pales beside what I take to be the dominant *conservative* white southern response to the civil rights movement. the substitution of religious narcissism for racial narcissism. See chapter 2.

8. Reed is of course making a joke, but jokes matter. As Žižek pointedly notes in just this context, "melancholy and laughter are not opposed, but *stricto sensu* two sides of the same coin: the much-praised ability to maintain an ironic distance to one's ethnic roots is the obverse of the melancholic attachment to those roots" ("Melancholy and the Act" 142).

9. Tellingly, Reed asks not about Holocaust guilt and its parallel with slavery guilt but about "the experience of defeat." What is important here is not what the Germans actually thought, but Reed's perception of their response as insufficiently melancholy: his bafflement that they did not identify with Nazis—here characterized passively as "the generation that had happened to"—as he identified with Confederates. I also wish to note here Reed's gracious help in locating for me the passage about those young Germans.

10. For a related, if broader, critique of academics' consumption not of melancholy but of trauma, see Yaeger's "Consuming Trauma."

11. See Lott, "First Boomer." Barack Obama has highlighted this distinction, not only in his inaugural call to "put away childish things," but also by distancing himself from boomer divisions in *The Audacity of Hope*, presenting the image of "no drama Obama," and referring to Wall Street as in need of "adult supervision." Adulthood, in Obama's writings and public persona, is not the object of fear, the disavowed mark of mortality, it has so often been for the boomers.

12. See Langbauer, "Ethics."

13. As late as 1987, Todd Gitlin could mention Bob Dylan's *Nashville Skyline* as "including a duo [sic] with no less a mainstream idol than Johnny Cash" (428).

14. "I was always aware of how important Johnny Cash was," declares Rubin in the *New York Times Magazine*. "But no one under 40 who didn't live in the South knew much about Johnny Cash besides a few hits and his name" (Hirschberg). Yet interviews with several alumni of the early 1990s Wicker Park/Chicago indie/alt-country scene, for example, confirm that "knowledge of Cash's career was pretty much de rigueur in the indie/punk scene [there] from at least the mid-1980s forward, if not sooner" (Diane Pecknold, personal communication).

15. See Howard's discussion of this matter in *Men Like That*.

Chapter Two. German Lessons

1. www.time.com/time/magazine/article/0,9171,954833-2,00.html.

2. The first was Rwanda.

3. See Sharlet, *The Family: The Secret Fundamentalism at the Heart of American Power*; for one report on the "proxy wars" that the U.S. religious Right is conducting in Africa, see Kapya Kaoma's *Globalizing the Culture Wars: U.S. Conservatives, African Churches, and Homophobia*—though the report is published by a progressive

American think tank and Kaoma sometimes seems as much a proxy of the American Left as the African bishops seem proxies of the Right.

4. Such an explanation might have been compelling ten or fifteen years ago; indeed, it is precisely Žižek's as set forth in his 1997 book *The Plague of Fantasies*: "Recall the election campaigns of Jesse Helms, in which the racist and sexist message is not publicly acknowledged (on the public level, it is sometimes even violently disavowed), but is instead inarticulated 'between the lines,' in a series of double-entendres and coded allusions" (25).

5. "In the 'authoritarian syndrome,' the liberal personality locates and organizes its enjoyment" (Žižek, *For They Know Not What They Do* 55n7). As ever, Scott Romine drives this home wittily: "I would, however, question whether Christian fundamentalists have a higher level of experienced assault than, say, the Modern Language Association. . . . I would put the efficacy of prayer up against the efficacy of MLA [Modern Language Association] resolutions any day, and I think both are serving roughly the same function" (personal communication). As I hope my introduction shows, I agree: MLA resolutions reflect a structure of feeling, not actual politics.

Despite the humor, Romine's underlying point is very serious: "it's pretty easy to prove irrationality, but harder to understand that our motives for doing so are often themselves irrational" (personal communication). On said point, Romine is, I think, a more consistently mindful psychoanalytic critic than I; moreover, his observation is in keeping with recent social intuitionist psychological research suggesting moral and political judgments tend first to be made intuitively, then retroactively justified with "reason." (Haidt, "Emotional Dog"). (The same body of research, by the way, suggests conservatives are more prone to the emotions of fear and disgust [Inbar et al., "Conservatives Are More Easily Disgusted"].) However, because of this perceived absence of rational grounding for any set of convictions, Romine would prefer "multiple spheres of unregulated and mutually exclusive fantasy wherein symptoms can be enjoyed without bothering the neighbors" (personal communication). Here we differ. For a detailed response to Romine's smart arguments on this point and in the conclusion of *The Real South*—particularly his "better a cyber-Confederacy than a real one" (236)—please see my forthcoming essay "Toward a Post-postpolitical Southern Studies."

I should also note here that in *The Civil Sphere* Jeffrey Alexander makes a relativist point similar to Romine's. For Alexander, oppositions such as rational/irrational are not grounded in reality but in the *structure* of civil discourse. The trick is to get your side identified with rationality. (See especially Alexander's chapter 4.) I actually disagree, and would cite Rebecca Mark's and Aaron Fox's equation of sentiment with authenticity (see my own chapter 1) as cases in which citizenship is, bizarrely but not atypically, associated with what Alexander calls "anticivil motives" (57).

6. I am not interested here in the queer theory issue of whether homosexuality is or is not, as a category, equivalent to race and gender as a category of civil rights; I am only interested in its function for the circling of a certain sort of conservative drive.

7. It wasn't just civil rights, either. As Douglas Smith notes, prior to the reapportionment cases—which Earl Warren later claimed had been more important than *Brown v. Board*—"widespread malapportionment across the United States ensured

the overrepresentation of rural and small-town areas while diluting the votes of metropolitan residents" (263).

8. Remarkably, the call for papers of the 2010 Society for the Study of Southern Literature biennial conference recuperated this enduring logic in a twenty-first-century context, pitting as it did "we Southerners" against "tourists and carpetbaggers . . . historians and theorists" (Ewell and Mark).

9. While there is no necessary connection between where one lives and teaches and what one thinks about evangelicals or "the South," on this matter both writers' perspectives do seem to be limited by their positions at relatively cosmopolitan universities of the sort where the majority of influential work in American studies is still produced—here, Cornell and Princeton. If Jonathan Culler taught at a university with a substantial percentage of evangelical students, for example, he would quickly find that "satire and mockery" are both pedagogically ineffective and, particularly in a freshman classroom, ethically cruel. Jeffrey Stout's romanticization of "real people" also seems to have been shaped largely by his own "situatedness." Because Stout explicitly notes in his acknowledgments that "except for college and some time traveling, I have spent my whole life in the same county" (xiv) and praises the impact on his book of "the local soccer community" (xv), which has had a big impact on "what democracy means to me" (xiv) and hence on his notion of the public sphere, one cannot help but observe that "real people" may look somewhat different in the Deep South (or at a Sarah Palin rally) than they do in the leafy, genial environs of Princeton, where, Stout claims, such people have taught him "much about virtue, ethical formation, and the art of tending to arrangements" (xiv–xv).

10. For a useful counterargument here—one that is rather rare in religious studies, because so many practitioners of the discipline are themselves religious—please see Steven Caton's discussion of Yemeni rain prayers in "What Is an 'Authorizing Discourse'?"

11. One might contrast the really rather normal American experiences (of both time and, for most of us, social class) of Gen X new southern studies scholars who grew up, chiefly in "the South," attended integrated schools, and participated in national mass culture, with those depicted in the anguished confessions of relatively privileged white baby boomer southernists, such as Diane McWhorter, Jefferson Humphries, and Patricia Yaeger, about passing their formative years with "Negro" domestic servants (McWhorter 143, 348–39; Humphries x–xii; Yaeger, *Dirt and Desire* 1).

Chapter Three. Our Turn

1. In 1998, Grant Alden and Peter Blackstock actually boasted that "the phrase 'No Depression' is now tossed around by many of the same hands that dealt 'grunge' when we started the magazine." "Out there in the margins," they went on, "that's where some of the most rewarding music is to be found" (*No Depression* 8).

2. As the phrase moved rapidly from marking resistance to a marketing buzzword, thereby illustrating how quickly style politics could be co-opted, it fell out of favor among Gen Xers. I use it deliberately and unfashionably to attempt to resist the logic of branding and style. *Not* to use it would be to endorse the illusion that style poli-

tics offered meaningful rebellion: would be, that is, at least marginally "hip" in a way this essay attempts to resist.

3. In 2000, Neil Howe and William Strauss, whose 1993 book *13th Gen: Abort, Retry, Ignore, Fail* served as the starting point of Sherry Ortner's argument, published *Millennials Rising: The Next Great Generation*, whose title largely says it all. They followed it up in 2006 with *Millennials and the Pop Culture*, aimed directly at entertainment industry executives.

4. Thanks to Matt Roth, one of my students and millennial informants, for directing me to the single—and for suggesting his own generation's embrace of the single's impatience with struggling to feel "hip."

5. For a thorough discussion of this process, see old issues of *The Baffler*, many of whose better articles were collected in *Commodify Your Dissent*, and Alan Liu's remarkable description of resistance and resignation among knowledge workers, in *The Laws of Cool: Knowledge Work and the Culture of Information*. At the risk of providing too much information, in 1998, when Ortner's article first appeared, I had (I thought) left a tenure-track job to teach middle-school English at a posh private school in the city where my wife was an English professor rather than endure the 900-mile commuter marriage forced on us by "the market." I had to sign out whenever I went off campus, and I had to wear a tie every day. I wore skinny ones. I sported a mustache that could have been interpreted as ironic. I could go on—the point is to admit guiltily that I am no stranger to Gen X-style politics, even if I no longer feel the need to deploy them.

6. *No Depression* is as thoroughly steeped in Gen X–style politics as any other aspect of 1990s alt-country. Co-editor Grant Alden is a graphic designer with his visual sense firmly rooted in retro. As he writes on one of the magazine's web pages, "Initially *No Depression*'s visual identity was meant to update the look of a magazine you might have found laying [sic] around in the waiting room of a muffler shop in the late 1950s. As a younger generation of designers has begun to plunder the moderne style of the 1950s, and as I've begun to develop new respect for the sounds of country music in the early 1960s, I have sought to move the magazine's visual identity a few years forward, say, to the Kennedy years." As soon as "a younger generation" of bourgeois creative-class professionals starts "plundering" the same visual vocabulary and look, Alden must move on, in his creative-class work at *No Depression*, to, er, "updating the look" of the early 1960s. And when those kids catch on to the 1960s gambit, he'll have to move again to stay on the graphic design cutting edge. It's all a bit reminiscent of the origins of the magazine itself. In an interview with the *Seattle Weekly*, Blackstock argues that, having grown up in Austin, he was a bit more into alt-country than Alden, who, however, was "tired of documenting the whole grunge thing—this was the early, mid-1990s in Seattle, remember, and Grant had written a *lot* about that" (Waggoner). And in an article in the *Puget Sound Business Journal*, Alden himself notes, "It just felt to me, based on music I'd been hearing, (and) the aging of the college radio audience, it felt like something that was right. I felt like I had been early on things in my life, with Seattle rock bands at *The Rocket*, and I looked around and decided to trust my instincts on this" (R. Smith).

7. For the definitive account of punk's roots in 1950s and 1960s surf and garage music, see Osgerby.

8. Consumption as protest carried over into the 2000s. Rob Walker writes about hipsters embracing Pabst Blue Ribbon precisely because they believed it was *not* being marketed to them: "The Plan B analysis even says that P.B.R.'s embrace by punks, skaters, and bike messengers make [sic] it a political, 'social protest' brand. These 'lifestyle as dissent' or 'consumption as protest' constituencies are about freedom and rejecting middle-class mores, and 'P.B.R. is seen as a symbol and fellow dissenter.' Eventually all of this sounds like satire, but the punch line is that it isn't really that far off from P.B.R.'s strategy" (Walker 44).

9. The earliest use of the term *post-hip* I have found comes from Boyd's *Life's Little Deconstruction Book*. It's also been applied to the ethos of *The Baffler*. I do not mean the term in John Leland's sense of "hip with ironic quotation marks" (338–56); I mean post-commodified distinction.

10. When Ching wrote "Acting Naturally," the angriest such performer she mentioned was Hank Williams Jr., who "enacts a grotesque country dandyism that may be one of the last effective ways to 'épater le bourgeoisie'" (116). Now that (as I first drafted this chapter in summer 2004) a grotesque country dandyism runs the nation, Williams seems decidedly middle-of-the-road compared to performers like Toby Keith and Darryl Worley. The tendency of country's once-benign camp to morph, when in power, into bullying is, however, outside the scope of this essay, except for a note that such a tendency in country's camp casts alt-country's irony, such as it is, in a somewhat better light. Speaking truth to power now appears to require épater les hicks.

11. Amazon.com's "customers who bought this CD also bought" feature is useful here. When I checked on July 28, 2004, customers who bought Case also bought the New Pornographers' two CDs, other Neko Case records, and an assortment of alt-country, chiefly Calexico. People who bought the New Pornographers also bought Death Cab for Cutie, the Shins, the Strokes, Fountains of Wayne, and so on. No traditional country musician appeared.

12. Robert Lanham identifies one sort of hipster as the "Bipster": "Blue-collar Hipsters who shun art-school pretension and have little patience with leisure-class Hipsters. . . . Bipsters are usually from middle-class to lower-middle-class backgrounds. They are a very common breed of Hipster and often grow up in the South or the Midwest" (112).

13. This is also, I suggest, how one should read the core of post-punk Gen X 1990s alt-country: Gillian Welch, Whiskeytown and its descendants, Uncle Tupelo and its descendants, Freakwater, the Gourds, Lambchop, and so on. However, as I have implied by contextualizing my argument in 1990s Gen X consumption politics, it is *not* the way to read late boomer acts that got their country starts in the 1980s and were retroactively labeled alt-country by the tastemakers in *No Depression*: Steve Earle, Dwight Yoakam, Lyle Lovett, and most importantly Jason and the Scorchers, each of whom, however hip, makes some kind of campy bargain with hickness (Earle, however, seems to have quit making it around the time he moved to New York City).

14. No longer flaccid, her songwriting gets better with each album. "Set Out Running" contains the great country couplet, "If I knew heartbreak was comin', I would've set out runnin'," and on other parts of *Furnace Room Lullaby*, she seems to

have been listening to a good bit of early Dylan. "We've Never Met" recalls "I Don't Believe You (She Acts Like We Never Have Met)"; "Whip the Blankets" invokes the humorous tall-tale surrealism of *The Freewheelin' Bob Dylan*.

15. In England, for example, the fashion magazine *The Face* offered its readers only the latest fashions in verbal as well as visual style. In September 2003, they helpfully explained to their readers that "fuck all y'all" was "classic Deep South abuse—use 'fuck y'all' to two or three people, but for a whole room you need this" (51).

Chapter Four. Two Ties and a Pistol

1. Holt himself, for example, discusses crises in "society" and sees solutions in smaller units such as the "bohemia community." In *Against the Romance of Community*—which is not really about the South, though the cover photo was taken in Tupelo—Miranda Joseph quite thoroughly deconstructs the false opposition between community and capitalism, arguing in part that "local heterogeneity does not necessarily imply resistance to globalization either in the form of authentic original otherness or excess" (150). The most masterful treatment of this concept in southern literary studies, of course, is Romine's *Narrative Forms of Southern Community*.

2. In Michael Kreyling's *Inventing Southern Literature* and Patricia Yaeger's *Dirt and Desire*. Kreyling's and Yaeger's metaphor of the literary critic as Luddite guerrilla obviously pertains to my argument about modernity in this essay. In the fifty years since Flannery O'Connor's original depiction of Faulkner as a relatively high-tech modernist express train, Faulkner's modernity has become, metaphorically, the problem itself. Yaeger's embrace of the metaphor, of course, is meant chiefly as a way of distancing herself from Kreyling's ultimate unwillingness to follow through on the implications of his own project. Kreyling's use is more complex. For the record, I *like* express trains, and wish the contemporary South had some.

3. The classic treatment is, of course, Dick Hebdige's *Subculture*, and most other works on punk style have followed Hebdige's lead, even as they increasingly dissent from Hebdige's idea of punk as subversively heroic.

4. See discussions of Ratliff's tie and Kohl's sculpture below.

5. According to a conversion table provided on the website of Oregon State University political science professor Robert Sahr: www.oregonstate.edu/cla/polisci/individual-year-conversion-factor-tables, July 20, 2011.

6. costing $11, or $175 today.

7. As if to reinforce an already obvious contrast, Faulkner almost anxiously repeats the line "This is New York" five times in six pages.

8. The pistol itself is also associated with Ratliff's ties. Both are bargained for; in a grim bit of class parody, the pistol comes out of the blue-jowled pawnshop owner's "private stock," and just as Ratliff and Allanovna attempt to soften the commerciality of their transaction, so too, through semantics, must Mink "reclaim" rather than "buy" the pistol (291). And when at the end of the novel Ratliff hesitates to walk right in on Mink's hiding place, he might not explicitly recall his own two-for-one tie purchase, but we do: "You never seen that pistol," he says to Stevens. "I did. It didn't look like no one-for-ten-dollars pistol. It looked like one of a two-for-nine-and-a-half pistols. Maybe he's still got the other one with him" (432).

9. For a full recent treatment of the importance of Ratliff's sentimental pilgrimage, see Boyagoda, "Imagining Nation."

10. In the mid-2000s, the Farmington Hunt Club website noted that "[i]n order to wear the colors, members must prove their ability in the hunting field, and must be awarded their colors by the master" (www.farmingtonhunt.org/history.html, August 30, 2005). However, given the social dynamics of Albemarle County—where I grew up—it's safe to say that the coat symbolizes more than hunting ability.

11. Good design is rarely *purely* aesthetic. For example, like line or shape, color draws some of its meaning from context: some colors look fresher for not having been used in design for a while—or, conversely, because they are currently "in." (Avocado and gold, for example, looked a lot better in 1970 than in 1980.) In 1960, pink had been "in" for a while, especially paired with black, and Faulkner may have been drawn to two or more incongruous combinations: first, an "in" mid-century modern tone paired with the coat's classic, conservative tailoring and expensive traditional materials—a coat that functions simultaneously as sign and symbol—and, second, the allegedly feminine pink's standing for his hunting prowess.

12. There is a world of difference between the most famous shop-window scene in American literature, Dreiser's account of Hortense Briggs ogling a fur coat in *An American Tragedy*, and Faulkner's version. Yet Walter Benn Michaels's now rather hoary observation about Dreiser, that he "didn't so much approve or disapprove of capitalism; he desired pretty women in little tan jackets with mother-of-pearl buttons, and he feared becoming a bum on the streets of New York" (*Gold Standard* 19), has not been taken sufficiently to heart by writers of the rather large body of critical work treating the Snopes trilogy as Faulkner's critique of *Gesellschaft* or capitalism, patriarchal or otherwise.

13. As Serge Guilbaut argues in *How New York Stole the Idea of Modern Art*, New York in the 1950s supplanted Paris as the center of the art world.

14. I exaggerate. According to Chick Mallison, Ratliff's parlor three or four years later holds, in addition to the tie and Kohl's sculpture, a "fireplace filled with fluted green paper in the summer but with a phony gas log in the winter" (231), a *Southern Living* tableau if ever there was one, especially along with "the spotlessly waxed melodeon in the corner and the waxed chairs."

15. Though such an affirmation can degenerate into the desperate ghetto pursuit of Air Jordans and other logoed products, the ghetto version suggests a different aesthetic, since it emphasizes conformity, not the individuality of dress espoused by Ellison, Faulkner, and others.

Chapter Five. Flying without Wings

1. If public affiliation can take on the attributes of private consumption, there is a good book to be written, somewhere between the intellectual history of Michael O'Brien and the economic history of David Carlton and Peter Coclanis, which might productively modify Jürgen Habermas by examining exactly what sort of public sphere emerged from the South's economic and racial conditions in the nineteenth century. I would also note that, practically speaking, there presently *is* no southern public sphere, and that (as Scott Romine argues on a related issue in *The Real South*)

this is a good thing. There are many smaller public spheres where citizens debate pertinent issues—Does Alabama need a new constitution? What should we in metro Birmingham do about congestion on Highway 280? Should we build a domed stadium?—but virtually none in which people debate issues pertaining to "the South." That realm has been wholly ceded to consumer culture—chiefly, in fact, to *Southern Living*. (In watching Fox News, as so many white southern conservatives do, those conservatives are always interpellated as Americans—"real Americans"—not as southerners.)

2. As noted in the introduction, Rubin himself was, of course, engaged in marketing the South as what marketing professor Douglas B. Holt calls a "populist world."

3. In April 2003, however, Alabama Governor Bob Riley and Mississippi Governor Ronnie Musgrove announced they would form a two-state industrial park in the Black Belt. They would thus have two congressional delegations working to land the site, and, as Riley put it, "instead of bidding against each other for large industrial projects, we can partner our resources and each spend less incentive dollars." See Dedrick, "Two-state Industrial Park."

4. Fantasia Barrino's win the following year largely put such charges to rest, perhaps too soon, given Paris Bennett's surprising early ejection in season 5.

5. Scott Romine's dictum in *The Narrative Forms of Southern Community* that "insofar as it is cohesive, a community will tend to be coercive" (2) should caution us here against too much happiness in merely cross-racial cohesion. According to a recent examination of UNC's Southern Focus Polls, "Asians, Hispanics, Jews, Catholics, Lutherans, and the unchurched"—a remarkable catchall—are less likely to identify as "southern" than black and white Protestants ("Southerners All," 15). In the polls, sexual orientation goes unaddressed. The very "family-friendly" approach of the video, however, reminds us that gay marriage was a more galvanizing issue in the 2004 election in the South than race, and while "Ten Commandments judge" Roy Moore lost the Republican gubernatorial primary to Riley in 2006, the comments of Len Gavin, a Moore volunteer and former Republican Party executive director, suggest that George Wallace's politics of narcissistic rage—to adapt Dan T. Carter's title—remain alive but may have shifted their target (see chapter 2). "For Wallace, the issue was race. For Moore, it's 'values,'" Gavin said. (Chandler 6A). Hysteria over gays almost exactly fits the role once played by hysteria over black people, and in 2012 hysteria over brown people (similarly invisible in the video, though a burgeoning demographic in the metropolitan area) seems not far behind. Curiously, even the most interesting reevaluation of the race hypothesis in southern voting, Shafer and Johnston's *End of Southern Exceptionalism*, merely shifts the question of southern politics from race to class, effectively ignoring the role of conservative evangelicalism.

6. For a discussion of this emblem's relation to commodity fetishism, see Smith, "Southern Culture," 82–83.

7. By May 2006, Aiken's first album had outsold Studdard's 3 million to 2 million.

8. Galloway, "Democrats Push";" idem, "Rebel Emblem"; idem, "Deal Let Both Sides Dodge Minié Ball"; idem, "Carter Smoothed Flag Deal"; Galloway and Baxter, "Flag Issue"; Tharpe, "Coleman's Seat Appears Secure."

9. For the definitive treatment of this theme, see Duck's *Nation's Region*, and Greeson's *Our South*.

10. For a trenchant critique of the cooptation of 1960s "radicalism" that suggests its inability to market to post-boomers, see, most notably, Frank's *Conquest of Cool*.

Chapter Six. In the Garden

1. My focus on a plant of such mediated authenticity is deliberate; I also saw plenty of native southern plants in London as well, from southern magnolias (*M. grandiflora*) to many, many hybridized descendants of the Catawba rhododendron (*R. catawbiense*).

2. We now live in North Vancouver, British Columbia, but—since we moved during the Great Recession—we were unable to sell our Birmingham house. I have opted, therefore, to continue using the present tense and referring to the place as "our house," especially because we own no other: in North Vancouver, we are renters.

3. Apparently they were not alone. As the leading book on dogwoods puts it: "Take a typical understory plant like *C. florida* that thrives in the partly shady wood with nice rich organic soils all moist and acidic. Once the plant leaves the nursery for that long trunk ride to its new home, the game is just about over. Despite all encouragement and direction, most homeowners run right home and find the sunniest, driest, and nastiest site with the poorest excuse for soil available to them" (Cappiello and Shadow 32).

4. For what is quite possibly the definitive treatment of diasporic gardening, see Sarah Casteel's remarkable recent book *Second Arrivals*.

5. On December 19, 2006, the National Arbor Day Foundation—hardly a political organization—published, based on the past fifteen years' climate data, its independent revision of the USDA's 1990 map of climate hardiness zones (www.arborday .org/media/zones.cfm), reinforcing what gardeners had been experiencing—"on the ground," as it were—for some time.

6. Frankly, as a modernist I'm not much concerned with accessibility, and, at the risk of sounding overly literal about it, most people seeing the garden from that direction will have had to walk at least half a mile to do so.

7. Louise Wrinkle's Mountain Brook garden, often cited in works like the Wasowskis' *Gardening with Native Plants of the South*, is a model here, or was until she paved her creekside walkway with asphalt. (In some cases, creating such an illusion is not difficult because people are not always very observant. In 2004, a group of non-neighborhood-residents calling themselves "Friends of the Vulcan Trail," on an annual and officious "trail-clearing" mission, veered several yards off the trail to destroy two of my rhododendrons, not to mention a small tree belonging to one neighbor and a mahonia belonging to another.) But the real impulse behind this sort of restorative gardening is what Ken Druse in *The Passion for Gardening* calls "giving back" (97–143). It's a different aesthetic and ethic from Schwartz's, which I deploy elsewhere in the garden. (Why choose?) Schwartz, notes Richardson, "does not try to manipulate the natural landscape in a subtle way, bending it to her ends by using nature's own palette of trees, shrubs, and flowers. For Schwartz, such an approach is lazy or even dishonest, since her argument is that even the notion that unsullied 'nature' exists out there is patently false" (7). Like most dogmatism, such orthodox postmodernism can overstate its point. Habitat restoration, subtly aestheticized or not, isn't about pretending unsullied nature exists, it's about ameliorating some of the sullying.

8. Partly because of gardening's perceived distance from urban youth subcultures and electronic media, no scholarly cultural studies treatment of its pleasures exists, and the present afterword is not intended to fill that void. For an impressionistic meditation intended to "inspire" other gardeners, see Druse.

9. "I wonder," asks Tom Rooks, a landscape designer in Michigan extensively quoted by Druse, "what do people do who are in love with things that are completely man-made? Like people who are in love with cars? What we're in love with is so complex and so never-ending, you can never feel you've done everything or learned everything about it" (Druse 22). Druse's own metaphor that nature is "the senior partner in this collaboration" (232) is schmaltzy but accurately depicts the basic ontological sense that gardening can resist fetishism.

10. For the classic postmodern-geography treatment of Atlanta, see Rutheiser.

11. See McClung, "Afterword."

WORKS CITED

Aaker, David A. *Building Strong Brands*. New York: Free Press, 1996.

Abrams, Vin. "Survey Finds Civic Pride, Lack of Positive Image." *Birmingham News*, February 28, 2003, 1B, 4B.

Advertisement. *American Quarterly* 61:2 (June 2009): 442.

Advertisement. *Parade. Atlanta Journal-Constitution*. March 2, 2003, 24.

Advertisement. *Parade. Birmingham News*. March 2, 2003, 24.

Advertisement. *Parade. Bloomington Hoosier Times*. March 2, 2003, 24.

Advertisement. *Parade. Boston Globe*. March 2, 2003, 24.

Advertisement. *Parade. Chicago Tribune*. March 2, 2003, 24.

Advertisement. *Parade. Greensboro News & Record*. March 2, 2003, 24.

Advertisement. *Parade. Mobile Register*. March 2, 2003, 24.

Advertisement. *Parade. Orlando Sentinel*. March 2, 2003, 24.

Advertisement. *Parade. San Francisco Chronicle*. March 2, 2003, 24.

Agamben, Giorgio. *Stanzas: Word and Phantasm in Western Culture*. Minneapolis: University of Minnesota Press, 1993.

Alden, Grant. "A Few Words about Philosophy." www.nodepression.net/adfaq.html. Accessed July 30, 2004.

Alden, Grant, and Peter Blackstock. *No Depression: An Introduction to Alternative Country Music, Whatever That Is*. Nashville: Dowling, 1998.

Alderman, Edwin A. "The Growing South." In *The Library of Southern Literature*, edited by Edwin Anderson Alderman and Joel Chandler Harris, 14: 6197–6218. 16 vols. Atlanta: Martin and Hoyt, 1910.

Alexander, Constance. Rev. of *Generation X. Louisville Courier-Journal*. www .geocities.com/SoHo/Gallery/5560/genx15.html. Accessed July 30, 2004.

Alexander, Jeffrey C. *The Civil Sphere*. New York: Oxford University Press, 2006.

Appadurai, Arjun. *Modernity at Large: Cultural Dimensions of Globalization*. Minneapolis: University of Minnesota Press, 1996.

"Arrivals/Departures." *The Face*. September 2003, 47–48.

Ayers, Edward J. *What We Talk About When We Talk About the South*. Athens: University of Georgia Press, 1996.

Badiou, Alain. "The Subject of Art." *The Symptom.* www.lacan.com/symptom6 _articles/badiou.html. Accessed July 4, 2011.

Bailey, Steve. "Faithful or Foolish: The Emergence of the 'Ironic Cover Album' and Rock Culture." *Popular Music and Society* 26, no. 2 (2003): 141–59.

Baker, Houston A., Jr. *Turning South Again: Re-thinking Modernism, Re-reading Booker T.* Durham: Duke University Press, 2001.

Baker, Houston A., Jr., and Dana D. Nelson. "Preface: Violence, the Body, and 'The South.'" *American Literature* 73, no. 2 (June 2001): 231–44.

Banet-Weiser, Sarah. "Editor's Note." *American Quarterly* 62, no. 4 (December 2010): v–vii.

———. "Editor's Note." *American Quarterly* 63, no. 1 (March 2011): ix–x.

Barnett, Pamela E. "James Dickey's *Deliverance*: Southern, White, Suburban Male Nightmare or Dream Come True?" *Forum for Modern Language Studies* 40, no. 2 (April 2004): 145–59.

Baym, Nina. Rev. of *Inventing Southern Literature*, by Michael Kreyling. *Mississippi Quarterly* 52, no. 4 (Fall 1999): 659–62.

Bender, Steve, ed. *The Southern Living Garden Book.* Birmingham: Oxmoor House, 1997.

Bennett, Stephen Earl, and Stephen C. Craig with Eric W. Rademacher. "Generations and Change: Some Initial Observations." In *After the Boom: The Politics of Generation X*, edited by Stephen C. Craig and Stephen Earl Bennett, 1–19. New York: Rowman and Littlefield, 1997.

Berelowitz, Lance. *Dream City: Vancouver and the Global Imagination.* Vancouver: Douglas & McIntyre, 2005.

Berlant, Lauren. *The Female Complaint.* Durham: Duke University Press, 2008.

———. *The Queen of America Goes to Washington City.* Durham: Duke University Press, 1997.

Blackstock, Peter. "Destiny Rides Again." *No Depression* 26 (March/April 2000): 50–59.

Blau, Herbert. *Nothing in Itself: Complexions of Fashion.* Bloomington: Indiana University Press, 1999.

Blight, David. *Race and Reunion: The Civil War in American Memory.* Cambridge: Harvard University Press, 2001.

Bone, Martyn. *The Postsouthern Sense of Place in Contemporary Fiction.* Baton Rouge: Louisiana State University Press, 2005.

Boultwood, Anne, and Robert Jerrard. "Ambivalence, and Its Relation to Fashion and the Body." *Fashion Theory* 4, no. 3 (2000): 301–22.

Bové, Paul. "Agriculture and Academe: America's Southern Question." *Boundary 2* 14, no. 3 (Spring 1986): 169–86.

Bowsher, Alice Meriwether. *Community in Alabama: Architecture for Living Together.* Montgomery: Alabama Architectural Foundation, 2007.

Boyagoda, Randy. "Imagining Nation and Imaginary Americans: Race, Immigration and American Identity in the Fiction of Salman Rushdie, Ralph Ellison, and William Faulkner." Ph.D. diss., Boston University, 2005.

Boyd, Andrew. *Life's Little Deconstruction Book: Self-help for the Post-hip.* New York: Norton, 1998.

Brooks, Cleanth. "William Faulkner." In *The History of Southern Literature*, edited by Louis D. Rubin Jr. et al., 333–42. Baton Rouge: Louisiana State University Press, 1985.

Brown, Bill. "Object Relations in an Expanded Field." Talk delivered at Universität Dortmund, June 2005.

Buchanan, Rita, and Roger Holmes, eds. *Taylor's Guide to Gardening in the South*. New York: Houghton Mifflin, 1992.

Butler, Judith. "Afterword: After Loss, What Then?" In *Loss*, edited by David L. Eng and David Kazanjian, 467–73. Berkeley: University of California Press, 2004.

Byrd, Kim. "Chilton County: Where Peaches Are Tops!" Unpublished graduate seminar paper, University of Montevallo, 2006.

Cappiello, Paul, and Don Shadow. *Dogwoods*. Portland: Timber Press, 2005.

Case, Neko. "Neko's Ladies." www.nekocase.com/ladies.html. Accessed July 30, 2004.

Cash, Johnny. With Patrick Carr. *Cash: The Autobiography*. New York: HarperSan-Francisco, 1997.

Cash, W. J. *The Mind of the South*. New York: Vintage, 1991.

Casteel, Sarah. *Second Arrivals: Landscape and Belonging in Contemporary Writing of the Americas*. Charlottesville: University of Virginia Press, 2007.

Castronovo, Russ, and Susan Gillman. "Introduction: The Study of American Problems." In *States of Emergency: The Object of American Studies*, 1–16. Chapel Hill: University of North Carolina Press, 2009.

Caton, Steven C. "What Is an 'Authorizing Discourse'?" In *Powers of the Secular Modern: Talal Asad and his Interlocutors*, edited by David Scott and Charles Hirschkind, 31–56. Palo Alto: Stanford University Press, 2006.

Chandler, Kim. "Moore Sees Self as Fighter Firm in his Convictions." *Birmingham News*, May 17, 2006, 1A, 6A.

Chappell, David L. *A Stone of Hope: Prophetic Religion and the Death of Jim Crow*. Chapel Hill: University of North Carolina Press, 2004.

Ching, Barbara. "Acting Naturally: Cultural Distinction and Critiques of Pure Country." *Arizona Quarterly* 49, no. 3 (Autumn 1993): 107–25.

Ching, Barbara, and Gerald W. Creed. *Knowing Your Place: Rural Identity and Cultural Hierarchy*. New York: Routledge, 1997.

Christgau, Robert. "Diffusion Rools." *Village Voice*, June 16, 2003. www.villagevoice.com/2003-06-17/music/diffusion-rools/ Accessed November 4, 2012.

Church, Thomas D. *Gardens Are for People*. 2nd ed. New York: McGraw-Hill, 1983.

Cohn, Deborah. *History and Memory in the Two Souths: Recent Southern and Spanish American Fiction*. Nashville: Vanderbilt University Press, 1999.

Cooppan, Vilashini. "Mourning Becomes Kitsch: The Aesthetics of Loss in Severo Sarduy's *Cobra*." In *Loss: The Politics of Mourning*, edited by David L. Eng and David Kazanjian, 251–77. Berkeley: University of California Press, 2003.

"Country Love Song." Interview with Neko Case. n.d. www.playboy.com/sex/features/indierock/. Accessed July 30, 2004.

Coupland, Douglas. *Generation X: Tales for an Accelerated Culture*. New York: St. Martin's, 1991.

———. "Picking Brains." *Wired*, April 1997. www.hotwired.wired.com/hardwired/wiredstyle/97/04/pickingbrains.html. Accessed July 30, 2004.

Craig, Stephen C., and Stephen Earl Bennett, eds. *After the Boom: The Politics of Generation X*. New York: Rowman and Littlefield, 1997.

Culler, Jonathan D. *Framing the Sign: Criticism and its Institutions*. New York: Blackwell, 1988.

Davis, Mike. *City of Quartz: Excavating the Future in Los Angeles*. New York: Verso, 1990.

de Grazia, Victoria, ed. *The Sex of Things: Gender and Consumption in Historical Perspective*. Berkeley: University of California Press, 1996.

de Moraes, Lisa. "Ruben Studdard Squeezes into the 'Idol' Pantheon." *Washington Post*, May 22, 2003, C01.

Dedrick, Patricia. "Two-state Industrial Park in the Works." *Birmingham News/Birmingham Post-Herald*, April 12, 2003, 1A, 10A.

Denning, Michael. "Work and Culture in American Studies." In *The Futures of American Studies*, edited by Donald E. Pease and Robyn Wiegman. Durham: Duke University Press, 2002.

Deusner, Stephen M. "Johnny Cash: 'Folsom Prison Blues (Live at Folsom Prison).'" *The 200 Greatest Songs of the 1960s*. www.pitchforkmedia.com/article/feature /37901-the-200-greatest-songs-of-the-1960s, August 18, 2006. Accessed December 17, 2008.

———. Rev. of *Johnny Cash at Folsom Prison: Legacy Edition*. www.pitchforkmedia .com/node/146684, October 23, 2008. Accessed December 17, 2008.

Dirr, Michael A. *Dirr's Trees and Shrubs for Warm Climates: An Illustrated Encyclopedia*. Portland: Timber Press, 2002.

Donaldson, Susan V. "Introduction: The Southern Agrarians and Their Cultural Wars." In *I'll Take My Stand: The South and the Agrarian Tradition*, ix–xl. 75th anniversary ed. Baton Rouge: Louisiana State University Press, 2006.

Donlon, Jocelyn Hazelwood. *Swinging in Place: Porch Life in Southern Culture*. Chapel Hill: University of North Carolina Press, 2001.

Drawbaugh, Kevin. *Brands in the Balance: Meeting the Challenges to Commercial Identity*. New York: Financial Times/Prentice Hall, 2001.

Dreiser, Theodore. *An American Tragedy*. New York: Signet, 2000.

Druse, Ken. *The Passion for Gardening: Inspiration for a Lifetime*. New York: Clarkson Potter, 2003.

Duck, Leigh Anne. *The Nation's Region: Southern Modernism, Segregation, and U.S. Nationalism*. Athens: University of Georgia Press, 2006.

Elias, Amy J. "Postmodern Southern Vacation: Vacation Advertising, Globalization, and Southern Regionalism." In *South to a New Place: Region, Literature, Culture*, edited by Suzanne W. Jones and Sharon Monteith, 253–82. Baton Rouge: Louisiana State University Press, 2002.

Eng, David L., and David Kazanjian. "Introduction: Mourning Remains." In *Loss*, edited by David L. Eng and David Kazanjian, 1–25. Berkeley: University of California Press, 2004.

Ewell, Barbara, and Rebecca Mark. "Everybody Loves You When You're Down and South: Cultural Capital in Hard Times." Call for Papers, Society for the Study of Southern Literature Conference, 2010. www.web.wm.edu/english/sssl/papers .php?svr=www. Accessed March 9, 2010.

Ewen, Stuart. *All Consuming Images: The Politics of Style in Contemporary Culture.* Rev. ed. New York: Basic Books, 1990.

Fabricant, Florence. "So Naughty, So Nice." *New York Times*, February 14, 2007, F1.

Faulkner, William. "Banquet Speech." www.nobelprize.org/literature/laureates/1949/faulkner-speech.html. Accessed July 17, 2011.

———. *Absalom, Absalom!* In *Novels 1936–1940.* Edited by Joseph Blotner and Noel Polk. New York: Library of America, 1990.

———. *The Hamlet.* New York: Random House, 1940.

———. *The Mansion.* New York: Random House, 1959.

———. *Novels 1936–1940.* Edited by Joseph Blotner and Noel Polk. New York: Library of America, 1990.

———. *Selected Letters of William Faulkner.* Edited by Joseph Blotner. New York: Random House, 1977.

Felski, Rita. "Modernist Studies and Cultural Studies: Reflections on Method." *Modernism/modernity* 10, no. 3 (2003): 501–17.

Foster, Hal. "Postmodernism: A Preface." In *The Anti-Aesthetic: Essays on Postmodern Culture*, edited by Hal Foster, ix–xvi. Port Townsend, Wash.: Bay Press, 1983.

———. *The Return of the Real: The Avant-Garde at the End of the Century.* Cambridge: MIT Press, 1996.

Fox, Aaron A. "'Ain't It Funny How Time Slips Away?' Talk, Trash, and Technology in a Texas 'Redneck' Bar." In *Knowing Your Place: Rural Identity and Cultural Hierarchy*, edited by Barbara Ching and Gerald Creed, 105–30. New York: Routledge, 1997.

———. "'Alternative' to What? *O Brother*, September 11, and the Politics of Country Music." In *Country Music Goes to War*, edited by Charles K. Wolfe and James E. Akenson. Lexington: University of Kentucky Press, 2005.

———. *Real Country: Music and Language in Working-Class Culture.* Durham: Duke University Press, 2004.

Fox, Pamela, and Barbara Ching, eds. *Old Roots, New Routes: The Cultural Politics of Alt.country Music.* Ann Arbor: University of Michigan Press, 2008.

Fraiman, Susan. *Cool Men and the Second Sex.* New York: Columbia University Press, 2003.

Frampton, Kenneth. "Towards a Critical Regionalism: Six Points for an Architecture of Resistance." In *The Anti-Aesthetic: Essays on Postmodern Culture*, edited by Hal Foster, 16–30. Port Townsend, Wash.: Bay Press, 1983.

Frank, Thomas. *The Conquest of Cool.* Chicago: University of Chicago Press, 1997.

Frank, Thomas, and Matt Weiland, eds. *Commodify Your Dissent: Salvos from* The Baffler. New York: Norton, 1997.

Frith, Simon. *Performing Rites: On the Value of Popular Music.* Cambridge: Harvard University Press, 1996.

Galloway, Jim. "Carter Smoothed Flag Deal." *Atlanta Journal-Constitution*, May 4, 2003, E1, E5.

———. "Deal Let Both Sides Dodge Minié Ball." *Atlanta Journal-Constitution*, April 27, 2003, C6.

———. "Democrats Push for Single Referendum." *Atlanta Journal-Constitution*, April 24, 2002. www.ajc.com/metro/content/metro/politics/0403/24legflag.html.

———. "Rebel Emblem Dropped from Flag Vote Options." *Atlanta Journal-Constitution*, April 26, 2003. www.ajc.com/metro/content/metro/politics/0403/26legflag.html.

Galloway, Jim, and Tom Baxter. "Flag Issue Likely to Flap Till Very End of Season." *Atlanta Journal-Constitution*, April 25, 2003. www.ajc.com/metro/content/metro/politics/0403/25legflag.html.

García Canclini, Néstor. *Hybrid Cultures: Strategies for Entering and Leaving Modernity*. Minneapolis: University of Minnesota Press, 1995.

Garreau, Joel. "Alt-Dominion: In the Virginia Piedmont, a Broadbanded Gentry Is Remaking the Cultural Landscape." *Washington Post*, July 30, 2006, DO1.

Gettleman, Jeffrey. "Americans' Role Seen in Uganda Anti-Gay Push." *New York Times*, January 3, 2010. www.nytimes.com/2010/01/04/world/africa/04uganda.html?scp=4&sq=gettleman%20uganda&st=cse. Accessed March 5, 2010.

Gillian T. Comment. www.realcountry.blogspot.com/2006/03/discuss-real-country.html#comments. Accessed June 1, 2006.

Gitlin, Todd. *The Sixties: Years of Hope, Days of Rage*. New York: Bantam, 1987.

Glendon, Mary Ann. "The Naked Public Square Today: A Secular Public Square?" In *The Naked Public Square Reconsidered: Religion and Politics in the Twenty-First Century*, edited by Christopher Wolfe. Wilmington: ISI Books, 2009.

Godden, Richard. "Earthing *The Hamlet*, an Anti-Ratliffian Reading." *The Faulkner Journal* 14, no. 2 (Spring 1999): 77–79.

———. *Fictions of Labor: William Faulkner and the South's Long Revolution*. New York: Cambridge University Press, 1997.

———. *William Faulkner: An Economy of Complex Words*. Princeton: Princeton University Press, 2007.

Goldman, Adam. "Big Buck Game Bags City Hunters." *Birmingham News*, July 26, 2006, 1D, 3D.

Greeson, Jennifer. *Our South: Geographic Fantasy and the Rise of National Literature*. Cambridge: Harvard University Press, 2010.

Griffin, Larry J., Ranae J. Evenson, and Ashley B. Thompson. "Southerners, All?" *Southern Cultures* 11:1 (Spring 2005): 6–25.

Griffith, R. Marie, and Melani McAlister, eds. *Religion and Politics in the Contemporary United States. American Quarterly* 59:3 (September 2007).

Grossberg, Lawrence. *Dancing in Spite of Myself: Essays on Popular Culture*. Durham: Duke University Press, 1997.

———. "Raymond Williams and the Absent Modernity." In *About Raymond Williams*, edited by Monika Seidl, Roman Horak, and Lawrence Grossberg, 18–33. New York: Routledge, 2010.

———. *We Gotta Get Out of This Place: Popular Conservatism and Postmodern Culture*. New York: Routledge, 1992.

Guilbaut, Serge. *How New York Stole the Idea of Modern Art*. Chicago: University of Chicago Press, 1983.

Gwin, Minrose. "Introduction: Reading History, Memory, and Forgetting." *Southern Literary Journal* 40, no. 2 (Spring 2008): 1–10.

———. "Mourning Medgar." *Southern Spaces*. www.southernspaces.org/contents/2008/gwin/1a.htm. Accessed January 25, 2010.

Habermas, Jürgen. "Modernity—An Incomplete Project." In *The Anti-Aesthetic: Essays on Postmodern Culture*, edited by Hal Foster, 3–15. Port Townsend, Wash.: Bay Press, 1983.

———. "Public Space and Political Pubic Sphere: The Biographical Roots of Two Motifs in my Thought." In *Between Naturalism and Religion: Philosophical Essays*, translated by Ciaran Cronin, 11–23. Malden, Mass.: Polity, 2008.

———. *The Structural Transformation of the Public Sphere: An Inquiry into a Category of Bourgeois Society*. Translated by Thomas Burger. Cambridge: The MIT Press, 1991.

Haidt, Jonathan. "The Emotional Dog and Its Rational Tail: A Social Intuitionist Approach to Moral Judgment." *Psychological Review* 108, no. 4 (2001): 814–34.

Handley, George. *Postslavery Literatures in the Americas: Family Portraits in Black and White*. Charlottesville: University Press of Virginia, 2000.

Hebdige, Dick. *Subculture: The Meaning of Style*. New York: Methuen, 1979.

Henninger, Katherine Renée. "How New? What Place? Southern Studies and the Rest of the World." *Contemporary Literature* 45, no. 1 (2004): 177–85.

Hill, Sam. "Fundamentalism in Recent Southern Culture." *Journal of Southern Religion* 1, no. 1 (1998). www.jsr.fsu.edu/essay.htm. Accessed March 5, 2010.

Hill, Trent. "Why Isn't Country Music Youth Culture?" In *Rock Over the Edge: Transformations in Popular Music Culture*, edited by Roger Beebe, Denise Fulbrook, and Ben Saunders, 161–90. Durham: Duke University Press, 2002.

Hirschberg, Lynn. "The Music Man." *New York Times Magazine*, September 2, 2007. www.nytimes.com/2007/09/02/magazine/02rubin.t.html. Accessed March 20, 2010.

Hobson, Fred. *The Southern Writer in the Postmodern World*. Athens: University of Georgia Press, 1991.

Holloway, Karla F. C. *Passed On: African American Mourning Stories*. Durham: Duke University Press, 2002.

Holt, Douglas B. *How Brands Become Icons: The Principles of Cultural Branding*. Cambridge: Harvard Business School Press, 2004.

hooks, bell. "Uniquely Toni Cade Bambara." *Black Issues Book Review* 2, no. 1 (January/February 2000): 14–16.

Hotchkiss, Sandy, and James F. Masterson. *Why Is It Always About You? The Seven Deadly Sins of Narcissism*. New York: Free Press, 2003.

Howard, John. *Men Like That: A Southern Queer History*. Chicago: University of Chicago Press, 1999.

Hulbert, Ann. "Look Who's Parenting." *New York Times Magazine*, July 4, 2004. www.nytimes.com/2004/07/04/magazine/04WWLN.html. Accessed July 13, 2004.

Humphries, Jefferson. "Introduction: On the Inevitability of Theory in Southern Literary Study." In *Southern Literature and Literary Theory*, edited by Jefferson Humphries, vii–xviii. Athens: University of Georgia Press, 1992.

Huyssen, Andreas. "High/Low in an Expanded Field." *Modernism/modernity* 9, no. 3 (2002): 363–74.

Inbar, Yoel, David A. Pizarro, and Paul Bloom. "Conservatives Are More Easily Disgusted than Liberals." *Cognition and Emotion* 23, no. 4 (2008): 714–25.

Jacobson, Joanne. "Exploding Plastic Inevitable." Rev. of *Tupperware: The Promise of Plastic in 1950s America*, by Alison Clarke. *The Nation*, December 27,

1999. www.thenation.com/article/exploding-plastic-inevitable. Accessed July 17, 2011.

Jameson, Fredric. "On Cultural Studies." *Social Text* 34 (1993): 17–52.

———. "Postmodernism and Consumer Society." In *The Anti-Aesthetic: Essays on Postmodern Culture*, edited by Hal Foster, 111–25. Port Townsend, Wash.: Bay Press, 1983.

———. *Postmodernism, or, The Cultural Logic of Late Capitalism*. Durham: Duke University Press, 1991.

———. *A Singular Modernity*. New York: Verso, 2002.

Joseph, Miranda. *Against the Romance of Community*. Minneapolis: University of Minnesota Press, 2002.

Kaoma, Kapya. Globalizing the Culture Wars: U.S. Conservatives, African Churches, and Homophobia. Somerville, Mass.: Political Research Associates, 2009. www .publiceye.org/publications/globalizing-the-culture-wars/pdf/africa-full-report.pdf. Accessed November 4, 2012.

Kipnis, Laura. "Adultery." *Critical Inquiry* 24, no. 2 (Winter 98): 289–327.

Klein, Kerwin Lee. "On the Emergence of *Memory* in Historical Discourse." *Representations* 69 (Winter 2000): 127–50.

Klein, Naomi. *No Logo*. New York: Picador, 2002.

Kreyling, Michael. *Inventing Southern Literature*. Jackson: University Press of Mississippi, 1998.

———. Rev. of *The Nation's Region*, by Leigh Anne Duck. *Southern Cultures* 14, no. 1 (Spring 2008): 111–13.

———. *The South That Wasn't There: Postsouthern Memory and History*. Baton Rouge: Louisiana State University Press, 2010.

———. "Toward 'A New Southern Studies.'" *Mississippi Quarterly* 54, no. 3 (Spring 2001): 383–91.

———. "Toward 'A New Southern Studies.'" *South Central Review* 22, no. 1 (Spring 2005): 4–18.

Kruse, Holly. "Subcultural Identity in Alternative Music Culture." *Popular Music* 12, no. 1 (1993): 33–41.

Kwon, Miwon. *One Place After Another: Site-Specific Art and Locational Identity*. Cambridge: The MIT Press, 2002.

Lacan, Jacques. *The Four Fundamental Concepts of Psycho-analysis*. New York: Norton, 1981.

Ladd, Barbara. "Literary Studies: The Southern United States, 2005." *PMLA* 120 no. 5 (October 2005): 1628–39.

Langbauer, Laurie. "The Ethics and Practice of Lemony Snicket: Adolescence and Generation X." *PMLA* 122, no. 2 (March 2007): 502–21.

Lanham, Robert. *The Hipster Handbook*. New York: Anchor, 2002.

Lanier, Lyle H. "A Critique of the Philosophy of Progress." In *I'll Take My Stand: The South and the Agrarian Tradition*. By Twelve Southerners. Baton Rouge: Louisiana State University Press, 1977. 122–54.

Lassiter, Matthew D., and Joseph Crespino. "Introduction: The End of Southern History." In *The Myth of Southern Exceptionalism*, edited by Matthew D. Lassiter and Joseph Crespino, 1–22. New York: Oxford University Press, 2010.

Leblanc, Laraine. *Pretty in Punk: Girls' Gender Resistance in a Boys' Subculture*. New Brunswick: Rutgers University Press, 1999.

Leland, John. *Hip: The History*. New York: HarperCollins, 2004.

Lippard, Lucy R. *The Lure of the Local: Senses of Place in a Multicentered Society*. New York: The New Press, 1997.

Lipsitz, George. *The Possessive Investment in Whiteness: How White People Profit from Identity Politics*. Rev. and expanded ed. Philadelphia: Temple University Press, 2006.

Liu, Alan. *The Laws of Cool: Knowledge Work and the Culture of Information*. Chicago: University of Chicago Press, 2004.

Lott, Eric. "The First Boomer: Bill Clinton, George W., and Fictions of State." *Representations* 84 (Autumn 2003): 100–122.

Mark, Rebecca. "Mourning Emmet." *Southern Literary Journal* 40, no. 2 (Spring 2008): 121–37.

Martin, Joel W. "All that is Solid (and Southern) Melts into Air: A Response to Sam Hill's Fundamental Argument Regarding Fundamentalism." *Journal of Southern Religion* 1, no. 1 (1998). www.jsr.fsu.edu/martin.htm. Accessed March 5, 2010.

Maychork, Jesse Fox. "Recalling the Twang That Was All Country." *New York Times*, July 16, 2006, B26.

McClung, William Alexander. *Landscapes of Desire: Anglo Mythologies of Los Angeles*. Berkeley: University of California Press, 2000.

McPherson, Tara. *Reconstructing Dixie: Race, Gender, and Nostalgia in the Imagined South*. Durham: Duke University Press, 2002.

McRobbie, Angela. "Second-hand Dresses and the Role of the Ragmarket." In *Zoot Suits and Second-hand Dresses*, edited by Angela McRobbie. London: Macmillan, 1989. Rpt. in *The Subcultures Reader*, edited by Ken Gelder and Sarah Thornton, 191–99. New York: Routledge, 1997.

McRobbie, Angela, and Jenny Garber. "Girls and Subcultures." In *Resistance Through Rituals*, edited by Stuart Hall and Tony Jefferson. London: Routledge, 1973. Rpt. in *The Subcultures Reader*, edited by Ken Gelder and Sarah Thornton, 112–20. New York: Routledge, 1997.

McWhirter, Cameron. "'Other Georgia' Is Split over Flag." *Atlanta Journal-Constitution*, February 23, 2003, C1, C7.

McWhorter, Diane. *Carry Me Home: Birmingham, Alabama: The Climactic Battle of the Civil Rights Revolution*. New York: Touchstone, 2001.

Michael, John. *Anxious Intellects: Academic Professionals, Public Intellectuals, and Enlightenment Values*. Durham: Duke University Press, 2000.

Michaels, Walter Benn. *The Gold Standard and the Logic of Naturalism: American Literature at the Turn of the Century*. Berkeley: University of California Press, 1988.

———. *The Trouble with Diversity: How We Learned to Love Identity and Ignore Inequality*. New York: Henry Holt, 2006.

Michna, Catherine. "A *New* New Urbanism for a *New* New Orleans." *American Quarterly* 58, no. 4 (December 2006): 1207–16.

Mitscherlich, Alexander, and Margarete Mitscherlich. *The Inability to Mourn: Principles of Collective Behavior*. New York: Grove, 1975.

Mumford, Lewis. *The South in Architecture*. New York: Harcourt, Brace, 1941.

Neuhaus, Richard John. "Can Atheists Be Good Citizens?" *First Things* (August/ September 1991). www.firstthings.com/article/2007/11/003-can-atheists-be-good -citizens-5. Accessed March 5, 2010.

———. *The Naked Public Square: Religion and Democracy in America*. Grand Rapids: Eerdmans, 1984.

Nonini, Donald M. "Critique: Creating the Transnational South." In *The American South in a Global World*, edited by James L. Peacock, Harry L. Watson, and Carrie Matthews, 247–64. Chapel Hill: University of North Carolina Press, 2005.

Obama, Barack. *The Audacity of Hope: Thoughts on Reclaiming the American Dream*. New York: Crown, 2006.

O'Brien, Michael. *Rethinking the South: Essays in Intellectual History*. Baltimore: Johns Hopkins University Press, 1988.

O'Connor, Flannery. "A Cartoon by Flannery O'Connor." *Vice* 13, no. 2 (December 2006): 50.

Olmsted Brothers. *A System of Parks and Playgrounds for Birmingham: Preliminary Report upon the Park Problems, Needs, and Opportunities of the City and its Immediate Surroundings*. Birmingham: Park and Recreation Board of Birmingham, 1925. Rpt. Birmingham Historical Society, 2005.

Ortner, Sherry. *Anthropology and Social Theory*. Durham: Duke University Press, 2006.

———. "Generation X: Anthropology in a Media-Saturated World." *Cultural Anthropology* 13:3 (August 1998): 414–40.

Osgerby, Bill. "Chewing Out a Rhythm on my Bubble-Gum': The Teenage Aesthetic and Genealogies of American Punk." In *Punk Rock: So What?* edited by Roger Sabin, 154–69. New York: Routledge, 1999.

Ownby, Ted. *American Dreams in Mississippi: Consumers, Poverty, and Culture, 1830–1998*. Chapel Hill: University of North Carolina Press, 1999.

Peacock, James L. *Grounded Globalism: How the U.S. South Embraces the World*. Athens: University of Georgia Press, 2007.

———. "The South and Grounded Globalism." In *The American South in a Global World*, edited by James L. Peacock, Harry L. Watson, and Carrie Matthews, 265– 76. Chapel Hill: University of North Carolina Press, 2005.

Peacock, James L., Harry L. Watson, and Carrie Matthews, eds. *The American South in a Global World*. Chapel Hill: University of North Carolina Press, 2005.

Pease, Donald. *The New American Exceptionalism*. Minneapolis: University of Minnesota Press, 2009.

Pease, Donald E., and Robyn Wiegman. "Futures." In *The Futures of American Studies*, 1–42. Durham: Duke University Press, 2002.

Polhemus, Ted. *Style Surfing: What to Wear in the 3rd Millennium*. New York: Thames and Hudson, 1996.

Polhemus, Ted, and Lynn Procter. *Fashion and Antifashion: An Anthropology of Clothing and Adornment*. London: Thames and Hudson, 1978.

Posner, Richard. "Is the Conservative Movement Losing Steam?" *The Becker-Posner Blog*. www.becker-posner-blog.com/archives/2009/05/is_the_conserva.html. Accessed March 10, 2010.

Poynor, Rick. *No More Rules: Graphic Design and Postmodernism*. New Haven: Yale University Press, 2003.

Ransom, John Crowe. "Reconstructed but Unregenerate." In *I'll Take My Stand: The South and the Agrarian Tradition*. By Twelve Southerners. Baton Rouge: Louisiana State University Press, 1977. 1–27.

Rapping, Elayne. "Daytime Utopias: If You Lived in Pine Valley, You'd Be Home." In *Hop on Pop: The Politics and Pleasures of Popular Culture*, edited by Henry Jenkins, Tara McPherson, and Jane Shattuc, 47–65. Durham: Duke University Press, 2003.

Reed, John Shelton. *The Enduring South: Subcultural Persistence in Mass Society*. Chapel Hill: University of North Carolina Press, 1975.

———. *My Tears Spoiled My Aim*. New York: Harcourt, 1993.

Reynolds, Richard. *Guerrilla Gardening*. www.guerrillagardening.org/. Accessed March 29, 2010.

———. *On Guerrilla Gardening: A Handbook for Gardening Without Boundaries*. New York: Bloomsbury USA, 2008.

Richardson, Riché. "'A House Set off From the Rest': Ralph Ellison's Rural Geography." *Forum for Modern Language Studies* 40, no. 2 (April 2004): 116–44.

Richardson, Tim, ed. *The Vanguard Landscapes and Gardens of Martha Schwartz*. New York: Thames and Hudson, 2004.

Romine, Scott. *The Narrative Forms of Southern Community*. Baton Rouge: Louisiana State University Press, 1999.

———. *The Real South: Southern Narrative in the Age of Cultural Reproduction*. Baton Rouge: Louisiana State University Press, 2008.

———. "Where is Southern Literature? The Practice of Place in a Postsouthern Age." In *South to a New Place: Region, Literature, Culture*, edited by Suzanne W. Jones and Sharon Monteith, 23–43. Baton Rouge: Louisiana State University Press, 2002.

Rosaldo, Renato. Foreword to *Hybrid Cultures: Strategies for Entering and Leaving Modernity*, by Néstor García Canclini, xi–xvii. Minneapolis: University of Minnesota Press, 1995.

Rowe, John Carlos. "Introduction." In *A Concise Companion to American Studies*, edited by John Carlos Rowe, 1–16. New York: Wiley-Blackwell, 2010.

"Royal Ascent." *The Guardian*, October 23, 2004. www.guardian.co.uk/arts/features/story/0,11710,1333648,00.html. Accessed October 23, 2004.

Rubin, Louis D. "Introduction to the Torchbook Edition." In *I'll Take My Stand: The South and the Agrarian Tradition*, by Twelve Southerners, xxiii–xxxv. Baton Rouge: Louisiana State University Press, 1977.

———. "The Trilogy of the Snopes Family Complete." *Baltimore Evening Sun*, November 27, 1959. Rpt. in *William Faulkner: The Contemporary Reviews*, edited by M. Thomas Inge, 449. New York: Cambridge University Press, 1994.

Rushing, Felder, and Jennifer Greer, eds. *Alabama and Mississippi Gardener's Guide*. Nashville: Cool Springs Press, 2005.

Rutheiser, Charles. *Imagineering Atlanta: The Politics of Place in the City of Dreams*. New York: Verso, 1996.

Sanneh, Kalefa. "In the Desert, a Festival of Country and Its Kin." *New York Times*, May 8, 2007, E1.

Santner, Eric. *Stranded Objects: Mourning, Memory, and Film in Postwar Germany*. Ithaca: Cornell University Press, 1993.

Sepsas, Niki. "Sharing the Spotlight." *Birmingham Magazine*, June 2003, 142–45.

Shafer, Byron E., and Richard Johnston. *The End of Southern Exceptionalism: Class, Race, and Partisan Change in the Postwar South*. Cambridge: Harvard University Press, 2006.

Sharlet, Jeff. *The Family: The Secret Fundamentalism at the Heart of American Power*. New York: HarperCollins, 2008.

"A Sign of Growth." *Birmingham News*, February 28, 2003, 5C.

Silverman, Jonathan. "'The Fool in the Mirror.'" Rev. of *Real Country: Music and Language in Working-Class Culture*, by Aaron A. Fox. *American Quarterly* 58, no. 2 (June 2006): 545–50.

Simpson, David. *Situatedness, or, Why We Keep Saying Where We're Coming From*. Durham: Duke University Press, 2002.

Smith, Douglas. "Into the Political Thicket: Reapportionment and the Rise of Suburban Power." In *The End of Southern Exceptionalism*, edited by Matthew D. Lassiter and Joseph Crespino, 263–85. New York: Oxford University Press, 2010.

Smith, Jon. "Postcolonial, Black, and Nobody's Margin." *American Literary History* 16:1 (Spring 2004): 144–61.

———. Rev. of *The Narrative Forms of Southern Community*, by Scott Romine. *Style* 34, no. 2 (Summer 2000): 329–32.

———. "Southern Culture on the Skids: Punk, Retro, Narcissism, and the Burden of Southern History." In *South to a New Place: Region, Literature, Culture*, edited by Suzanne W. Jones and Sharon Monteith, 76–95. Baton Rouge: Louisiana State University Press, 2002.

———. "Toward a Post-Postpolitical Southern Studies." In *Creating and Consuming the South*, edited by Martyn Bone. Gainesville: University of Florida Press, forthcoming.

Smith, Jon, and Deborah Cohn. "Introduction: Uncanny Hybridities." In *Look Away! The U.S. South in New World Studies*. Durham: Duke University Press, 2004. 1–19.

Smith, Rob. "Founders Upbeat over No Depression's Growth." *Puget Sound Business Journal*, July 24, 2000. www.bizjournals.com/seattle/stories/2000/07/24/focus2.html. Accessed December 16, 2003.

Smith-Nonini, Sandy. "Federally Sponsored Mexican Migrants in the Transnational South." In *The American South in a Global World*, edited by James L. Peacock, Harry L. Watson, and Carrie R. Matthews, 59–79. Chapel Hill: University of North Carolina Press, 2005.

Soja, Edward W. *Postmetropolis: Critical Studies of Cities and Regions*. Malden, Mass.: Blackwell, 2000.

Spacks, Patricia Meyer. *Boredom: The Literary History of a State of Mind*. Chicago: University of Chicago Press, 1995.

Stout, Jeffrey. *Democracy and Tradition*. Princeton: Princeton University Press, 2005.

Striffler, Steve. "We're All Mexicans Here: Poultry Processing, Latino Migration, and the Transformation of Class in the South." In *The American South in a Global*

World, edited by James L. Peacock, Harry L. Watson, and Carrie R. Matthews, 152–65. Chapel Hill: University of North Carolina Press, 2005.

Tharpe, Jim. "Coleman's Seat Appears Secure." *Atlanta Journal-Constitution*, June 8, 2003, C1, C9.

Thornton, Sarah. *Club Cultures: Music, Media, and Subcultural Capital*. Hanover: Wesleyan University Press, 1995.

Tracey, David. *Guerrilla Gardening: A Manualfesto*. Gabriola Island, British Columbia: New Society, 2007.

Travasos, Gabino. "Neko Case." Interview. *Mote Magazine*, August 1999. www .moregoatthangoose.com/interviews/neko.htm. Accessed July 30, 2004.

Travis, Daryl. *Emotional Branding: How Successful Brands Gain the Irrational Edge*. Roseville, Calif.: Prima, 2000.

Tuan, Yi-Fu. *Space and Place: The Perspective of Experience*. Minneapolis: University of Minnesota Press, 1977.

Tullos, Allen. *Alabama Getaway: The Political Imaginary and the Heart of Dixie*. Athens: University of Georgia Press, 2011.

Turkle, Sherry. Letter to the Editor. *New York Review of Books*, May 31, 1979. www.nybooks.com/articles/archives/1979/may/31/lacan-an-exchange/?pagination=false. Accessed November 4, 2012.

Twelve Southerners. *I'll Take My Stand*. Baton Rouge: Louisiana State University Press, 2006.

Upshaw, Lynn B. *Building Brand Identity: A Strategy for Success in a Hostile Marketplace*. New York: John Wiley and Sons, 1995.

Vale, V. *Swing! The New Retro Renaissance*. San Francisco: V/Search, 1998.

van Ham, Peter. "The Rise of the Brand State: The Postmodern Politics of Image and Reputation." *Foreign Affairs* 80, no. 5 (September/October 2001): 2–6.

Villa, Raúl Homero, and George J. Sánchez. "Introduction: Los Angeles Studies and the Future of Urban Culture." *American Quarterly* 56, no. 3 (September 2004): 499–505.

Waggoner, Eric. "Profile: Radio Cure." *Seattle Weekly*, April 2–8, 2003. www.seattle weekly.com/features/0314/music-waggoner.php. Accessed June 12, 2004.

Wald, Priscilla. "Atomic Faulkner." In *Faulkner's Inheritance: Faulkner and Yoknapatawpha 2005*, edited by Joseph R. Urgo and Ann J. Abadie, 35–52. Jackson: University Press of Mississippi, 2007.

Walker, Rob. "The Marketing of No Marketing." *New York Times Magazine*, June 22, 2003, 42–45.

Wasowski, Sally. *Gardening with Native Plants of the South*. With Andy Wasowski. New York: Taylor Trade Publishing, 1994.

Watson, Jay. "Mapping out a Postsouthern Cinema: Three Contemporary Films." In *American Cinema and the Southern Imaginary*, edited by Deborah Barker and Kathryn McKee, 219–52. Athens: University of Georgia Press, 2010.

Weinzierl, Rupert, and David Muggleton. "What is 'Post-subcultural Studies' Anyway?" In *The Post-Subcultures Reader*, edited by David Muggleton and Rupert Weinzierl, 3–23. New York: Berg, 2003.

Williams, Raymond. *The Country and the City*. New York: Oxford University Press, 1975.

Williams, Roy L. "Tourism Officials Hope to Build on Image Set by 'Idol' Studdard." *Birmingham News*, July 3, 2003, 1D, 2D.

Williamson, Joel. *William Faulkner and Southern History*. New York: Oxford University Press, 1993.

Wilson, Edward O. *The Future of Life*. New York: Vintage, 2003.

Wise, Gene. "'Paradigm Dramas' in American Studies: A Cultural and Institutional History of the Movement." In *Locating American Studies: The Evolution of a Discipline*, edited by Lucy Maddox, 166–210. Baltimore: Johns Hopkins University Press, 1999.

Witt, Elaine. "History Did Not End With Bombing." *Birmingham News*, February 22, 2003, 1C, 3C.

Woodham, Jonathan. "A Brand New Britain?" In *Brand.new*, edited by Jane Pavitt, 56–57. Princeton: Princeton University Press, 2000.

Woodward, C. Vann. *The Burden of Southern History*. 3rd ed. Baton Rouge: Louisiana State University Press, 1993.

Wyatt, Kristen. "Flag Flap Taints Atlanta's Image." *Birmingham News*, February 28, 2003, 1E.

Yaeger, Patricia. "Consuming Trauma; or, The Pleasures of Merely Circulating." *Journal X* 1, no. 2 (Spring 1997): 255–51.

———. *Dirt and Desire: Reconstructing Southern Women's Writing, 1930–1990*. Chicago: University of Chicago Press, 2000.

———. "Editor's Note: The Almost-All-Asian Issue: Channeling Ai Weiwei and the Grass-Mud Horse." *PMLA* 126, no. 3 (May 2011): 553–54.

Zanes, R. J. Warren. "A Fan's Notes: Identification, Desire, and the Haunted Sound Barrier." In *Rock over the Edge: Transformations in Popular Music Culture*, edited by Roger Beebe, Denise Fulbrook, and Ben Saunders. Durham: Duke University Press, 2002.

Žižek, Slavoj. *Did Somebody Say Totalitarianism? Five Interventions in the (Mis)use of a Notion*. New York: Verso, 2001.

———. *For They Know Not What They Do: Enjoyment as a Political Factor*. 2nd ed. New York: Verso, 2008.

———. *In Defense of Lost Causes*. New York: Verso, 2008.

———. *Living in the End Times*. New York: Verso, 2010.

———. *Looking Awry: An Introduction to Lacan through Popular Culture*. Cambridge: The MIT Press, 1991.

———. "Melancholy and the Act." In *Did Somebody Say Totalitarianism? Five Interventions in the (Mis)use of a Notion*. New York: Verso, 2001. 141–89.

———. *The Plague of Fantasies*. New York: Verso, 1997.

———. "A Plea for a Return to Différance (with a Minor Pro Domo Sua)." *Critical Inquiry* 32, no. 2 (Winter 2006): 226–49.

———. *Tarrying with the Negative: Kant, Hegel, and the Critique of Ideology*. Durham: Duke University Press, 1993.

———. *Welcome to the Desert of the Real! Five Essays on September 11 and Related Dates*. New York: Verso, 2002.

Žižek, Slavoj, and John Milbank. *The Monstrosity of Christ: Paradox or Dialectic?* Cambridge: MIT Press, 2009.

INDEX

Aaker, David A., 75, 108, 110

Abrams, Vin, 113

Absalom, Absalom! (Faulkner), 92, 102, 126, 130

Adams, Ryan, 67, 68, 75

Adkisson, David, 113

adulthood: and Case's career, 81–96 passim; Gen-X, melancholy for, 39–40, 43, 68–69, 86; narcissistic youth, compared with, xi; mentioned, 7, 23, 73, 141n7, 141n11

After the Boom (Craig and Bennett), 69

Agamben, Giorgio, 140n5

agrarians, Nashville: and alienation in the modern metropolis, 92, 100; and community, 63, 113; modernity, disavowal of, 8, 10; and slavery, 110

Aiken, Clay, 115, 116, 119, 120, 148n7

Alabama: constitution of, 121; rebranding of, 111, 112; shopping culture of, 89–90; as site of alternative modernities, 21–22; mentioned, 124, 148n1, 148n3. *See also* Birmingham; *Sweet Home Alabama*; "Sweet Home Alabama"; *specific landmarks*

Alabama Theatre, 116, 120

Alden, Grant, 143n1, 144n6

Alderman, Edwin, 39

Alexander, Constance, 70

Alexander, Jeffrey C., 142n5

alt-country music: and authenticity, 65–67, 84; and branding, 96–97; and camp, 80, 82, 145n10; contested meanings of, 71–72; and cultural capital, 46, 68, 80; and Gen X, fantasies of, 67, 85; and Gen X, melancholy of, 38, 40–41; and graphic design, of, 144n6; narcissism of, 71–72, 81; and swing, shared genealogy of, 75. *See also* Case, Neko

"Alt.Everything" (Klein), 65

American Idol (television series): 107, 113–18 passim. *See Also* Studdard, Ruben

American Quarterly, 2, 8, 11, 123–24, 137n1, 138n4

American studies: and American exceptionalism, x, 1–2; and branding, 107, 122–24, 143n9; modernity, disavowal of, 8–9; and narcissism of, 6, 9, 15–16; and radicalism, fantasized, 2–4, 11–13, 138n4; and rationality, standards of, 59–62; and southern studies, marginalization of, x–xi, 124; therapeutic approach of, 16–17. *See also* cultural studies, American; southern studies, new; southern studies, old

country music (*continued*)
46–47; and hipsters, appeal for, 38–
39, 41–43, 66, 79; and loss fetish, 30,
41, 48–49; as performed authenticity,
45–48, 66, 79, 81. *See also* alt-country
Coupland, Douglas, 1, 38, 67–68, 69–
70, 76
Court, U.S. Supreme, 56–57, 116
Craig, Stephen, 69, 71
Creed, Gerald W., 9
Crespino, Joseph, xi, 15, 55, 56
crisis, fantasy of, 3–4, 6, 30, 35
Crosby, Bing, 83
Culler, Jonathan, 59, 143n8
cultural studies, American, x, 1–2; and
baby boomers, 5–7, 71; and com-
plications of, feminist and minority,
13; and melancholy, 31, 35, 68; and
modernity, disowning, 8–9, 13, 20,
139n13; and narcissism, 15–16; and
southern studies, 21–22, 26, 31; and
trendiness, 94, 96–97, 138n5

das Trieb. *See* drive
Davis, Mike, 10–11, 134–35
deep (periodical), 24
de Grazia, Victoria, 102
Democracy and Tradition (Stout), 57–58
de Moraes, Lisa, 114, 115, 116
Denning, Michael, 8
desire: of American studies scholars,
xi–xiii, 2–3, 9–14; contradictions of,
127, 134; for dialectical synthesis, 21–
26; Lacanian perspectives on, 3–4, 5,
· 37; and melancholy, white southern,
34–39. *See* drive
Deusner, Stephen M., 44–45
Dirr, Michael, 126, 129
Dirt and Desire (Yaeger), 15, 110,
143n11, 146n2
Diva Citizenship, limits of, 60
Donaldson, Susan, 140n3
Dreiser, Theodore, 100, 102, 147n12
drive: and American exceptionalism,
xi, 3–4; circular structure of, 41–

42, 53, 58; desire, compared to,
3–4; disruption of, 42, 52–53; and
melancholy, hipster, 41–42; and
melancholy, white southern, 32–39,
58, 105
Duck, Leigh Anne, 15, 61, 67
Dylan, Bob, 82, 145–46n14
dynamiting the rails, x, 34, 63, 91

Earwax Records, 24
Eggers, Dave, 76
Electric Version (New Pornographers), 82
Elias, Amy J., 15
Ellison, Ralph, 91–92, 97, 105, 147n15
Eng, David L., 48–49
enjoyment: disrupting academic
enjoyment, xi, 4–6, 142n5; and drive,
32–33, 64; ignorance, as product of,
61; new southern studies, challenge
to, 7, 16; theft of, 40, 53, 54, 56
Evers, Medgar, 33
exceptionalism, American: and drive,
xi, 3–4; Pease's reinscription of, x–xi;
and radicalism, fantasies of, 1–2; and
the South, exclusion through, xi
exceptionalism, southern: academic
reinscription of, 13–15, 17, 123–
24; critical challenges to, 55–56; as
ideological fantasy x–xi, 23

Fabricant, Florence, 24
"Family, The" (religious organization),
50
fantasy, 139n13; and community,
disruption of, 5–7, 14–15, 22–23; and
conservative secessionists, 53–54; and
exceptionalism, x–xi; and hipness,
disruption of, 8–9, 22–23, 26; and
narcissistic radicalism, 2–4, 11–13,
72. *See also* desire; drive; enjoyment;
objet petit a
fashion: 18, 73–76, 96; ambivalence
toward, 19; and dignity, 105; in the
south, 23–25. *See also* Faulkner,
William; *Mansion, The*

Go-Gos, the, 77
Goldman, Adam, 24
Goldwater, Barry, 50
Greeley, Andrew, 71
Greenwich Village, 90, 92, 94, 100, 104
Greeson, Jennifer, 15, 67
Griffith, R. Marie, 59
Grossberg, Lawrence, 13, 14, 39, 85, 137n2
Grounded Globalism (Peacock), 16, 25, 51
Gwin, Minrose, 33

Habermas, Jürgen, 52, 62–63, 138–39n9
Handley, George, 26
Hebdige, Dick, 7, 73–74
Henninger, Katherine Renée, ix
Hill, Sam, 54
Hill, Trent, 38–39, 68, 72
hipness: as academic "structure of feeling," 1–4; Faulkner, in context of, 91; and southern identity 18–19. *See also* hipsters; subcultural capital
Hipster Handbook, The (Lanham), 4, 14, 70
hipsters: and authenticity, fetish for, 21, 24, 38, 46, 145n8; class privilege, disavowal of, 46, 145n12; generational perspectives on, 1–2, 70; and irony, 83–85; Johnny Cash as object of, 24, 41–42, 45, 81; and melancholia, 41, 42–43; and subcultural capital, 14, 68, 74, 80, 91
Hirsch, Marianne, 37
Hobson, Fred, 13, 29
Holloway, Karla F. C., 140–41n7
Holmes, Roger, 128
Holt, Douglas B., 9–10, 91
hooks, bell, 20
Hoop Roots (Wideman), 114–15
Hulbert, Ann, 80
"Hurt" (Cash), 41–43

icons, 9–10, 121, 127–28
I'll Take My Stand (Twelve Southerners), 30, 91

Inventing Southern Literature (Kreyling), 33, 91, 146n2
Invisible Man (Ellison), 91–92, 97, 105

Jackson, Alan, 71
Jackson, Wanda, 77
Jacobs, Harriet, 35
Jacobson, Joanne, 93
Jameson, Fredric, 15, 19–20, 39, 40
Jayhawks, 70
Jerrard, Robert, 19, 127
Johnny Cash at Folsom Prison (Cash), 44–45
Johnston, Richard, 148n5
Joseph, Miranda, 146n1
jouissance. See enjoyment

Kaoma, Kapya, 141–42n3
Kazanjian, David, 48–49
"Kill the Gays" bill (Uganda), 50, 52–53
King, Martin Luther, Jr., 22, 55, 111, 116, 121
King, Rodney, 112, 134
Klein, Naomi: and bourgeois ennui, 65–67; on brand identity, 67, 76, 107, 108, 109; on generational tyranny, 70–71
Kreyling, Michael, 109, 146n2; on Faulkner, 91; on memory in Southern studies, 30, 33–34
Kruse, Holly, 71
Kwon, Miwon, 21, 127, 129, 134

L.A. *See* Los Angeles
Lacan, Jacques, 137n2; atheism, nothing permitted under, 57; on the drive, concept of, 32, 53; and narcissism, opposition to, 3; on *objet a*, function of, 34; on the Real, concept of, 30–31, 139n13. *See* Žižek, Slavoj
Ladd, Barbara, 8, 13, 30
Landscape Architecture (periodical), 127
Lanham, Robert, 4, 70, 71, 76, 145n12
Lasch, Christopher, 39
L.A. school, 10–11, 134–35
Lassiter, Matthew, xi, 15, 55, 56

The New Southern Studies

*The Nation's Region: Southern Modernism, Segregation, and
U.S. Nationalism*
by Leigh Anne Duck

Black Masculinity and the U.S. South: From Uncle Tom to Gangsta
by Riché Richardson

Grounded Globalism: How the U.S. South Embraces the World
by James L. Peacock

*Disturbing Calculations: The Economics of Identity in Postcolonial
Southern Literature, 1912–2002*
by Melanie R. Benson

American Cinema and the Southern Imaginary
edited by Deborah E. Barker and Kathryn McKee

*Southern Civil Religions: Imagining the Good Society in the
Post-Reconstruction Era*
by Arthur Remillard

*Reconstructing the Native South: American Indian Literature and the
Lost Cause*
by Melanie Benson Taylor

*Apples and Ashes: Literature, Nationalism, and the Confederate States
of America*
by Coleman Hutchison

*Reading for the Body: The Recalcitrant Materiality of Southern Fiction,
1893–1985*
by Jay Watson

*Latining America: Black-Brown Passages and the Coloring of Latino/a
Studies*
by Claudia Milian

*Finding Purple America: The South and the Future of American
Cultural Studies*
by Jon Smith

The Signifying Eye: Seeing Faulkner's Art
by Candace Waid